An ACTIVITY-BASED APPROACH to
DEVELOPING YOUNG CHILDREN'S
Social Emotional
Competence

An ACTIVITY-BASED APPROACH to DEVELOPING YOUNG CHILDREN'S Social Emotional Competence

by

Jane Squires, Ph.D.

and

Diane Bricker, Ph.D.

University of Oregon
Eugene

·P·A·U·L·H·
BROOKES
PUBLISHING CO.®

Baltimore • London • Sydney

Paul H. Brookes Publishing Co.
Post Office Box 10624
Baltimore, Maryland 21285-0624

www.brookespublishing.com

Typeset by Barton, Matheson, Willse, and Worthington, Baltimore, Maryland.
Manufactured in the United States of America by
Versa Press, East Peoria, Illinois.

Most individuals described in this book are composites, pseudonyms, or fictional
accounts based on the authors' actual experiences. Individuals' names have been changed
and identifying details have been altered to protect their confidentiality.

Library of Congress Cataloging-in-Publication Data

Squires, Jane.
  An activity-based approach to developing young children's social emotional competence /
  by Jane Squires and Diane Bricker.
     p.   cm.
Includes bibliographical references and index.
ISBN-13: 978-1-55766-737-3 (pbk. with cd-rom)
ISBN-10: 1-55766-737-3
1. Children with disabilities—Education (Preschool)   2. Education, Preschool—Activity programs.
I. Bricker, Diane D.   II. Title.
LC4019.2.S66 2006
371.9'0472—dc22   2006031798

British Library Cataloguing in Publication data are available from the British Library.

Contents

CD-ROM Contents vii
About the Authors ix
Preface xi
Acknowledgments xiii
Introduction xvii

I The Need for the Activity-Based Intervention: Social Emotional Approach
1   Background and Overview   3
2   The Mental Health Status of Young Children   11
3   Conceptual Principles and Framework   25

II The Activity-Based Intervention: Social Emotional Approach
From Screening to Evaluation
4   Overview of the Activity-Based Intervention: Social Emotional Approach   41
5   Screening for Social Emotional Problems   55
6   Assessment to Determine Social Emotional Goals and Intervention
Content   71
7   Developing Intervention Goals   89
8   The Intervention Process   99
9   Evaluating Intervention Outcomes 117

Afterword: Our Closing Perspective 131

References 139

Appendices
    A   Environmental Screening Questionnaire (ESQ™),
        Experimental Edition
    B   Social Emotional Assessment/Evaluation Measure (SEAM™),
        Experimental Edition
        Infant
            Child Benchmarks and Assessment Items
            Child Benchmarks and Assessment Items (professional version
              with age intervals)
            Adult/Caregiver Benchmarks and Assessment Items
            Summary Form
        Toddler
            Child Benchmarks and Assessment Items
            Child Benchmarks and Assessment Items (professional version
              with age intervals)
            Adult/Caregiver Benchmarks and Assessment Items
            Summary Form

Preschool-Age
    Child Benchmarks and Assessment Items
    Child Benchmarks and Assessment Items (professional version
      with age intervals)
    Adult/Caregiver Benchmarks and Assessment Items
    Summary Form
C   Resources
    Guide to Early Childhood Curricula
    Guide to Social Emotional Screening Instruments
    Functional Behavioral Assessment and Behavior Support Planning
      with Deborah Russell and Robert Horner

Index 271

CD-ROM Contents

Welcome

Environmental Screening Questionnaire (ESQ™),
    Experimental Edition
Social Emotional Assessment/Evaluation Measure (SEAM™),
    Experimental Edition
    Infant
        Child Benchmarks and Assessment Items
        Child Benchmarks and Assessment Items (professional version with
          age intervals)
        Adult/Caregiver Benchmarks and Assessment Items
        Summary Form
    Toddler
        Child Benchmarks and Assessment Items
        Child Benchmarks and Assessment Items (professional version with
          age intervals)
        Adult/Caregiver Benchmarks and Assessment Items
        Summary Form
    Preschool-Age
        Child Benchmarks and Assessment Items
        Child Benchmarks and Assessment Items (professional version with
          age intervals)
        Adult/Caregiver Benchmarks and Assessment Items
        Summary Form

Licensing Agreement

About the Authors

Jane Squires, Ph.D., Professor, Early Intervention Program, Center on Human Development, College of Education, 5253 University of Oregon, Eugene, Oregon 97403

Dr. Squires directs doctoral and master's level early intervention/special education personnel preparation programs and teaches graduate courses in the College of Education at the University of Oregon. In addition to her work with the Center on Human Development at the university, she is Associate Director of the University of Oregon Center for Excellence in Developmental Disabilities. Dr. Squires has directed several research studies at the university on the *Ages & Stages Questionnaires®(ASQ): A Parent-Completed, Child Monitoring System, Second Edition,* and the *Ages & Stages Questionnaires®: Social-Emotional (ASQ:SE): A Parent-Completed, Child Monitoring System for Social-Emotional Behaviors* (available from Paul H. Brookes Publishing Co., www.brookespublishing.com). In addition, she has directed national outreach activities related to developmental screening and the involvement of parents/caregivers in the assessment and monitoring of their child's development. Additional research efforts focus on research and systems change projects related to assessing and improving social emotional competence in young children and their families.

Diane Bricker, Ph.D., Professor Emerita, Early Intervention Program, Center on Human Development, College of Education, 5253 University of Oregon, Eugene, Oregon 97403

Dr. Bricker received her bachelor's degree from the Ohio State University, her master's degree in special education at the University of Oregon, and her doctoral degree in special education at Vanderbilt University, Peabody College. Her initial work focused on improving the language skills of children with severe disabilities in institutions. That work led to the development of one of the first community-based integrated early intervention programs in the early 1970s. Since then, her work has continued in the area of early intervention, including her work on the ASQ and the ASQ:SE with Dr. Squires and *An Activity-Based Approach to Early Intervention, Third Edition* with Dr. Kristie Pretti-Frontzcak (Paul H. Brookes Publishing Co., 2004). Dr. Bricker has directed a number of national demonstration projects and research efforts focused on examining the efficacy of early intervention; the development of a linked assessment, goal development, intervention, and evaluation system; and the study of a comprehensive, parent-completed screening measure. Dr. Bricker has also directed a graduate training program focused on preparing early interventionists. More than 300 students have received their master's or doctoral degrees from this program and have gone on to practice in the field. Dr. Bricker served as Associate Dean for Academic Programs, College of Education, University of Oregon, for 8 years.

Preface

When we began work on a screening tool in the early 1980s, our expectations about where the development of the *Ages & Stages Questionnaires® (ASQ): A Parent-Completed, Child Monitoring System* (now available in a second edition from Paul H. Brookes Publishing Co., www.brookespublishing.com) might lead us were modest. The initial work on the ASQ led to a relatively negative reaction from many of our colleagues, who were skeptical that parents or other caregivers could be relied on to assess their own children accurately. Yet in the ensuing years, the accumulation of data has convinced all but the most severe critics that the majority of caregivers can accurately assess their child's developmental skills if given a straightforward, easy-to-complete tool such as the ASQ.

Feedback on the ASQ has been remarkably positive over the years except in one important area. Our professional colleagues repeatedly called to our attention the need for a more detailed screening tool focused on social emotional behavior. Those requests sent us off on another adventure—the development of *The Ages & Stages Questionnaires®: Social-Emotional (ASQ:SE): A Parent-Completed, Child Monitoring System for Social-Emotional Behaviors* (available from Paul H. Brookes Publishing Co., www.brookespublishing.com). At the outset, we were skeptical that we could develop a reliable screening tool that addressed difficult-to-define and measure social emotional behaviors. With strong encouragement and help from our doctoral students and early intervention/early childhood special education personnel, however, we did create the ASQ:SE. Much to our amazement and delight, we found that caregivers and child care workers can reliably use the ASQ:SE to identify infants, toddlers, and preschool-age children who may have social emotional or mental health problems.

As might be expected, the dissemination and use of the ASQ:SE solved some problems; however, the use of the tool also brought to our attention new challenges. Now that young children with social emotional problems were being reliably identified, early intervention and child care personnel were confronted with new, legitimate intervention needs. Repeated pleas have come from personnel in the field seeking help in formulating intervention efforts to prevent and/or reduce social emotional problems in their young charges.

Our initial reaction to these pleas was to empathize and to indicate that we would search for resources in the professional literature. To this end, for 2 years we dedicated our doctoral research seminar to first understanding the early development of social emotional behavior and then to exploring the mental health literature for empirically based intervention approaches. We located two types of interventions: those that suggested general intervention strategies and those delivered by mental health specialists.

Although we came to learn much about the social emotional competence of young children and what can go wrong when children do not achieve competence in this area, our findings concerning intervention efforts were extremely disappointing. The general intervention types posed two problems. First, the recommended strategies were extremely broad and almost impossible to operationalize (e.g., "Engage in reflective listening"). Second, the recommended interventions were almost never accompanied by any evidence of their value. The more technically defined and supported interventions offered a different problem in that the interventions required mental health experts.

The recognition that the literature offers little help for non–mental health experts who are confronted with a range of young children with social emotional problems led us to consider the development of this book. Again, we approached the challenge with significant trepidation; however, the need for carefully operationalized intervention efforts was so great that we overcame our initial reluctance to venture forth.

Acknowledgments

The Activity-Based Intervention: Social Emotional (ABI:SE) Approach, described in this book, evolved from our belief that early childhood and early intervention/early childhood special education practitioners are concerned about the social emotional development of the children that they serve. These professionals clearly recognize the importance of children's social emotional competence for their future interpersonal adjustments and academic success; however, the importance of this recognition often is not accompanied by the experience or knowledge necessary to assist young children in the development of social emotional competence. In our judgment, university preparation programs have not offered students adequate training in the social emotional area nor are useful assessment and curricular materials available to assist in helping practitioners detect and intervene with social emotional problems. This lack of appropriate training and useful materials in the social emotional area has been the inspiration for this book.

The ABI:SE Approach was developed to assist practitioners and families in creating responsive environments that facilitate the development of social emotional competence in young children by offering a coordinated, comprehensive system that permits early detection of problems and offers early preventative and intervention strategies.

The ABI:SE Approach evolved over time from discussions and experimentation conducted by the authors in conjunction with a cadre of doctoral students in the Early Intervention Program at the University of Oregon. These students were instrumental in the creation of the Environmental Screening Questionnaire (ESQ™), Experimental Edition, and the Social Emotional Assessment Measure (SEAM™), Experimental Edition. We are grateful to Hyeyoung Bae, Elizabeth Benedict, Jantina Clifford, Hollie Hix-Small, Mona Ivey-Soto, Karen Lawrence, Suzanne Bells McManus, Jin Ai No, Juli Pool, Deborah Russell, Helen Sharp, Krista Swanson, Hasnah Toran, and Jennifer Westover, who spent countless hours writing and rewriting assessment items and trying these items with friends, families, and local intervention programs. We would also like to acknowledge the assistance provided by Deborah Russell and Robert Horner, who created the positive behavioral support (PBS) materials contained in Appendix C.

In addition, we wish to acknowledge the ongoing clerical and technical support provided by Annette Tognazzini, James Jacobson, and Eva Quinby. Finally, our expert colleagues at Paul H. Brookes Publishing Co. made this edition possible. Our sincere thanks go to Jessica Allan, Melissa Behm, Leslie Eckard, Sarah Shepke, and Heather Shrestha.

To our family members
Paul, Jensena, and Lonnie
for their support and love

Introduction

Historically, professionals working with young children have come a long way in researching, assessing, and intervening with young children and families in the areas of early childhood development. Data and services targeted toward children's social emotional development are sadly lacking, however. An array of critical indicators point to a growing mental health crisis in populations of young children—a crisis that begs for attention and effective solutions. Professionals and paraprofessionals working with young children have seen a significant number of infants, toddlers, and preschool-age children who display troubling social emotional behavior or appear to be headed for the development of such problems. It has been their voiced concern to us that led to the development of the Activity-Based Intervention: Social Emotional Approach, hereafter referred to as the ABI:SE Approach. The need for effective solutions is paramount and serves as the major impetus for this book, which describes an intervention approach specifically designed to meet the substantial mental health needs of many young children.

The ABI:SE Approach, presented in this volume, differs from other approaches in two important ways. First, the approach was designed to be used by non–mental health specialists. The ABI:SE Approach is designed for use by a range of interventionists, teachers, and child care workers who are not mental health specialists. A rationale for this focus on non–mental health experts is addressed in detail later in this book.

Second, the ABI:SE Approach differs in its focus on embedding intervention efforts into daily activities experienced by young children and their caregivers. Rather than requiring a set of activities and events apart from children's play and daily routines, the ABI:SE Approach uses the many daily routine events in children's lives as times when their social emotional competence can be addressed.

The book is composed of two sections: 1) The Need for the Activity-Based Intervention: Social Emotional Approach, which presents a background and introduction to the ABI:SE Approach, and 2) The Activity-Based Intervention: Social Emotional Approach: From Screening to Evaluation, which provides a description of the steps of the approach and accompanying assessments.

Chapter 1 opens with an introduction focused on the need for and purpose of the book. A brief introduction to the ABI:SE Approach is offered and critical terms are defined to orient the reader.

Chapter 2 addresses the pertinent recent literature related to 1) the state or status of mental health in the United States, with a focus on young children; 2) the importance of early detection; and 3) barriers to early identification.

Chapter 3 offers a conceptual framework and set of foundational principles that underlie the ABI:SE Approach. Salient features of emotional and social development are discussed, as are the regulation and dysregulation of social emotional behavior, to provide a foundation for understanding the proposed paradigm for social emotional learning.

Section II is composed of six chapters, 4–9. Each chapter in Section II is dedicated to a discussion of these processes as defined and employed by the ABI:SE Approach.

Chapter 4 begins with a description of a linked system that provides the broad framework for the ABI:SE Approach. The linked system is composed of five critical processes: 1) screening, 2) assessment, 3) goal development, 4) intervention, and 5) evaluation.

Chapter 5 defines screening, explores barriers to early identification, and presents the steps involved in the ABI:SE Approach screening process. Next, it describes an assessment tool for providing information on a child's environment that can be helpful for targeting intervention efforts. This assessment is called the Environmental Screening Questionnaire (ESQ™), Experimental Edition.

Chapter 6 addresses assessment with a particular emphasis on the curriculum-based measure developed for the ABI:SE Approach. This measure yields outcomes directly relevant to goal development and intervention planning. This chapter describes the assessment tools referred to in the rest of the chapters: the Social Emotional Assessment/Evaluation Measure (SEAM™), Experimental Edition, tool for three different age intervals: 1) infant, 2), toddler, and 3) preschool-age.

Chapter 7 discusses key mental health concepts and their associated social emotional goals that have been selected to serve as the primary intervention targets for the ABI:SE Approach. These key concepts have been operationalized into a set of social emotional goals.

Chapter 8 discusses how to develop and use authentic prevention and intervention activities. These activities are designed to target the social emotional goals identified during the assessment process.

Chapter 9, the final chapter, discusses evaluation of intervention efforts and is followed by an Afterword that briefly summarizes the major principles and processes that underlie the ABI:SE Approach and reviews the five processes of the approach. It also offers our personal thoughts on the state of children's mental health interventions and future directions in this area.

Three appendices complete the book:

- Appendix A: Environmental Screening Questionnaire (ESQ), Experimental Edition

- Appendix B: Social Emotional Assessment/Evaluation Measure (SEAM), Experimental Edition, for three different age intervals: 1) infant, 2), toddler, and 3) preschool-age.

- Appendix C: Resources such as a guide to early childhood curricula in table form, with contact information and a brief description of relevant curricula centered on social emotional development; and a similar table on screening instruments related to social emotional development. This appendix also includes a section on Functional Behavioral Assessment (FBA) and Positive Behavior Support (PBS), both of which look at preventing or ameliorating children's problem behaviors related to social emotional development.

I

The Need for the Activity-Based Intervention: Social Emotional Approach

1

Background and Overview

All children have a range of basic requirements that need to be fulfilled if they are to thrive and grow into reasonably well-adjusted, productive adults. For our purposes, these requirements are classified as *biological* (i.e., genetic/physiological) and *environmental* (i.e., stimulation and responsive feedback). Furthermore, it is clear that children can and do experience significant variation in their biological endowments and their environmental surroundings. Biologically, these variations can produce conditions that range from death or severe impairments to outstanding abilities. Comparable ranges can be found to describe environments that can fall on a continuum from abusive and destructive to nurturing and supportive.

As Sameroff and Chandler (1975) noted in the mid-1970s and have recently revisited (Sameroff & MacKenzie, 2003), the dimensions of reproductive risk and caretaker risk predict children's developmental outcomes. Children endowed with "good" genes and strong physiological constitutions thrive if they live with reasonably nurturing and responsive caregivers. These same children are likely to experience poorer outcomes if they grow up with caregivers who do not consistently attend to their safety, nutritional, cognitive, linguistic, and social emotional needs. Children who are genetically or physiologically compromised may experience even poorer outcomes if they reside with caregivers who do not attend consistently to their unique and often multiple needs. Many children in this country continue to grow up in environments that can and do compromise even the sturdiest of children (Children's Defense Fund, 2005). Such environments affect development in all areas, but may be particularly devastating to children's mental health.

Many authorities (e.g., Drotar, 2002; Knitzer & Leftkowitz, 2006; Lally, 2003; Shonkoff & Phillips, 2000) believe that this nation is facing a crisis in the care of its young children. We have begun to recognize that large numbers of children are living with caregivers who, without help, have great difficulty providing safe and nurturing environments (Bricker, Schoen Davis, & Squires, 2004). Families living in poverty sometimes find themselves with such limited personal and material resources that they cannot consistently provide a supportive, stimulating, and nurturing environment for their young children. Children who live in non-nurturing environments are particularly vulnerable. These children often live with parents or other caregivers who are not able to attend to even their most basic health, safety, and mental health needs. Children growing up in such environments experience neither adequate cognitive and linguistic stimulation necessary for becoming competent nor necessary support and positive feedback that would permit them to grow into mentally healthy individuals (Qi & Kaiser, 2003).

Children who experience biological risks that can impede their development, such as low birth weight, prematurity, and in utero exposure to drugs and alcohol, are particularly vulnerable when living in impoverished and nonsupporting environments (Fifer, Monk, & Grose-Fifer, 2004; Sameroff, 2000; Sameroff & Chandler, 1975). These so-called "doubly vulnerable" children may require substantial supports and stimulation to acquire typical developmental and social emotional skills. Without supports such as parent–child groups, home visits, and specialized instruction, these children may enter school without the academic and social skills needed for success.

Growing numbers of practitioners, researchers, and policy developers have drawn attention to the perils facing many infants and young children and their families that, if not corrected, can lead to serious learning and/or social emotional problems. The federal government has acknowledged the increasing numbers of children at risk for learning difficulties with the passage of the No Child Left Behind Act of 2001 (PL 107-110). This important legislation has focused attention on the cognitive and linguistic needs of minority and poor children. In particular, considerable attention and resources are being directed to the creation of reading programs for young children. The goal of these programs is to ensure that all children become competent readers during their early elementary years. This national effort has drawn much needed attention to the development of approaches and curricular materials that may assist a wide range of children in learning basic skills that will permit them to, if not flourish, at least progress satisfactorily through the public education system.

Improvement in the cognitive and linguistic skills of young children is an important national goal that should receive substantial support from individuals and institutions and agencies assigned the responsibility of caring for the nation's young. However, the assembling of nationwide support to assist young children should have a focus that accounts for all critical dimensions of early development. The majority of children who confront difficulty in successfully negotiating the preschool years have social emotional problems that often interfere with the learning of basic skills such as reading. Adopting programs that address only academic problems is not likely to be totally successful because these programs do not address basic adjustment problems of young children (Knitzer, 2000).

The substantial number of young children with significant social emotional difficulties highlights the need for intervention efforts in the early childhood mental health area. Unfortunately, no unified national program exists that raises the nation's awareness of the significant mental health needs of young children living in non-nurturing environments or those with a developmental disability (Fenichel, 2000). We believe overlooking the mental health needs of the very young is a serious omission in federal and state policy and practice that will compromise much of the current work focused on assisting children to improve their math and linguistic skills. Can children be ready to learn if they have been raised to think of themselves as unworthy or incompetent and lack social skills? Can children who experience little positive nurturing or responsive feedback from at least some caregivers feel secure and/or motivated to learn effectively? We think not.

Just as evidence is accumulating that recognizes the effects of environmental conditions on children's brain development (Shore, 1997), evidence is also accumulating that children's perceptions of themselves and of their social world (i.e., that which forms their mental health) has a fundamental impact on their developmental outcomes (Osofsky & Fitzgerald, 2000; Raver, 2002). Furthermore, it has become clear that early caregivers' interactions with their infants and young children form, in part, the basis of children's subsequent mental health status (Sameroff, 2000; Shonkoff & Phillips, 2000).

Rana and her 6-month-old infant son, Lorenzo, live with Rana's family in a modest home located in a rural agricultural area. Rana is 17 years old and Lorenzo is her first child. Both of Rana's parents work and so, on most days, she is home alone with her baby. Rana loves her baby but finds Lorenzo often nonresponsive. There are many times when he does not make eye contact and he often turns his head away when Rana coos to him and strokes his face. Lorenzo frequently cries when she picks him up and he stiffens his body when she holds him for awhile. The baby's responses hurt Rana's feelings because she wants him to look at her and smile so she can cuddle and love him. Rana has shared her concern about Lorenzo with her mother; however, her mother tells Rana the baby is fine and not to worry. But Rana is unsure and, week after week, she feels less inclined to hold and talk to Lorenzo. She thinks something may be wrong but she is not sure what it is, and she does not know where to seek help.

The fact that many young children in this country are at risk for developing mental health problems has been made even more salient for us through conversations with many teachers, child care workers, and therapists. The essence of these conversations suggests that these professionals see many children who appear to be headed for serious mental health problems. These workers are, however, unsure as to the appropriate measures for documenting such mental health problems, and once these problems are detected, what types of intervention may be effective. The major impetuses for this book have been these two powerful realities: 1) the increase in children with mental health problems and 2) the uncertainty of early intervention/early childhood special education and child care worker personnel about how to help these children and their families.

PURPOSE AND APPROACH

This book has two purposes. The first is to bring attention to the significant mental health needs of many young children in this country. In particular, the content of this book is directed to paraprofessionals and professionals who work with infants, toddlers, and preschool-age children who have disabilities or who are at risk for developing problems. We focus on these children because considerable evidence indicates that the prevalence of social emotional problems in these populations is higher than in populations of young children who do not have disabilities or who live in nurturing environments (Bricker, Schoen Davis, & Squires, 2004).

The Growing Need

Since the 1990s, there has been a surge of interest in the mental health needs of young children and particularly of infants (Osofsky & Fitzgerald, 2000; Zeanah, 1993, 2000). However, many child care workers, teachers, interventionists, nurses, social workers, and other personnel who offer services to young children and their families are not well prepared to understand and address the social emotional needs of young children and their families (Eggbeer, Mann, & Gilkerson, 2003). Consequently, early indicators may go undetected or unnoticed and minor social or emotional problems may escalate into serious disorders. Most child care personnel are far better prepared to plan effective interventions focused on motor, cognitive, and linguistic development than on social emotional development. We believe an effective first step in addressing this deficiency is to focus needed attention on the mental health needs of young children who have disabilities and who are at risk because of compromised caregiving.

Designed for Ease of Use

The second and perhaps more vital purpose of this book is to offer an approach to social emotional intervention that has been designed to be delivered and used by agencies and personnel who are NOT mental health experts. Most early intervention programs would benefit greatly by having a full time or even part time mental health consultant, and useful models exist for including a mental health expert on the early intervention team (see for example, Donahue, Falk, & Provet, 2000). However, as appealing as the addition of a mental health consultant is, we believe that most child care programs, community-based play or educational programs, early intervention, and early childhood special education programs will be unable to add this expertise to their teams on a regular basis for two important reasons. First, it is unlikely that an adequate supply of mental health professionals—particularly those prepared to focus on young children and their families—will be forthcoming from higher education. Second, given the current and likely long-term economic conditions of the educational enterprise in the United States, it is unlikely that most child care, early intervention, and early childhood special education programs will have the financial resources to hire mental health consultants.

Given the reality that few mental health experts are available to work in child care and early intervention/early childhood special education programs and that most programs lack the resources to hire such personnel, we have targeted two criteria for the approach. The first criterion is that the approach can be integrated into existing community-based programs, whether these programs are focused on groups of individuals who are environmentally at-risk or who have disabilities or both. The second criterion is that personnel who do not have extensive mental health preparation are able to use the approach. Our desire is to expand the expertise of early intervention, early childhood special education, and early childhood workers and thereby augment existing services rather than create new, specialized programs.

In keeping with our two criteria, the Activity-Based Intervention: Social Emotional (ABI:SE) Approach described in this book is designed to be integrated into daily routines and to use existing personnel and services. Rather than develop techniques that require special instruction or materials, we have created an approach that can be used in the context of child care programs, classrooms, and the daily routines and authentic activities of family life (e.g., meal time, bath time). To that end, the book contains a variety of prevention and intervention activities that target key mental health concepts (e.g., self-image). The hallmark of these activities is that they can be adapted to match or fit the individual needs, values, and/or capabilities of a range of programs and families.

The ABI:SE Approach is guided by a linked systems framework. This framework first identifies the components or processes that compose a "system" and then articulates the connection or linkage between these processes (Pretti-Frontczak & Bricker, 2004). The linked systems framework that provides the structure for the ABI:SE Approach is composed of five processes: 1) screening, 2) assessment, 3) goal development, 4) intervention, and 5) evaluation. These processes and their connections or relationships are discussed in detail in Chapter 4 of Section II. The linked systems framework for the ABI:SE Approach is discussed in detail in Section II as well.

How These Strategies Depart from Tradition

We believe this book can make a significant contribution by suggesting prevention and intervention strategies that differ from traditional mental health approaches in three important ways:

1. The prevention/intervention strategies are designed to be used by personnel on the front line who already deliver direct services to young children and their families.

2. The intervention approach is designed so that "therapeutic" activities can be integrated into the fabric of program and family life.

3. The approach is composed of five linked processes that can be used to target social emotional goals and associated prevention and intervention activities that address each goal.

BOOK OVERVIEW

This section offers information and definitions that should be useful in orient-
ing the reader to the ABI:SE Approach. As noted earlier, the intended audience
includes individuals with varying educational and experiential backgrounds
who provide services to young children and their families. Specifically, this book
is intended for child care workers, early intervention/early childhood special education teachers and interventionists, Head Start personnel, and public health
personnel who are associated with projects focused on risk and disabilities. We
neither intend nor can turn such workers into mental health specialists. Rather,
we seek to help our readers to develop simple and effective strategies that can
assist them in successfully addressing social emotional problems or potential
problems that they may encounter in the young children they serve. Helping
these personnel address social emotional problems is necessary because currently, and likely well into the future, community-based programs do not receive adequate or ongoing assistance from mental health experts.

Also, as noted earlier, this book is particularly focused on infants, toddlers,
and preschool-age children who have disabilities or who are at risk because they
live in non-nurturing environments. This focus is appropriate for two reasons.
First, the personnel (e.g., teachers, public health nurses) for whom this book is
intended are the primary service providers for these groups of children. Second,
these children have a higher incidence of mental health problems than do children who have not experienced biological or environmental risk factors. However, it seems important to note that we believe the approach described in this
book is appropriate for all children. Many children who are typically developing and who have not been identified as having social emotional problems may
also receive significant benefits from the strategies and activities associated with
the ABI:SE Approach.

Definition of Terms

At the outset, it is useful to explain how the terms *mental health, emotions,* and
social emotional are used in reference to young children in this volume. Defining and understanding the term *mental health* is not an easy or straightforward
task. As Fitzgerald and Barton noted, "Infant mental health is difficult to define
because it is such a pervasive concept" (2000, p. 21). The far-reaching nature of
the concept makes setting parameters and establishing clear criteria a significant
challenge. Zeanah and Zeanah also viewed infant mental health as a broad concept, but nonetheless defined infant mental health as ". . . the state of emotional
and social competence in young children who are developing appropriately
within the interrelated contexts of biology, relationships, and culture" (2001,
p. 14). Knitzer has suggested using the terminology *early childhood mental
health* rather than *infant mental health* in order to emphasize "the need for a ser-

vice system that deals with the emotional, social, and behavioral needs of young children from birth to 6 . . ." (2000, p. 417). Knitzer sets the scope of early childhood mental health through the listing of four initiatives:

1. Promoting the emotional and behavioral well-being of young children

2. Helping families of young children address barriers to healthy emotional development

3. Assisting nonfamilial caregivers in promoting the emotional well-being of young children

4. Ensuring that young children with social emotional needs have access to needed services (p. 417).

This book embraces Knitzer's focus on children from birth to age 6, and the four initiatives she suggests set the parameters for early childhood mental health.

Defining the terms *emotions* and *social emotional* is no less daunting than addressing the term *mental health*. As with the latter, the reader should appreciate the lack of clarity and the inconsistencies that surround the terms *emotions* and *social emotional*. To reduce confusion, we present definitions of emotions and social emotional development that we believe best capture these elusive constructs. In addition, we emphasize the features that we think will help the reader to grasp the essence of these terms.

Witherington, Campos, and Hertenstein defined emotions as ". . . the processes by which an individual attempts to establish, change, or maintain his or her relation to the environment on matters of significance to the person [child]" (2001, p. 429). This definition suggests, and many other authorities agree (e.g., Sroufe, 1996), that emotions come into play only when the internal or external event is of real importance to the child. In contrast, many definitions of social emotional development do not focus on a child's evaluation of events but rather focus on the child's interactions and relationships with others (which clearly can be affected by emotions). For example, Wittmer, Doll, and Strain suggested, "Social development is composed of the behaviors, attitudes, and affects integral to a child's interactions with adults and peers" (1996, p. 301). Raver and Zigler defined social competence as, ". . . children's ability to engage in positive relationships with parents, peers, siblings, and teachers" (1997, p. 366).

Thus, authors do make distinctions between emotions and social responding; however, the social emotional processes and behaviors are so intertwined that it is often difficult, if not impossible, to sort children's responses into meaningful categories of *social* or *emotional*. At a general level, these two terms refer to children's adjustment to internal processes, social interactions and relationships, and environmental demands inherent in most people's lives. How well or poorly children are able to accommodate to a range of events, negotiate environmental demands, adjust to meet needs, and evaluate the emotional salience of events dictates in large measure their social emotional or mental health status.

When children are unable to satisfactorily meet their needs, negotiate demands, develop healthy relationships, and/or regulate their emotional responses, difficulties will ensue. In these cases, the literature speaks of social emotional or mental health problems, disabilities, deviancy, or other similar terms and indicates that the child's behavior (even indices of internal states) exhibits significant and consistent signs that all is not well. A child who has mental health or social emotional problems or who has early signs of such problems requires timely and effective intervention.

In this book, the terms *mental health* and *social emotional* refer to children's reactions and responses that produce satisfying interactions to the individual and his or her social world, comfortable self-images and perceptions by others, and matching and modulation of emotional and social responses to internal and external events. Mental health or social emotional problems or disabilities can be attributed to those children who consistently emit behaviors that produce unpleasant, unsatisfying, or unacceptable consequences to the child and/or social environment.

Primary Focus and Audience

The ABI:SE Approach is designed as a primary mental health prevention—that is, "an intervention intentionally designed to reduce future incidence of adjustment problems in currently normal populations as well as efforts directed at the promotion of mental health functioning" (Durlak & Wells, 1997, p. 117). Those children and families at increased risk for social emotional problems are the primary focus, including children from environments with increased risk factors such as teenage parents, substance abuse, parental mental disorders, and abuse and neglect. A second target group is children served in early intervention/ early childhood special education programs who are receiving intervention for delays or disorders in motor, cognitive, language, and other developmental areas. Specifically, ABI:SE is designed to enhance protective factors in a child's environment, such as supportive caregiving interactions, while enhancing specific social emotional skills in children, such as self-regulation and cooperative interactions. Through increased protective factors as well as improved social emotional competence, children in the target group should be better able to deal with factors that could otherwise lead to maladjustment. It is important to emphasize that the ABI:SE Approach is not designed to be used with young children who have significant and/or long-standing social emotional problems or disabilities. In most cases, these children require interventions directed by mental health experts.

The ABI:SE Approach is designed to promote "wellness" in young children and families through enhanced social emotional competence and environmental support. Wellness in children and families and long-term prevention of mental health disorders are the ultimate goals; short-term or proximal outcomes include improving or developing specific social emotional skills.

2

The Mental Health
Status of Young Children

T he quality of children's early care sets the stage for how children fare as adults. Children whose development is robust and untroubled will likely become healthy citizens who will be prepared to make positive contributions to our nation's welfare. Children whose development is compromised and who do not flourish are likely to drain resources rather than enhance the society in which they live. In light of these assumptions, a report from the Children's Defense Fund (2004) about the prevalence of risk factors challenging this nation's children is particularly sobering:

One in 4 lives with only one parent.

One in 8 is born to a teenage mother.

One in 13 was born with a low birth weight.

One in 6 lives in poverty.

One in 16 lives in extreme poverty.

One in 8 has no health insurance.

One in 141 will die before their first birthday.

The economic conditions of the United States leave many young children without supportive, nurturing environments; without parents who can attend to their developmental needs; without equal educational opportunities; and without adequate medical services. These unmet and unfilled developmental, educational, and medical needs introduce substantial risk into the lives of children. The mental health well-being of children who are exposed to multiple risk factors appears particularly vulnerable. The more numerous the risk factors and the longer these risk factors operate, the more likely children's developmental outcomes are compromised (Sameroff & MacKenzie, 2003).

The World Health Organization reported that by 2020, childhood neuropsychiatric disorders will be among the five most common causes of morbidity, mortality, and disability among children throughout the world (U.S. Surgeon General, 2000). Young children's vulnerability for mental health problems may occur in part because this vitally important dimension of development is often overlooked. Social emotional problems in young children are often ignored and undiagnosed for three important reasons. First, mental health systems were developed to focus on adolescent and adult pathology. Second, existing mental health services systems are woefully underfunded and thus, expanding their service base is challenging. Third, most mental health service providers have little training and experience in working with young children and conversely, personnel prepared to deliver services to young children have little, if any, background in dealing with social emotional problems.

Mental health intervention services in this country are often inadequately funded, fragmented, and unable to address the needs of families who have young children who may show signs of distress but whose emotional problems have not reached crisis proportions (Kataoka, Zhang, & Wells, 2002; President's New Freedom Commission on Mental Health, 2003; Walker, Ramsey, & Gresham, 2003). In most states, social emotional and mental health problems will not qualify an infant or toddler as eligible for federal IDEA services because of state eligibility definitions that require substantial developmental delay in two or more domains (Bricker, Schoen Davis, & Squires, 2004; Federal Interagency Coordinating Council, 2002; Walker, Nishioka, Zeller, Bullis, & Sprague, 2001). More often than not, young children with mental health problems and their families languish outside of the mental health and advocacy systems until they enter public school. By then, children's problems are likely to be considerably more challenging and costly to address (Abbott & Hill 1999; Duncan, Forness, & Hartsough, 1995; Hawkins, Catalano, Kosterman, Zigler, Taussig, & Black, 1992; Walker et al., 1996).

As a contextual foundation and rationale for the ABI:SE Approach, this chapter reviews the mental health status of this country's young children. The prevalence rates of atypical social and emotional development among children residing in the United States are examined, specifically children who live in poverty, who are in the foster care system, and who have a disability. An argument is then made for developing a system of early identification and intervention with social emotional difficulties to focus community resources efficiently. Finally, barriers to early identification are discussed.

ESTIMATES OF MENTAL HEALTH PROBLEMS IN YOUNG CHILDREN

Mental health problems or disorders have been reported across the age spectrum; however, until the decade of the 1990s, little attention was given to the prevalence of mental health problems in infants, toddlers, and preschool-age children. Recent prevalence figures and estimates of rates, discussed next, provide significant fuel to fan the fires of concern about the growing numbers of young children with significant mental health challenges.

Since the mid-1990s, both independent researchers and agencies of the federal government have focused their attention on the alarming numbers of children in all age groups with psychological problems. Based on their findings, Jellinek and Murphy (1999) have estimated that 13% of all children living in the United States have an emotional or behavioral disorder—and this prevalence figure swells in groups of children who are risk. For example, Dawes (1994) reported prevalence rates of disorder as high as 20% for children who are from economically disadvantaged groups. A report from the United States Surgeon General (2000) noted that one in five children and adolescents has signs or symptoms of a disorder listed in the *Diagnostic and Statistical Manual of Mental Disorders–Fourth Edition* (American Psychiatric Association, 1994). United States Department of Health and Human Services reports from 1999 and 2000 (NIH, 1999; NIMH, 2000) estimated that at least 5% of all children experience "extreme functional impairment" due to an emotional problem or behavioral disability.

The societal institution most affected by children and adolescents with social emotional disorders is the public school. Wagner (1995) reported that approximately 12% of all school-age children were eligible for Individuals with Disabilities Education Act (IDEA) Amendments of 1991 (PL 102-119) services based on the definition of social emotional disturbances. A National Institute of Mental Health (2000) report indicated that 2.5 to 5 million children had significant learning problems associated with identified emotional or behavioral disabilities, and of all disability categories, children with severe emotional disturbance fare least well in our educational system (Catron, 1997; Shinn, Walker, & Stoner, 2002). Children diagnosed with severe emotional disturbance have the lowest graduation rate of all IDEA disability categories (U.S. Department of Education, 1999).

As Knitzer (2000) noted, until the 1990s, reporting of prevalence rates for social emotional disabilities was focused on school-age populations (cf., Lavigne et al., 1993; Lavigne et al., 1996). The few prevalence studies from the 1970s and 1980s centering on preschool-age children reported mental health problems in 3.3% to 5.4 % of children in this age group (Goldberg, Regier, McInerny, Pless, & Roghmann, 1979; Goldberg, Roghmann, McInerny, & Burke, 1984). However, more recent estimates indicate that the percentage of young children receiving a psychosocial diagnosis is consistent with the numbers reported for school-age children. For example, Campbell (1995) found that the prevalence rates for mild to moderate social emotional problems were between 10% and 15% for the sample of preschool children in her study. A statewide survey conducted in Illinois reported that 16% of newborn to 3-year-old children displayed social emotional behaviors that were of concern to parents and/or child care providers (Culter & Gilkerson, 2002). In this study, 42% of the surveyed child care programs indicated that staff had asked at least one family to withdraw an infant or toddler because of inappropriate aggressive behaviors such as biting and hitting.

ESTIMATES OF MENTAL HEALTH PROBLEMS IN RISK GROUPS

The estimated rates of problems and disorders reported for general preschool populations pale when compared with estimates for high-risk groups. The next section of this chapter reviews the estimates for social emotional disorders for three high-risk groups: children living in poverty, children living in the foster care system, and children with disabilities.

Children Living in Poverty

Although being poor does not automatically produce poor outcomes for children, poverty is a convenient indicator variable that may signal the presence of an array of risk factors (e.g., inadequate child care, poor nutrition) in families. A functional translation of poverty may mean that children's nutrition, safety, and development is significantly compromised. The probability of poor child outcomes is particularly disturbing given that nearly one-fifth of the young children in the United States live in families whose income is below the government established poverty level (Children's Defense Fund, 2006). As Hart and Risley (1995) noted in their book, *Meaningful Differences in the Everyday Experience of Young American Children,* children raised in low-income homes are often so linguistically disadvantaged by the time they reach first grade that without extraordinary resources, these children will not catch up to their more economically advantaged peers. In fact, the authors predict that over time, the gap between children raised in poverty and those raised in advantaged homes is more likely to grow than to diminish.

The accumulating data also suggest that children living in poverty are considerably more likely to have mental health problems than their economically advantaged peers. Children in low-income homes were found to have a higher incidence of behavior problems: 30% as compared with 3%–6% in the general population (Qi & Kaiser, 2003). The interaction of child, parent, and socioeconomic characteristics may produce and sustain these behavior problems. Data from Head Start populations are revealing. Kupersmidt, Bryant, and Willoughby (2000) noted that more than 50% of Head Start preschoolers in their sample exhibited aggressive behaviors, as measured by their classroom teachers. Mowder, Unterspan, Knuter, Goode, and Pedro (1993) reviewed the records of 510 3- and 4-year-old children who were attending Head Start programs in the Denver area. These records indicated that 55% of these children at high risk had been referred because of social emotional concerns. A study by Webster-Stratton (1995) found that children attending the Head Start programs in Seattle were at high risk for mental health problems.

A second Webster-Stratton study (1997) offers further corroboration by noting that 25% of surveyed Head Start parents reported that their children had problem behaviors of clinical significance. Feil and colleagues (2000) found that 30% of 954 Head Start children in their study met the cutoff criteria for externalizing problems (e.g., aggression) and 31% were rated as having internalizing problems (e.g., depression) on the Teacher Report Form (TRF) of the Child Behavior Checklist (Achenbach, 1991). Harden and colleagues (2000) also identified 24% of Head Start children in their sample as having externalizing behavior problems but only identified 6.5% with internalizing difficulties. Finally, in a survey of 1,326 Head Start Centers serving over 58,000 children, staff identified the greatest training need as assistance in managing social emotional problems in participating children (Buscemi, Bennett, Thomas, & Deluca, 1995).

A mother's mental health has important implications for the social emotional welfare of her children (Landy, 2002). Unfortunately, women living in poverty present with significantly more mental health disturbances than women who are not poor. For example, the National Center for Children in Poverty (2002) reported that women from low-income circumstances experience clinical depression at twice the rate of other women. In a national survey, nearly 50% of Early Head Start mothers reported experiencing symptoms of depression (Head Start National Survey, 2003). A number of investigations have reported an important link between maternal depression and child behavior in that young children exposed to maternal depression are at high risk for exhibiting conduct disorders and aggression (Beck, 1999; Murray, Sinclair, Cooper, Docournau, & Turner, 1999; National Institutes of Health, 1999).

Living in poverty is not only a matter of economic deprivation but also it may be accompanied by poor parenting due to the stresses poverty brings to many families. Parents who are mentally troubled, depressed, or who lack emotional stability cannot provide optimal or often even minimal levels of nurturing and support for their children through beginning and ongoing interactions. There is little doubt, then, that many children living in poverty are at significant risk for poor social emotional outcomes.

Children Living in the Foster Care System

Children who are removed from their families and placed into foster care are at extreme risk for social emotional problems for a least two reasons. First, children are not usually removed from their families unless their home conditions are life threatening (e.g., extreme neglect, extreme physical violence). In order for the state to seek removal from their parents, children living in such conditions usually have endured repeated severe attacks on their physical and mental well-being. (Bilaver, Jaudes, Koepke, & Goerge, 1999).

A second reason that children in foster care are at high risk for social emotional disturbances is that removal from their home—no matter how destructive the environment—is at best upsetting and at worst traumatic for them (Lowenthal, 2001). Placement with strangers, no matter how caring, requires a significant adjustment by children who often lose not only their parents but also their siblings and familiar surroundings (Bornstein & Tamis-LeMonda, 2001). The initial trauma of removal from the family is often compounded for children because child protection agencies often need time to find an appropriate foster care placement, which may necessitate that children experience several moves and concurrent adjustments. Unfortunately, for many children, disrupted placements are the rule and not the exception. A U.S. House of Representatives Report (1994) incorporating data from a 15-state survey found that more than 57% of the children in foster care had been placed in multiple homes, and nearly 30% had had three or more placements. Children living in the foster care system are at great risk for social emotional disturbance, and the growing number of young children requiring legal protection is cause for great concern (Berrick, Nedell, Barth, & Johnson-Reid, 1998).

Perhaps one of the most salient indicators of a nation's well-being is the number of children who require legal protection to ensure their physical and psychological safety. If the number of children referred to child protection agencies is a valid indicator, then this nation has serious problems. In 2000, state child protection services received reports of suspected abuse or neglect for an estimated 2.8 million children, of which more than 900,000 were confirmed (Children's Defense Fund, 2004). The majority of children in this group experienced neglect (55%), with the remainder experiencing other types of maltreatment such as physical, sexual, or psychological abuse. Children under age 6 were the subjects of approximately 40% of the confirmed reports of maltreatment, even though they represent only one-third of the child population (Berrick et al., 1998). Reports of child abuse among the young appear to be escalating, with the youngest children most likely to be the victims of severe injury or death resulting from the abuse. According to an estimate by Berrick and colleagues, ". . . nearly 3% of all young children will experience such grave threats to their well-being that they will be placed in foster care at some point before age six" (1998, p.4). These researchers pointed out that children are entering the foster care system at younger ages, with the incidence of admission from birth to age 4 now twice what it is for children from ages 5 to 17.

As noted, children living in the foster care system are prime candidates for developing social emotional problems, and particularly those who experience repeated placements (Bornstein & Tamis-LeMonda, 2001). Children in foster care were found to be 16 times more likely to receive mental health services and 8 times more likely to experience an inpatient psychiatric hospitalization than children not in the foster care system but who were receiving Aid to Families with Dependent Children (Bilaver et al., 1999). Consequently, children in foster care should also be considered likely candidates for prevention and/or intervention services (Behrman, 2004) and are one of the target groups addressed in this book.

Children with Disabilities

Children with disabilities are 4 to 5 times more likely to be reported to have deficits in social emotional functioning than are children without disabilities (Merrell & Holland, 1997; Squires, Bricker, & Twombly, 2004). Approximately 50% of parents with children enrolled in early intervention programs indicated that their child had behavior and social emotional problems for which they needed help to manage (Culter & Gilkerson, 2002). This rate, if reflective of national trends, suggests that social emotional problems are more prevalent in groups of individuals with disabilities than in, for example, children attending Head Start programs.

Many children who begin life with a disability develop into well-adjusted adults who lead satisfying lives; however, being born with or acquiring a disability during the early years can pose serious challenges to a child's developmental integrity and social emotional health (Roberts, Mazzucchelli, Taylor, & Reid, 2003; Wolery, 2000). The impact of a disabling condition on a child's mental health is related to a number of important interdependent variables that include the seriousness and pervasiveness of the problem, the characteristics of the child, the support and resources of the family, the accessibility to compensatory interventions, and the quality of those interventions. On the one hand, a child with a disability such as cerebral palsy who lives with supportive parents and siblings and who is enrolled in a quality early intervention program, may show no or few signs of social or emotional disturbance. With help from family members and professional staff, the child may learn to cope well with his motor disorder by developing compensatory social responses that permit him to develop appropriate and satisfying relationships with peers and adults. On the other hand, a disability—whether mild or serious—may threaten a child's mental health adjustments by inhibiting or interfering with social interactions. Thus, the development of healthy relationships and the learning of emotional regulation and independence may be disrupted, as well as the development of a healthy self-image and relationships with others (Crnic, Hoffman, Gaze, & Edelbrock, 2004).

Fraiberg's vivid descriptions of parental struggles to adapt to their sightless infants provide poignant examples of the challenges some disabilities pose to parents and their children (Fraiberg, 1971, 1974). Kelly and Barnard (1999) have also provided an insightful review of studies focused on the interaction between parents and children with disabilities. These authors concluded that there are certain differences in mother–child interactions—such as infants' slower response time and difficult-to-read cues—that often occur when an infant has a disability or is at risk for disabilities. These differences could well set the stage for the onset of social emotional problems in young children.

In addition to threatening the development of healthy social relationships, disabilities may also interfere with the acquisition of independence and important communicative functions. For example, an infant who cannot move her arms and legs is dependent on others for feeding, positioning, and social interactions. Thus, exploration of the physical environment is severely impaired, as is her ability to manipulate objects. A preschool child with limited language skills may be unable to contribute to communicative exchanges with peers, may find it difficult to gather information, and may endure frequent episodes of unmet needs. These conditions are not conducive to the acquisition of a healthy self-concept.

For such children, the effects of their disability may increase over time, causing growing discrepancies with their peers. These differences may result in less social acceptance and greater stigmatization, which is likely to further impair already shaky social emotional functioning and lead to serious mental health problems. The developmental nature of social emotional competence suggests that without effective intervention, problems may compound over time, posing increasingly greater challenges to children's mental health (Bricker et al., 2004; Butterfield, Martin, & Pratt Prairie, 2004; Cicchetti & Cohen, 1995).

Of note, a relationship appears to exist between disability and children in foster care. In discussing data provided by the National Center on Child Abuse and Neglect, Lowenthal wrote,

> A child with a disability is 1.7 times more likely to be abused than a child without a disability. The rate for emotional abuse in children with disabilities is 2.8 times higher than for that for children without disabilities. (2001, p. 23)

These findings strongly suggest that children with disabilities are at significant risk for developing serious mental health problems. Given this reality, the field of early intervention must move forward in developing effective prevention and intervention approaches to address this important challenge.

BENEFITS OF EARLY IDENTIFICATION AND INTERVENTION

The prevalence studies and associated estimates of mental health problems in young children described earlier emphasize what child care and early intervention/ early childhood special education personnel already know: Many young children they see have mild to serious behavioral or social emotional problems. These problems interfere with a child's daily social and environmental interactions and may produce at least two unwanted outcomes. First, mental health problems may diminish the development of healthy relationships with peers and adults, and second, mental health problems may hinder or compromise the acquisition of important adaptive, cognitive, and communication skills.

Given the potentially large number of young children (i.e., prevalence rates range from 13% to 30%) who may develop mental health or social emotional problems, early identification and intervention becomes urgent to ensure reasonable developmental outcomes. Without timely identification, children and caregiver and/or peer interactions can disintegrate over time and may become costly and difficult to remediate (Walker et al., 1996). Once maladaptive behaviors become part of children's repertoires, they tend to be resistant to change and often grow into more serious problems (Kaufman, 1999; Loeber & Farrington, 1998; Squires, 2000). The ABI:SE Approach offers a comprehensive system that addresses early identification, timely referral, and functional assessment focused on caregiver–child interactions, family-appropriate intervention, and the ongoing monitoring of program effectiveness (e.g., child and caregiver change).

The Key: Early Identification

Nurturing, constructive, and developmentally appropriate early experiences are the essential bedrock for infants and young children to 1) acquire important processes such as self-regulation, 2) shape positive views and expectations about their social world, and 3) permit necessary neural growth and organization. Many children served in early childhood programs and especially those living in poverty, foster care, or with a disability, are at risk for having early experiences that may hinder or interfere with the acquisition of critical skills and the acquisition of healthy perceptions about their social milieu. The longer children experience environments that do not facilitate the development of positive and constructive self-image, emotion regulation, and social perceptions, the greater the potential harm. Thus, it seems imperative as well as entirely sensible for communities to put in place strategies for prevention, early identification, and early intervention if they are to maximize children's potential to be contributing members of society.

The key to young children's social emotional well-being is to offer families a range of services that can be matched to the seriousness of their particular problem or need. Service options should include offering community-based prevention strategies, ferreting out problems before they become intractable, and providing appropriate interventions to children/family units who show clear signs of troubled interactions. This hierarchy of service options has been represented as a pyramid of services (see for example, Fox, Dunlap, Hemmeter, Joseph, & Strain, 2003; Horner, Sugai, Todd & Lewis-Palmer, 2005) that begins with a broad base of prevention activities and moves to progressively more specialized and costly interventions.

Figure 2.1 displays a three-level pyramid of service options focused on the prevention of, and early intervention to alleviate, social emotional problems. In

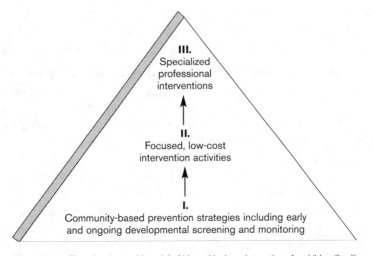

Figure 2.1.   Three-level pyramid model of hierarchical service options for children/families at risk for social emotional problems.

this figure, Level I represents low-cost prevention strategies that can be used with large groups of individuals. Examples of Level I activities include community support groups, well baby clinics, educational classes, quality child care and media (e.g., books, manuals, television programs), and low-cost screening programs focused on early identification of social emotional problems in young children and monitoring of targeted groups (e.g., children in the foster care system) over time. Level II represents more focused intervention strategies for groups of children and families who have significant environmental risk factors and/or show early signs of maladaptive interactions. Examples of Level II activities might include specialized parenting classes, play groups focused on relationship building, and therapeutic child care settings. Level III represents the most costly service options that are designed to target a limited number of children/families who show clear and persistent signs of mental health disturbances. Interventions that occur at Level III are focused on individual families, are specialized, and are managed by professionals.

This pyramid approach, if employed properly, should result in an efficient use of community resources and comprehensive identification and prevention activities. A clear requisite to the development of coordinated and graduated systems of service options is early identification. Despite the economic value, appeal, and demonstrated effectiveness of this hierarchical offering of service options (e.g., Metzler, Biglan, Rusby & Sprague, 2001), most communities do not have in place coordinated models of this type for the early detection of and intervention with young children who are at risk for social emotional problems.

Barriers to Early Identification

Significant barriers to the early identification of social emotional problems in young children exist and include 1) lack of clarity in defining the parameters of acceptable or appropriate social emotional behavior, 2) service providers poorly equipped to detect early signs of social emotional disorders, 3) few valid screening measures, particularly for infants and toddlers, and 4) limited mental health service options (Bricker et al., 2004). Each of these barriers is discussed next.

Lack of a Clear Definition of What Is Acceptable   The lack of clarity in defining or operationalizing acceptable or discrepant social emotional behavior interferes with early identification of children who would likely profit from some form of intervention. Except in cases in which a disorder is obvious (e.g., a child who will not make eye contact, a child who only engages in repetitive behavior), it is often difficult to determine if a child's behavior is disordered or merely immature, or whether the frequency and intensity of a behavior requires intervention. For example, determining if a child's temper tantrums are a social emotional problem is likely dependent on a number of variables such as the child's age, the frequency of occurrence, and the intensity of the response. Although defining some behaviors as aberrant can be done with relative ease, many behaviors, such as shyness, can be considerably challenging in terms of setting parameters of appropriateness. Much progress is being made toward operationalizing social emotional problems, and perhaps in the future this difficulty will no longer be a significant barrier to early identification.

Poorly Equipped Professionals   Given the difficulty in the valid detection of early signs of social emotional problems, it may not be surprising that many professionals are poorly equipped to identify troubling behaviors early in children's lives. More than 76% of children living in the United States receive health care from medical professionals, and it would appear that these well-trained personnel are ideally situated to detect developmental and social emotional problems and refer families to appropriate services (Costello et al., 1988; Dulcan, et al., 1990; Kemper, Osborn, Hansen, & Pascoe, 1994). However, physicians and other medical personnel often fail to identify mental health problems and thus do not refer children to mental health services (Jellinek, Patel, & Froehle, 2002). In a recent mental health survey, more than half of the parent respondents indicated that their child's primary care physician did not recognize serious mental health problems in their child (National Alliance for the Mentally Ill, 2000). This survey's findings are consistent with other studies that report that pediatricians recognized half or fewer of the children in need of mental health referrals (Horowitz, Leaf, Leventhal, Forsyth, & Speechley, 1992; Jellinek, 1998), and the rate of detection is lowest for the youngest children (Stancin & Palermo, 1997; Wildman, Kinsman, Logue, Dickey, & Smucker, 1997). Clearly, considerable work is necessary to educate medical and other professionals to recognize early signs of social emotional disorders in young children.

Few Valid Screening Measures   A third barrier to early identification has been the availability of family-focused, psychometrically sound screening measures, particularly for infants and toddlers (Greenberg, Domitrovich, Bumbarger, 1999; Squires & Nickel, 2003). Until relatively recently, professionals were faced with the dilemma of either using a low-cost screening measure with questionable or undetermined reliability and validity or using psychometrically sound instruments (e.g., *Child Behavior Checklist,* Achenbach & Rescorla, 2000) that require professional administration and interpretation and are prohibitively costly to use with large groups of children.

Fortunately, this barrier is being overcome since the development of several new screening measures that are psychometrically sound and family-focused, that target infants and toddlers as well as preschool-age children, and that are low-cost to use. These measures include *Temperament and Atypical Behavior Scale (TABS): Early Childhood Screener* (Bagnato, Neisworth, Salvia, & Hunt, 1999); *Brief Infant–Toddler Social and Emotional Assessment* (Briggs-Gowan & Carter, 2001; Briggs-Gowan, Carter, Irwin, Wachtel, Cicchetti, 2004); and *Ages & Stages Questionnaires®: Social-Emotional* (ASQ:SE) (Squires, Bricker, & Twombly, 2002). These tools can be completed by parents or other caregivers and can be scored quickly, making them appropriate to assess and monitor large groups of children.

Lack of Community-Based Mental Health Services for Young Children and Their Families   Lack of community-based mental health services for young children and their families constitutes a final barrier to early identification. Some practitioners may avoid identifying young children because few mental health resources are available to help families. Families are often put on waiting lists because of a significant shortage of mental health professionals who are knowledgeable about young children (Gilkerson, 2000).

Although 1 in 10 children and adolescents is estimated to have a mental health disturbance that causes impairment, only about 1 in 25 receives mental health services in a given year (U.S. Surgeon General, 2000). Of children and adolescents from 6 to 17 years old who were found to need mental health services, nearly 80% received no care (Kataoka, Zhang, & Wells, 2002). The percentage of children under age 6 who do not receive care is likely much higher.

Other Potential Barriers   Besides the few available community-based mental health services, it is also difficult for young children to qualify for mental health services under IDEA (Duncan et al., 1995; U.S. Surgeon General, 2000). Under Part C of IDEA, states are required to develop their own eligibility guidelines, and, for the most part, states have not adopted guidelines or criteria that address mental health problems in infants and toddlers. For 3- to 5-year-olds, eligibility guidelines for the category of behavior disorders can be used; however, the match between early childhood mental health problems and these guidelines is often poor (Conroy & Brown, 2004). For example, a child with emotion regulation problems may also have attentional and motor processing difficulties, may be awkward, and may perseverate over arranging his physical environment. The category of emotional disorder does little to capture the nature of this child's problems.

Little will be accomplished if children are identified early but then cannot obtain effective services. Unfortunately, expanded services are not likely to appear until the need for such services cannot be ignored. Thus, early identification is a fundamentally important motivator to the establishment of mental health service options for young children and their families.

SUMMARY

Mental health is a critical component of children's learning and general health. Fostering social and emotional health in children as a part of healthy development must be a national priority. Both promoting mental health in children and intervening and treating mental disorders should be major public health goals (U.S. Surgeon General, 2000, p. 2). Much effort will be required to push young children's mental health to the top of this country's priorities list.

Early identification is an important key to obtaining timely mental health services for young children and their families. Progress toward overcoming barriers to early identification has been uneven. Headway is being made on defining social emotional behaviors and expectations: Valid and low-cost screening measures are now available for use in large-scale screening efforts. However, substantial work still remains to affect change in medical personnel's ability and interest in early identification of social emotional problems and to expand the number and range of available mental health community-based service options.

With the increasing numbers of children at risk and those with identified social emotional disturbances, a critical need has emerged for an integrated prevention/intervention approach. To be effective, we believe that social emotional problems should be identified early, that caregivers should be provided the necessary support for addressing problems, that intervention should be linked or mapped into everyday family activities, and that effectiveness should be monitored. The ABI:SE Approach incorporates each of these dimensions. The conceptual underpinnings for the approach is described in the next chapter, whereas an overview and the five processes that compose the approach are described in detail in Section II of this volume.

3

Conceptual
Principles and Framework

This chapter offers a framework for understanding the ABI:SE Approach. We begin by presenting an overall view of early development, then move to a discussion of social and emotional areas of development—in particular, definitions of these constructs and how they relate to each other and other developmental areas. We offer illustrations of how foundational principles are related. Finally, we propose a learning model that incorporates the previously discussed developmental principles and how their relationship might explain how children arrive at either a satisfactory or unsatisfactory mental health status.

CONCEPTUAL PRINCIPLES
UNDERLYING THE FRAMEWORK

The ABI:SE Approach described in this volume is based on the overriding theoretical perspectives often referred to as *transactional* and *organizational*. The transactional position posits that development is the result of ongoing transactions or interactions that occur between children and their environment (Sameroff & Chandler, 1975). These back-and-forth transactional exchanges permit children to learn. The organizational perspective, based on the writings of Cicchetti and his colleagues, present an important complement to transactional theory:

> According to the perspective, development is [seen] as a series of qualitative reorganizations among and within behavioral and biological systems. Through the processes of differentiation and hierarchical integration, individuals move from a relatively diffuse, undifferentiated condition to a state of increasingly differential and hierarchically organized behavior complexity (Werner, 2000). During this process, intrinsic or organismic factors and extrinsic and environmental factors dynamically interact to determine a person's developmental outcome (Cicchetti, Ganiban, & Barnett, 1991, p. 15).

These theories of development account for, at least in part, the evolution of most infants from having few directed or organized behaviors to having increasingly complex and interrelated repertoires of mental processes and overt behaviors.

25

For example, an intentional reach-and-grasp response does not exist in the repertoire of a 1-month-old (neonates have reflexive grasps); however, as infants' nervous systems mature and the environment offers objects and people of interest, most infants begin making outward swiping moves with their arms and hands. Initially, these swipes are uncoordinated, may appear random, and may often be unsuccessful (i.e., may not reach the intended target).

With practice and feedback, an infant becomes able to reorganize diffuse swiping moves into more direct reaches that result in the systematic capturing of objects. Once clutched, the infant can explore the features or characteristics of the grasped object. The milestone of reach and grasp reflects a qualitative change and reorganization in the infant's motor responses and in beginning cognitive (i.e., problem-solving) processes. This qualitatively new type of exploratory behavior, in turn, leads to further qualitative reorganization of the infant's motor repertoire as well as subsequent reorganization of the infant's understanding of the physical world.

Sroufe's (1996) description of the evolution of smiling offers an insightful example of qualitative reorganizations of emotional responses that occur for infants who are typically developing. The earliest smiles, often called *endogenous*, are associated with the biological state of the neonate. That is, some internal stimulation (e.g., gastric activity) produces an upturn in the corners of an infant's mouth rather than the infant's smiling in response to some external stimulation. An important change occurs during the first months when the first alert smiles (i.e., eyes brighten, eyes crinkle, and lips are pulled into a grin) emerge. Alert smiles generally are evoked by environmental events (e.g., mild tactile or auditory stimulation) rather than by a response to internal stimulation.

By 4–6 weeks, feedback from ongoing environmental transactions permits infants to direct their attention to events of interest, and infants at this stage produce active smiles often accompanied by vocalizations (e.g., cooing). Active smiles are evoked by patterns of environmental stimulation (e.g., caregiver's voice) and subsequent feedback, rather than by single events. Repetition of an activity (e.g., clapping hands) often elicits smiling that is, in turn, followed by the caregiver's positive response (e.g., repeats hand claps, tickles the baby's tummy). These changes in the smiling response and evoking stimuli clearly suggest qualitative reorganizations in development. It is also clear that associated changes in environmental feedback are instrumental in the development of qualitative changes in young children.

As Sroufe (1996) noted, at approximately 8–10 weeks of age, infants begin to smile at visual events (e.g., stationary faces) not accompanied by movement or noise. A smile response to a stationary face indicates that infants have sufficient cognitive functioning to match the stationary face to an internal visual scheme. This stage suggests that infants' responses are produced by some cognitive activity rather than by sensory stimulation alone. As infants mature, smiles are increasingly elicited by "meaningful" stimuli (e.g., playing simple games, repeating events); novel events can also produce smiles. Again, the social feedback received by infants is critical in shaping their smiling responses. Smiling at meaningful as well as novel activity and visual stimuli indicates the existence of

Table 3.1. Foundational principles of the ABI:SE Approach

Principle	Description
Child characteristics	The genetic/biological/physiological characteristics of children that affect their development.
Environmental context	The social and physical environments that surround children and affect their development.
Ongoing transactions	The ongoing interaction between children and their environment that produces developmental change.
Qualitative reorganizations	The ongoing transactions between children and their environment that produce qualitative reorganizations in development over time.
Goodness of fit*	The match or congruence between children's characteristics and environmental demands and expectations that helps to determine developmental outcomes.
Risk/protective factors	The multiplicity of risk and/or protective factors that affect development.

*A concept introduced by Chess and Thomas (1977).

cognitive activity associated with memory and discrimination processes and again suggests a qualitative reorganization of the infant's repertoire.

Inspection of the organizational perspective of development and other interactional or transactional theories of development (e.g., Sameroff, 2000) reveals four principles that are essential to their understanding: 1) biological basis of the child, 2) environmental effects, 3) interactions between the child and environment, and 4) qualitative reorganizations in development or in children's repertoires that these transactions produce over time. To these important principles we would add the following: 5) the goodness of fit between the child and the environment, and 6) the impact of risk and protective factors. These six principles serve as the foundation for the ABI:SE Approach. Brief descriptions of these foundational principles are contained in Table 3.1. We believe that these principles work together, resulting in developmental change and growth in most children.

The putative (i.e., assumed) relationship between the six principles contained in Table 3.1 is shown in Figure 3.1. The child characteristics principle is illustrated by the words *infant, toddler,* and *preschool-age child* placed at the center of each circle. Dual outer lines that surround the infant, toddler, or preschool-age child represent the environmental context principle, indicating that a child is embedded in his or her environmental context. The small arrows represent the ongoing transactions that show the bi-directionality of effects between the infant, toddler, and preschool-age child and the environment. The principle of qualitative reorganizations is captured by the three circles, and the longest arrow illustrate their connectivity. The goodness of fit principle is shown as an interface between the environment and the infant, toddler, and preschool-age child, and is meant to indicate that the transactions between a child and his or her environment are effected by the goodness of fit between the child's temperament, personality, or reactivity and environmental feedback. The final

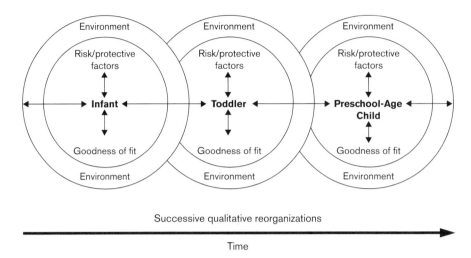

Successive qualitative reorganizations

Time

Figure 3.1.   Putative relationship between the six foundational principles that underlie the ABI:SE Approach.

principle, risk and protective factors, is also shown as an interface between the child and environment that affects the transactions that occur between the child and his or her environmental context.

As noted, the three circles represent successive qualitative reorganizations of a child's internal and external repertoires as development proceeds over time. The longest arrow underlines the presumed relationship between early and subsequent development. That is, later development is predicated on, at least in part, the earlier repertoire of the child. Thus, what occurs during the period of infancy affects development during toddlerhood and likewise, development during toddlerhood provides the basis for development during the preschool period.

Although Figure 3.1 shows only three qualitative organizational changes, it is likely that within each of these developmental periods a number of qualitative changes occur.

Of course, development does not occur in precise, tidy phases or stages; nevertheless, these developmental periods in the center of each oval represent major qualitative changes. In each developmental period, as mentioned earlier, children are embedded in their environmental context. The arrows going between the infant, toddler, and preschool-age child and the environment represent the ongoing transactions that occur between children and their environment.

These transactions not only shape and build children's repertoires but also affect subsequent environmental reactions. The insertion of the concept of goodness of fit on the smaller arrows linking the child and environment suggests that ongoing transactions are affected by how well the environment can adjust to characteristics of the child and/or how well the child is able to adjust to environmental demands or conditions. The concepts *risk/protective factors* and *goodness of fit* are included to indicate that interactions may be significantly mediated by these two concepts. Risk/protective factors refer to the many internal and external factors that may affect a child's development (e.g., newborn biological status, quality of parenting, nutrition), whereas goodness of fit refers to how well the child is able to adjust to environmental demands.

It is important to note that the quality and attained developmental status of one period, or stage, does not ensure subsequent outcomes. For example, an infant who meets developmental expectations during the first 12 months of life may fare much less well if his or her subsequent care deteriorates significantly during the next 12 months of life. Conversely, a premature infant with serious medical problems may overcome a poor start with quality care and intervention and thus, become a robust and competent toddler. However, as Sroufe noted, "If a developmental/organizational perspective is taken seriously, then the roots of healthy emotional development may be laid out even in the first year" (1996, pp. 155–156).

To summarize, Figure 3.1 provides a visual display of the relationship between the six principles that provide the foundation or framework for the ABI:SE Approach. For an intervention approach to be successful, it must recognize the qualities inherent in the child and his or her environment and how these qualities are affected by an array of important factors. For the approach to produce change it must be designed to address the many different factors or variables that are salient in children's lives.

Defining Social Emotional Development

As noted repeatedly by leaders in the field of mental health and developmental psychology (cf., Fitzgerald & Barton, 2000; Shonkoff & Phillips, 2000), there is a growing need to examine young children's social and emotional development and competence; however, defining the social and emotional domains as well as their behavioral indexes is a complex undertaking (Sroufe, 1996; Thompson, 1994). Why is the defining of emotions and, in some instances, social behavior more difficult than defining and examining, for example, gross motor behavior? The following are four of the main reasons or challenges:

First, much of emotional behavior is internal (i.e., physiological reactions) making it challenging to observe and monitor. However, it is important to note that most emotional responses are indexed by overt, observable, and measurable behavior and physiological reactions. For example, a fear reaction produces an internal reaction (e.g., heart rate may increase) and usually registers on an individual's face as well.

A second challenge to understanding and mapping emotional and social development is the variety and variability in social and emotional reactions and responses. This variability makes capturing these concepts under consistent and cohesive rubrics difficult (e.g., fear may produce flight, crying, or other reactions).

Third, separating emotional and social behavior from each other and other domains of behavior (e.g., cognitive) is an artificial rendering of a child's behavior (Dodge & Garber, 1991). For example, when a child displays anger by turning red, screaming, and throwing an object, he or she is also displaying a phys-

iological reaction and motor responses. The "triggering" event that produced
the anger was mediated by cognitive processes such as memory and discrimination. Emotional and social behavior does not occur in a vacuum but rather, it is
a part of dynamic and complex repertoire available to most children.

Fourth and finally, social and emotional behaviors have strong family and
cultural ties. That is, acceptable and/or permissible responses are determined to
an extent by family and cultural values or standards. These and other possible
reasons make the defining and examination of social and emotional development a challenging undertaking.

Social and emotional development and competence are clearly connected;
however, we as well as others believe that social and emotional development and
outcomes represent distinct though overlapping areas of behavioral functioning.
Grappling with definitional problems associated with social and emotional behavior has concerned a number of important contributors to developmental psychology (Campos, Mumme, Kermoina, & Campos, 1994; Emde, Korfmacher,
& Kubicek, 2000; Sroufe, 1996; Thompson, 1994). A review of this work suggests that the areas of social and emotional development can be usefully (although artificially) separated, with the understanding that overlap exists between
these two very connected domains.

In addition to defining and understanding early social and emotional development, it is important to appreciate the concept of emotional regulation.
The regulation of emotional responses is paramount to the development of
healthy, satisfying and acceptable social emotional behavior.

Defining Emotions, Social
Development, and Emotional Regulation

Three major concepts are addressed next: social development and competence,
emotions, and emotional regulation. As noted earlier, many writers have com-
mented on the difficulty of defining the areas of social competence and emotions and of arriving at a consensus concerning these concepts. In fact, many
writers carefully note that the concept of emotion, in particular, is complex and
multifaceted (Dodge & Garber, 1991; Thompson, 1994). Keeping these definitional challenges in mind, this section offers a brief examination of emotions,
social development, and emotional regulation.

Emotions   Numerous definitions of emotions and emotional behavior have been offered (Dodge, 1991; Witherington, Campos, & Hertenstein,
2001). For example, Sroufe defined emotion as ". . . subjective reaction to a
salient event, characterized by physiological, experiential, and overt behavioral
change" (1996, p.15). Sroufe also pointed out: "Regardless of focus or theoretical orientation, virtually all investigators of emotion emphasize that emotions
must be viewed as complex transactions with the environment" (p. 12).

Dodge and Garber (1991) underlined the complexity of defining emotion
by describing three systems that may be involved in emotional responding:

- Neurophysiological–biochemical

- Cognitive–subjective–experiential

- Motor–behavioral–expressive

That is, an emotional response may involve activation of a biological system (e.g., increased heart rate), cognitive processing (e.g., remembered previous fear), and a behavioral reaction (e.g., facial change). Dodge stressed the inseparability of emotion from cognitive functioning.

Using a functional orientation, Witherington, Campos, and Hertenstein referred to emotions as ". . . the processes by which an individual attempts to establish, change, or maintain his or her relation to the environment on matters of significance to the person" (2001, p. 429). These writers stressed that the difference between emotional and nonemotional responding is the "value, importance, or relevance" of the environmental encounter for the child or adult—that is, "what is potentially damaging or beneficial to oneself is emotional; what is routine is not" (p. 430). The functional perspective held by Witherington and colleagues (2001) emphasizes the concept of relational meaning. The type of exchange between person and event and the meaning attributed to the event is the basis for emotional responding. This phenomenon explains why different events can produce the same emotion or why the same event can produce different emotions across time, people, and settings. It is the relational meaning assigned to the event that will or will not produce an emotional response.

Thus, it seems that emotions are subjective reactions (i.e., the individual assigns meaning) that occur in response to an internal or external triggering event. The interpretation (i.e., assigning meaning) of the event by the individual requires at least some cognitive activity and most likely previous history. Emotional responses can be both overt (e.g., crying) and internal (e.g., increasing blood pressure) and can change over time depending on environmental support and feedback. For example, around 9 to 11 months of age, most infants and toddlers display a fear reaction to strange adults who they may encounter. A stranger's approach may cause a child to turn her head, cry, and flee to a familiar caregiver. For most children, the fear of strangers disappears or at least dissipates as caregivers use a variety of strategies to reassure children (i.e., environmental support and feedback). A caregiver may approach the strange adult, indicating to the child that the stranger is acceptable, and/or the caregiver may soothe the child by talking or touching while approaching the stranger. Over time, as children encounter strangers, they reduce and usually eliminate their crying or fleeing responses and replace them with more adaptive responses such as verbal exchanges and/or wariness. Thus, over time, children's internal and overt responses can change in relation to the triggering event, such as a stranger.

It is important to note that environmental feedback may also result in a child maintaining an emotional response. A toddler who laughs at incongruity and whose social environment supports the response (e.g., caregivers also laugh) may continue to do so throughout life. Thus, over time the emotional development of most children becomes more psychologically based—that is, more meaning based. In addition, emotions become more specific rather than global, and more complex. Finally, emotional reactions become more precise rather than diffuse.

The challenge associated with the evolution of emotional responding in children is to become emotionally competent. *Emotional competence* has been defined as the ability to effectively regulate emotions to accomplish one's goals (Campos et al., 1994). Therefore, to be emotionally competent, children should have developed a range of emotional responses that they can manage and modulate to produce desired outcomes and adjustments satisfying to themselves and to their social environments.

Social Development and Competence As with emotions, social development and responding is complex and multifaceted. Child development textbooks (e.g., Berk, 2003; Landy, 2002) place a range of specific developmental phenomena and constructs under the general rubric of social development. These phenomena and constructs can include attachment, temperament, self-image, self-control or behavioral regulation, empathy, social interactions, morality, and social knowledge (e.g., gender). Attempts to coordinate this range of important developmental constructs into more global and cohesive descriptions have engendered definitions such as the one suggested by Wittmer, Doll, and Strain, "Social development is composed of the behaviors, attitudes, and affect integral to a child's interaction with adult and peers" (1996, p. 301). Along a similar vein, Raver and Zigler (1997) defined social competence as an array of behaviors that permits one to develop and engage in positive interactions with peers, siblings, parents, and other adults. These and similar definitions often encompass some but clearly not all the phenomena and constructs listed previously; the deficiencies likely reflect the challenge of developing a comprehensive and meaningful definition of social development.

As we noted earlier, it is a relatively artificial exercise to parse social and emotional development into separate areas, even when overlap is noted. In addition, the younger the child, the more difficult it is to separate social and emotional developmental phenomena. When concepts such as self-image and temperament are addressed, the distinction becomes even more blurred. Nevertheless, it seems useful to examine the unfolding of social development apart from emotions.

The areas in social development may include 1) responding to and initiating interactions between caregivers, siblings, other adults, and peers; 2) meeting physical and social needs; 3) participating in cooperative and social activities; 4) managing behavior and resolving conflict; 5) knowing about self and others; 6) showing empathy; and 7) developing self-image and self-worth. Initially, infants demonstrate only reflexive or rudimentary responding in these areas; however, ongoing transactions with their social environment produce significant change over time. Preschoolers who are typically developing can

- Manage peer and adult interactions

- Generally meet their own needs

- Successfully participate in a range of home and community activities

- Accurately report information about self and others

- Show appropriate empathic reactions

- Demonstrate a well-developed sense of self

In other words, at this age, preschoolers are becoming socially competent.

Similar to the evolution of increasingly differentiated and sophisticated emotions based on environmental feedback (i.e., deriving relational meaning), so too does social behavior become increasingly mature. The systematic differentiation and integration of social behavior leads to successive qualitative reorganizations that permit children to cope with increasingly complex needs and transactions. One-year-old babies may observe the behavior of other infants, and may, if given the opportunity, physically explore other children, but they do not display the ability to "play" jointly with toys. If given sufficient opportunity to interact with siblings and peers, toddlers will display early signs of rudimentary interactive play. For example, toddlers may chase or be chased by older children and may snatch desired toys from other toddlers. From 24 to 36 months, most toddlers can successfully engage in parallel play. That is, they can engage in separate play activities but within clear view of each other. By the time they are 3 years old, if given adequate experience, most children can engage in social or interactive play in which the sharing and coordination of responses occurs (e.g., two children run their small cars in and out of toy garage).

Thus, social development spans a range of related and yet quite different phenomena. Nurturing and supportive social environments help children to acquire increasingly satisfying and successful strategies to interact with others, to meet needs, and to develop a healthy self-image. Intertwined with and fundamental to social and emotional development is emotion regulation. The development of emotion regulation is discussed next.

Emotion Regulation   Not surprisingly, defining emotion regulation has proven as challenging as defining emotion. Thompson (1994) noted that many developmental specialists "may 'know' emotion regulation when they see it," but trying to capture the phenomena in words presents a difficult task. An early definition was formulated by Kopp: "Emotion regulation (ER) is the term used to characterize the processes and the characteristics involved in coping with heightened levels of positive and negative emotions including joy, pleasure, distress, anger, fear, and other emotions" (1989, p. 343).

She further suggests that three foundational principles underlie emotional regulation. Emotional regulation involves an action system or behavioral scheme, is adaptive, can be activated by different mechanisms, and requires external support in young children.

Thompson has proposed a similar but more inclusive definition: "Emotion regulation consists of the extrinsic and intrinsic processes responsible for monitoring, evaluating, and modifying emotional reactions, especially their intensive and temporal features, to accomplish one's goals" (1994, p. 27–28). Thompson highlighted five features of this definition. First, emotional regulation not only dampens responses but also may enhance and maintain emotional responding. Second, emotional regulation is managed by the self and by the social context in which the response occurs. Third, emotion regulation is particularly focused on intensity and temporal features of a response. Fourth, emotion regulation is associated with reaching personal goals. Fifth and finally, Thompson noted that, "Emotion regulation does not refer to a unitary phenomenon but is rather a broad conceptual rubric encompassing a range of loosely related processes" (1994, p. 30).

The separation of emotion and emotion regulation can only occur at the conceptual level. In effect, regulation or dysregulation cannot occur unless a child produces an emotional response. Emotional regulation usually modulates the immediacy and intensity of an emotion. For example, if another preschool child takes a toy away from 3-year-old Todd and he appears to evaluate this event as meaningful (i.e., he does not disregard or ignore losing the toy and thereby obviate an emotional response), he may respond in anger (i.e., an emotion). The rapidity and the intensity of the response is a function, at least in part, of Todd's emotional regulation processes. If Todd responds verbally in a loud voice, saying something like "Don't do that!" his anger response will likely be considered appropriate (i.e., well regulated). On the other hand, if Todd hits and bites the offending child, the anger response may be considered poorly regulated. Of course, it is essential when evaluating emotional regulation to appreciate the child's goals (e.g., to retrieve the toy) and the broader social context in which the emotional responses occur. For example, if the offending child had repeatedly snatched toys from Todd all morning or if the child was considerably older and taunted Todd as the toys were taken, a heightened (i.e., more rapid and more intense) anger response might be seen as, if not appropriate, at least acceptable. Of course, the anger response will not occur at all if Todd is uninterested in retrieving the toy.

Witherington and colleagues emphasized that emotion regulation is a complex process that cannot be understood apart from the function that the response plays for the individual as well as the social context in which the emotion occurs. As these authors noted, "The emotion system is inherently regulatory, and to study it we must look at the functional relationship between person and environment" (2001, p. 456). To understand emotion and its regulation, these authors believe that it is essential to understand what a child is trying to do (i.e., his or her goals); it is only by evaluating the child's goals and his or her social context that emotions and their regulation can be understood. Examples are offered in Table 3.2 and are also described next.

When confronted with an event a child evaluates as joyful (e.g., playing Pat-a-Cake with mom), the child's goal may be to maintain the interaction, whereas when confronted with an interaction a child evaluates as fearful (e.g.,

Table 3.2. Emotion regulation in a young child

Event	Child's reaction	Child's likely goal
Playing Pat-a-Cake with Mom	Joy	Maintain the interaction
Approach of an unfamiliar adult	Fear	Seek comfort, reassurance

the approach of an unfamiliar adult), the child's goal may be to make the situation change. The regulation of the fear response will be related to the larger social context. A child may be able to regulate her fear response to an unfamiliar adult if the child can flee to a trusted parent, whereas confronting an unfamiliar adult without having the perceived safety of a parent nearby may produce a less well-regulated fear reaction (e.g., crying, hiding).

These relatively brief descriptions of emotions, social development, and emotional regulation are included for two purposes. First, these descriptions should clarify the contents of this book. That is, the approach is designed to address problems or potential problems in the social emotional area. Second, these descriptions should help to clarify the nature of emotional and social development and their interrelationship to each other and to other critical areas of development as well (e.g., cognitive, communication, adaptive areas).

Social and Emotional Learning Model

A model of how we believe social and emotional learning occurs and thus how social and emotional development proceeds is presented in Figure 3.2. This illustration focuses on emotional responding but is equally applicable for social development. At the far left of the figure is a box that represents the internal condition or external antecedent event that elicits or triggers a reaction from the child. Internal conditions refer to a rise in blood pressure or thirst for example, whereas external events might be seeing a dog or falling on the floor. If the antecedent event crosses the child's sensory or input threshold and is processed, a reaction can occur. The reaction can be internal (e.g., the heart rate increases), external (e.g., face shows fear), or both. Initially, children have available a range of short-term or immediate response options.

In Figure 3.2, four different types of response options are listed: a) functional and appropriate, b) functional but inappropriate, c) chaotic, and d) nonfunctional and inappropriate. The following examples illustrate these options.

When Lea falls and calls a caregiver for help, this response can be both functional (i.e., help will likely be forthcoming) and appropriate (i.e., it is a socially acceptable way to seek assistance). Furthermore, it is likely that the "seeking help" response will be acceptable in the long term because Lea has adopted a response that will bring needed attention in a socially acceptable manner.

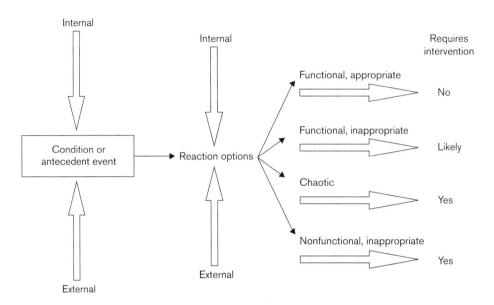

Figure 3.2. A model of social and emotional learning. An internal condition or external antecedent may elicit a reaction from a child that possesses characteristics of functionality and appropriateness.

If, after falling, Paul screams loudly and repeatedly, this response will likely be functional (draws assistance from the caregiver) but inappropriate (in all but the most dire cases it is not socially acceptable to scream for help). If Paul persists in screaming in situations in which he needs assistance, the long-term effect is generally unacceptable.

Jensena produces an array of disorganized, chaotic responses after falling. She alternates between laughing and crying, sometimes but not always calls a caregiver, and sometimes waits before seeking help. Thus, Jensena does not learn consistent functional and appropriate strategies for seeking assistance. In the long term, this inconsistency is likely to be unacceptable.

Annette, after falling, gets up and hits a peer or adult. This response is neither functional (i.e., does not elicit help) nor appropriate, thus making it unacceptable to her social environment in the long term.

Parent responses, too, determine both short- and long-term outcomes for children. If a parent continually fails to respond to an infant's cries, the infant may stop making bids for attention and may turn to self-stimulation actions. If an infant's cries are instead met with adult screaming and an occasional slap across the face, the infant may stop making eye contact with adults and cease looking to adults for soothing and vocal interactions. As children learn to habituate emotional responses to events and conditions, they can develop repertoires that are generally self-satisfying as well as acceptable to their social community or they can learn responses that produce trouble for them personally as well as difficulty for their social milieu (e.g., family life, school). If this paradigm is correct, the importance of learning functional and appropriate social and emotional response options is evident. If nonfunctional and inappropriate responses are allowed to persist, the child will likely suffer as will those who interact with him or her.

SUMMARY

This learning model, based on transactional and organizational principles of children's interactions with their environments, has important implications for the prevention and early intervention of social and emotional problems. Getting a child started on the right track should be the first priority. This entails encouraging functional and appropriate responding and reducing or eliminating responses that are in the long run personally and socially unacceptable. Further implications of this model are addressed in Section II.

II

The Activity-Based Intervention: Social Emotional Approach

From Screening to Evaluation

4

Overview of the Activity-Based Intervention: Social Emotional Approach

ection I provides the reader with three types of foundational information: the theory and principles that assist in understanding and appreciating social emotional development and regulation in young children, the importance of social emotional development and regulation in the lives of young children and their families, and the need for prevention and intervention efforts to address the growing numbers of young children whose mental health status may be in jeopardy. This important background information is offered to assist the reader in coming to understand and, if appropriate, to use the Activity-Based Intervention: Social Emotional (ABI:SE) Approach described in this chapter.

The name ABI:SE was selected for the approach to reflect its procedures and the content focus. Activity-based intervention refers to an intervention procedure that relies on integrating teaching and change efforts into the daily routines and activities (e.g., dressing, eating, playing) of children's and caregiver's lives (Pretti-Frontczak & Bricker, 2004). Activity-based intervention makes use of children's interests and motivation to promote the acquisition of needed developmental skills.

The ABI:SE Approach incorporates the elements of activity-based intervention with a particular content focus on social emotional development. The content of this approach is primarily directed to behaviors and responses that compose the social emotional competence of young children. However, as noted in Chapter 3, the complete separation of social emotional development from social-communication, cognitive, and adaptive domains is neither possible nor desirable.

The social emotional content for the ABI:SE Approach is derived from, and guided by, a set of key social emotional benchmarks. These key benchmarks address areas of great importance to the mental health well-being of young children. The benchmarks that provide the content focus for the ABI:SE Approach are described later in this chapter.

The ABI:SE Approach was designed especially for use by parents, caregivers, home visitors, teachers, and other child care personnel. Rather than re-

41

quiring mental health experts, the ABI:SE Approach relies on the adults and others (e.g., peers) who participate with children in their daily living activities. Intervention efforts are integrated with, or mapped onto, routine activities by the very individuals who share these activities with children. The success of this pragmatic approach is heightened because children can be provided with consistent, effective, therapeutic interventions by those who share their social milieu on a daily basis (Neisworth & Bagnato, 2004).

The ABI:SE Approach focuses not on determining a diagnosis or establishing an etiology but on what those who interact with children can do to ensure or improve the social emotional competence of their young charges. It is, of course, essential to determine the nature of children's problems or to uncover deficiencies in their environment so that effective interventions can be formulated. To that end, the focus of assessment in this approach is on targeting goals that will improve, directly or indirectly, children's social emotional adjustments rather than on determining or describing the etiological roots of the problem(s).

Another emphasis of the ABI:SE Approach is on prevention. We are convinced that early intervention is essential to the development of positive and appropriate social and emotional behavior. For many caregivers (perhaps the majority), providing caring, supportive interactions occurs "naturally." That is, caregivers are able to provide safe, nurturing environments for infants and young children in their care. However, not all caregivers are able to provide physically or emotionally safe environments, nor are they able to provide the necessary stimulation and feedback for their infants and young children to learn appropriate social behavior. Without early identification and intervention, habituated or ingrained social emotional problems may develop in young children (Bricker, Schoen Davis, & Squires, 2004). To address serious social emotional problems frequently means high-cost interventions that may not be available and, if available, they may have limited success. It is much easier, less costly, and more successful to assist caregivers in developing and maintaining healthy, supportive, nurturing, dyadic relationships early in children's lives than it is to "fix" relationships that are and have been troubled for months or years (Walker et al., 1998).

As noted previously, the procedures associated with the ABI:SE Approach are adopted from activity-based intervention, whereas the content focuses on the social emotional area. The linked system that provides the framework for the ABI:SE Approach is discussed next.

FRAMEWORK FOR THE APPROACH

The ABI:SE Approach is situated in the larger linked system framework that has been described in detail elsewhere (e.g., Bricker & Cripe, 1992; Pretti-Frontczak & Bricker, 2004). The linked system is presented in Figure 4.1 and is composed of five distinct processes: screening, assessment, goal development, intervention, and evaluation. Although the processes are distinct, the information generated by each process is directly related or relevant to the subsequent

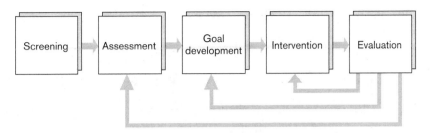

Figure 4.1. Five processes of the linked system framework and their relationship to each other.

process. That is, screening outcomes are directly relevant to assessment and the outcomes from assessment are directly relevant to goal development, whereas goal development, in turn, drives intervention efforts. Finally, the evaluation process is critical to determining the effectiveness of the previous assessment, goal development, and intervention processes. The relationship between processes is depicted in Figure 4.1 by the connecting arrows. These five processes provide a comprehensive context that should help to ensure an efficient and effective approach.

The linked system shown in Figure 4.1 provides a broad framework for the ABI:SE Approach that requires further expansion and refinement to make it applicable to the area of social emotional development. Figure 4.2 illustrates how the linked systems framework has been adapted to guide the ABI:SE Approach. The screening, assessment, goal development, intervention, and evaluation processes that compose the linked system framework appear in Figure 4.2 with arrows showing the relationship between the linked system processes and the processes that compose the ABI:SE Approach. As dictated by the linked system framework, each process in the ABI:SE Approach is directly related to the

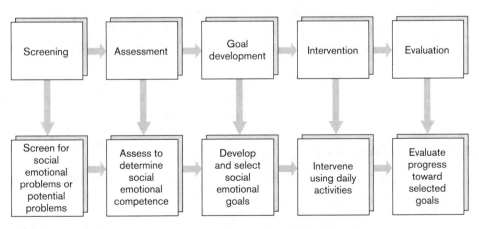

Figure 4.2. The relationship between the linked system framework and the ABI:SE Approach.

subsequent process. The ABI:SE processes shown at the bottom of Figure 4.2 include:

- Screen for social emotional problems or potential problems

- Assess to determine social emotional competence

- Develop and select social emotional goals

- Intervene using daily activities

- Evaluate progress toward selected goals

Screening

As shown in Figures 4.1 and 4.2, screening is the initial step or process of the ABI:SE Approach as well as for the broader linked system framework. In the ABI:SE Approach, screening can be thought of as taking a quick snapshot of the child to determine if further, more comprehensive evaluation is necessary. Children whose performance suggests a delay or problem are referred for more in-depth assessment designed to generate information directly relevant to goal development (e.g., the Social Emotional Assessment/Evaluation Measure (SEAM), described later in this volume).

Once social emotional goals are formulated, intervention efforts can begin, followed by periodic evaluation of children's and caregiver's progress toward selected goals.

Assessment

In both the linked system framework and the ABI:SE Approach, the second process is assessment directed toward gathering information that is relevant to goal development and intervention efforts. In most cases this requires administering a curriculum-based measure. The assessment process associated with the ABI:SE Approach entails the use of a curriculum-based measure that was developed specifically for this approach and is described in Chapter 6. The content of the assessment measure was chosen specifically to focus on the area of social emotional development. Having outcomes from a curriculum-based measure is essential to developing functional, appropriate, and important developmental goals and intervention targets that can be integrated into daily activities (Neisworth & Bagnato, 2004; Pretti-Frontczak & Bricker, 2004).

Goal Development

Parents or other primary caregivers should be intimately involved in goal development, the third process, to ensure that family desires and values are addressed. Selected social emotional goals should drive intervention efforts. Goals that are unimportant, inappropriate, nonfunctional, or that violate family values will lead intervention efforts astray and will likely result in little progress. It is, therefore, imperative to administer an assessment that will yield outcomes that can be used directly to develop functional goals and objectives.

Intervention

Intervention is the fourth process in the ABI:SE Approach and refers to activities offered to caregivers and children that address the selected social emotional goals developed during the previous goal development process. In the ABI:SE Approach, intervention efforts are mapped onto the many daily activities that occur in the lives of children and their caregivers. For example, if a selected goal is to increase the dyadic interaction between a mother and her infant, intervention efforts can focus on helping the mother learn to use diapering, feeding, bathing, and travel time activities to initiate interactions with her infant.

Evaluation

The final process, evaluation, is essential to understanding if intervention efforts are producing desired outcomes. For example, caregivers and child responses are measured on selected social emotional goals prior to intervention, and then are monitored consistently throughout intervention. The information gleaned from evaluating the targeted caregiver and child responses is used to adjust, as necessary, the assessment, goal development, and intervention processes.

The following section discusses the target populations for whom the ABI:SE Approach is intended. These groups include children with disabilities and children who are at risk for acquiring social emotional problems.

THE TARGET POPULATION OF THE APPROACH

As we noted in earlier chapters, the ABI:SE Approach is appropriate for use with two different (but often overlapping) populations of young children and their families. The first group is composed of children who are eligible to receive Individuals with Disabilities Education Act (IDEA) Amendments of 1997 (PL 105-17) services either under Part B or C. Before receiving services, state agencies require, for the most part, that children participate in a formal assessment process to determine if they meet established criteria for early intervention or early childhood special education services (Danaher & Armijo, 2004). This group of children is targeted because a number of studies have reported that the prevalence of young children with disabilities who also have social emotional problems is significantly higher than for typically developing children (Bricker et al., 2004; Squires, Bricker, Heo, & Twombly, 2001).

The second target population is children considered to be at risk for developing serious social emotional problems (e.g., children in foster care). Some of the children in this group show early signs that indicate potential social emotional problems if action (i.e., change or intervention) is not taken. A toddler who is excessively shy or the preschooler who bites or hits other children on occasion are examples of children who may develop more serious problems if timely change or intervention does not occur. The other children who compose the risk group are those who live in environments that do not provide adequate safety, nurturing, and/or stimulation. For example, children who live in homes with domestic violence or who suffer neglect may also develop serious social emotional problems if change or intervention is not forthcoming. This group is also targeted because they show a higher prevalence of social emotional problems than children from nonrisk groups.

Young children for whom the ABI:SE Approach is NOT appropriate are those who have serious social emotional or behavioral problems such as children with autism or psychiatric disorders, or those who commit serious acts of aggression (e.g., setting fires, inflicting bodily harm). Children with serious social emotional problems require mental health experts to diagnosis the problem and develop and deliver therapeutic interventions. The ABI:SE Approach was developed for use by early interventionists, early childhood teachers, caregivers, and other personnel who do not have extensive training in mental health or counseling. Therefore, this approach should only be used with children who show mild problems or the potential to develop social emotional problems.

For the disability and risk groups, screening is an essential first step to determine which of the children require more comprehensive social emotional assessment. Given the prevalence levels of social emotional problems in young children with disabilities, we recommend that all of these children undergo social emotional screening. Risk groups tend to include large numbers of children and most agencies or programs have limited resources that may require that screening is provided only to children who meet preset criteria (e.g., exposure to abuse, teen parent, depressed parent).

The assessment process is also essential for the disability and risk groups. In most cases, children who are assigned to the disability group must qualify for services. Qualification usually requires that children undergo a formal diagnostic assessment to ascertain if they meet eligibility guidelines for IDEA services. Assessing to determine a diagnosis of eligibility is undertaken separately from the ABI:SE Approach and is not part of its assessment process. Rather, the ABI:SE assessment process is focused on administering a curriculum-based measure that produces information that is directly relevant to developing quality social emotional goals and intervention content.

Paying attention to situational context and/or recent traumatic events occurring in the life of the child is critical in deciding the utility of the ABI:SE Approach. For example, if a toddler or preschooler has just witnessed a violent crime in their neighborhood, their behavior following that will most likely display signs of this intense experience. The child may be clingier, highly sensitive to loud noises, and possibly agitated if other children or adults get too close to her. These behaviors may be manifestations of the recent trauma and it is key to pay close attention and provide a safe and secure environment for this child to process her emotional turmoil. It is important that the caregiver and interventionists involved in the child's life discuss this event and pay careful attention to see whether these behaviors change and lessen as time goes on or if more intensive intervention is necessary. Paying attention to factors of duration and intensity of behaviors and observing the child in both the school and home environments will provide an important view into the emotional world of that child. If symptoms do not seem to change within a reasonable amount of time, the caregiver and staff may decide to make a referral for additional, more intensive services.

Sometimes, however, it is necessary to refer a child for mental health services immediately and not wait to see if symptoms will change or lessen. Such characteristics of conditions that would require intervention by a mental health expert include behaviors that present a danger to the child and/or those around him. Another example may be a parent–child relationship issue. If a parent is unable to read her infant's cues and, as a result, does not attend to the child's needs of comfort and care, and the child is at risk for physical and emotional problems, additional expertise would be necessary. If a depressed parent repeatedly seeks comfort from her infant, actively seeking out caregiving behavior from her child, again a referral may be in order (DC: 0–3, Zero to Three, 1995).

In addition, it is crucial to be aware that if more mild, commonly occurring social emotional behaviors occur in young children, and the ABI:SE Approach is followed with little improvement in the child's ability to function and properly develop, consulting with a mental health expert may be the logical next step. Often, issues or concerns in a child's social emotional development and/or the child's relationship with primary caregivers can be identified and ameliorated through using the ABI:SE Approach. It is critical, though, to pay close attention to and engage in ongoing assessment and observation of the child and the parent–child relationship to see if further, more intense intervention is needed.

Becoming aware of and building connections with local mental health providers in the community, especially those with expertise and knowledge in early childhood development, is an important activity for early childhood professionals. Building collaboration and partnerships with key mental health experts is critical for professionals' ongoing growth and also for the benefit of the children and families being served.

The following section addresses the content focus of the ABI:SE Approach. The targeted social emotional content is derived from a set of key social emotional benchmarks culled from the literature on social emotional development in young children.

CONTENT FOCUS OF THE APPROACH

The social emotional content focus of the ABI:SE Approach is based on a set of key child and adult/caregiver benchmarks. These benchmarks were derived from the vast literature on social emotional development of young children being raised in a western culture. We extracted from the literature those concepts that were repeatedly labeled by experts in the field as essential or as critically important to the mental health competence of young children and then formulated them into benchmarks to guide assessment and intervention efforts.

Table 4.1. Child and adult/caregiver benchmarks that provide the content focus for ABI:SE assessment items and intervention activities

Child benchmarks

 1. Child demonstrates healthy interactions with others.

 2. Child expresses a range of emotions.

 3. Child regulates social emotional responses.

 4. Child shows empathy for others.

 5. Child shares attention and engagement.

 6. Child demonstrates independence.

 7. Child displays a positive self-image.

 8. Child regulates attention and activity level.

 9. Child complies with requests and demands.

10. Child shows a range of adaptive skills.

Adult/caregiver benchmarks

 1. Caregiver provides safe home and play environment.

 2. Caregiver provides predictable schedules/routines.

 3. Caregiver is responsive.

 4. Caregiver provides appropriate type and level of activity.

The benchmarks we have targeted are likely not inclusive; however, we believe that they encompass many (perhaps most) of the critical social emotional behaviors that should be encouraged in children as well as identifying the critical caregiver benchmarks.

Table 4.1 presents the basic benchmarks that underlie the content of the ABI:SE Approach. The benchmarks address three developmental levels expressed in age ranges: 3–18 months, 18–36 months, and 36–63 months. Each benchmark is operationalized by one or more assessment items. These items are presented and discussed in detail in Chapter 6 (see Tables 6.1–6.3).

Child Benchmarks

The first child social emotional benchmark addresses the need for young children to develop a range of healthy relationships with caregivers and siblings or other children. Children must learn to trust and enjoy interactions with their caregivers—at least some of the time—if they are to develop social emotional competence. Healthy relationships likely incorporate a considerable range of options, but at a minimum the concept refers to interactions that result in positive growth in children.

The second benchmark focuses on the need for children to express a range of emotions. Infants should be able to show different emotions (e.g., laughing, crying, fear). Toddlers should be able to express a range of emotions through both verbal and nonverbal means and preschoolers should be able to accurately label their emotions, and, of course, they may express their emotions nonverbally as well. Although the form of expression may change as children get older, they should be able to indicate a variety of emotions at each stage of development, including anger, fear, and joy.

In addition to expressing a range of emotions, it is essential that children learn how to regulate or modulate their social emotional responses, the third child benchmark. For example, most infants are initially poor at managing crying. They may cry loudly for an extended period and only cease crying with exhaustion and sleep. Most babies learn to control their crying after a few months and most toddlers and preschoolers can quickly regulate their crying or other emotions even when hurt. Children must learn to regulate their emotional responses if they are to develop social emotional competence.

A social expectation for most children is that they can respond appropriately to the emotions of other adults and children; therefore, the fourth benchmark is that children can show empathy for others. The social referencing research finds that even infants can, and do, respond to their caregivers' emotions. Empathy for others can be displayed by toddlers and is present in most preschoolers, and showing a lack of empathy by preschool age is generally an indicator of social emotional disturbance.

The fifth benchmark, *Child shares attention and engagement,* reflects another constellation of behaviors essential for social emotional competence. Although the quality of the attention and engagement changes with development, even infants should be able to attend to events highlighted by caregivers and they should be able to engage in the event or activity for at least some minimal time. Children who have difficulty with shared attention and engagement are likely children whose social emotional competence is in jeopardy.

By age 3, children should demonstrate early stages of independence, which is the sixth benchmark. It is important to note that the roots of independence can be encouraged during the period of later infancy. Autonomy or independence can be displayed in many ways, such as a child taking responsibility for completing a task. Lack of autonomy by age 3 is a sign that a child's social emotional development is not typical.

Children's self-image, made up of the thoughts and feelings they have about themselves, is critical to social emotional competence and is the focus of the seventh benchmark. A child who frequently and consistently evaluates her performance and worth as "poor" may be a child in need of help. It is difficult to have a positive view of others if one's self-image is negative and wanting. Children need to have optimistic views about their worth and their competence if they are to be mentally healthy.

The eighth benchmark focuses on a children's ability to regulate attention and activity level. Caregivers and other adults generally expect that by age 3 to 4, children should be able to successfully manage their attention. That is, when asked to attend to an event or task, a child will able to do so most of the time. Most 3-year-olds can sit and listen to a story being read without fidgeting and getting up. In concert with attention is the regulation of activity level, so while listening to the story, a 3-year-old should also be able to sit still (more or less). Preschool children who have difficulty sustaining attention and regulating their activity level to match environmental expectations are children whose social emotional competence is at risk.

Children's ability to comply with requests and demands is the ninth benchmark. Even very young children should be able to inhibit at least some of their behavior when told to stop doing something. As children grow older they need to learn how to follow rules and directions both at home and in other settings. Children who have difficulty complying with reasonable requests and demands are likely to have significant adjustment problems.

The final child benchmark addresses children's need to engage in a range of adaptive skills for their own welfare as well as for the welfare of those around them. Children who have eating, sleeping, and/or elimination problems that persist over time are likely to be troubled children in need of intervention.

Adult/Caregiver Benchmarks

The first adult/caregiver benchmark focuses on the need for young children to have a safe home and play environment. Because they are less self-sufficient and more vulnerable, infants and toddlers have a far greater need for protection than do preschoolers; however, even preschoolers must be protected from an array of potentially dangerous objects and situations (e.g., ingesting poisons, running into the street). Although children must be protected, it is important that they have frequent opportunities to explore a range of settings so they can enrich both their cognitive and motor repertoires. Children left in cribs or playpens for extended periods have little opportunity to explore and learn about their environment.

The second benchmark is separate from but closely associated with child safety. Children who reside in homes that lack safety precautions may also experience conditions that offer little, if any, predictability. Meals may occur at odd times or not at all, naps and bedtimes may fluctuate dramatically as might the attention children receive from their caregivers. Chaotic days that lack predictable schedules are difficult for young children to manage, and may lead to the development of negative emotional responses. Children's lives do not have to be rigidly scheduled but they do require some minimal predictability in order to thrive emotionally.

Children may develop relatively unscathed when exposed to chaotic days if they interact consistently with responsive caregivers, the third benchmark. A caregiver who is responsive to a young child's needs may, in effect, provide some predictability even if the other conditions in the child's life remain relatively unstable. Few conditions supersede the importance of caregivers who consistently provide comfort, support, and encouragement to young children. The mental health of children raised by non-nurturing caregivers is surely at risk.

The fourth caregiver benchmark is focused on caregiver's providing appropriate type and level of activity. Caregivers should provide children with toys and materials that are appropriate for their developmental level as well as engage them in simple games that can become more sophisticated as children mature.

The content embodied in these key social emotional benchmarks has, in turn, been translated into a series of assessment items that constitute the ABI:SE curriculum-based assessment measure. This assessment, called the Social Emotional Assessment/Evaluation Measure (SEAM), is described in Chapter 6 and the actual SEAM is provided in Appendix B at the end of the book and on the accompanying CD-ROM. This measure is designed to generate the necessary information to develop functional, appropriate and important social emotional goals that can be integrated into the daily activities of infants, toddlers, and preschool-age children.

The next section provides a further discussion of the five processes that compose the ABI:SE Approach. Specifically, the steps associated with each process are described.

Purpose and Steps of the Processes

A further expansion of the ABI:SE linked system approach is contained in Figure 4.3. Under each of the five processes are listed the purpose as well as the steps required to meet the stated purpose. The purpose and steps subsumed by each process are discussed briefly in this section, whereas subsequent chapters provide extensive descriptions of each process and how they are conducted in the ABI:SE Approach.

As noted in Figure 4.3, the purpose of screening is to identify children who may have potential social emotional problems. Screening large groups of children and their environments efficiently requires measures that can be completed quickly and accurately and at low cost. Parent-completed measures such as the ASQ:SE and the Environmental Screening Questionnaire (ESQ), which is described in Chapter 5 and included in Appendix A at the end of the book and on the accompnaying CD-ROM, are particularly useful in meeting these criteria. Results from the screening process are used to classify children and environments into two groups: those children and environments that appear stable and positive (i.e., do not appear to have behaviors or deficiencies that could lead to the development of social emotional problems) and those children and environments that do not appear stable and positive. Children who fall into the latter group should be referred for a more comprehensive social emotional assessment.

In Figure 4.3, assessment refers to the administration of a curriculum-based assessment (CBA) to determine children's social emotional strengths and needs. The SEAM was designed to meet this purpose by yielding outcomes that are directly relevant for formulating goals. As indicated in Figure 4.3, the information generated by this CBA permits the development of appropriate social emotional goals for children and their caregivers. To effectively drive or guide intervention efforts, goals should be important (e.g., *Child responds to familiar caregivers*), functional (e.g., *Child displays a range of appropriate emotions*), objective (i.e., target overt behaviors) (e.g., *Child does not cry excessively*), and developmentally appropriate (i.e., target goals that are at the skill level of the child).

Screening	Assessment	Goal Development	Intervention	Evaluation
	Social Emotional Behavior Profile ⇩			
Purpose: To identify children who may have social emotional problems	To determine social emotional strengths and needs	To write and prioritize appropriate social emotional goals	To implement intervention plan designed to address selected goals	To determine progress toward goals
⇩	⇩	⇩	⇩	⇩
Steps: • Administer screening test • Determine if further assessment is warranted • Refer as appropriate • Continue periodic screening/ monitoring • Conduct prevention activites as appropriate	• Administer social emotional curriculum-based measure • Analyze results to determine social emotional needs	• Develop social emotional goals that are functional, important, objective, and developmentally appropriate • Prioritize goals • Write intervention plan	• Select intervention activities to address selected goals • Embed opportunities to address goals in routine activities across the day	• Collect data on progress toward goals • Compare performance over time

Figure 4.3.   The purpose and major steps associated with the ABI:SE Approach: screening, assessment, goal development, intervention, and evaluation.

Once goals are developed and prioritized, intervention activities can be planned and implemented. Intervention efforts should be focused on addressing the goals that were selected for the child and family. Intervention should be woven into the families' daily routines and activities (e.g., bath time, meal time) in order to ensure that the intervention occurs under authentic (i.e., meaningful) conditions.

The final process shown in Figure 4.3 is evaluation, which refers to monitoring the child and family's progress toward selected goals. It is essential to determine if intervention efforts are producing desired outcomes if time and resources are to be used effectively and responsibly. Systematic evaluations can be accomplished by administering the CBA used during the assessment process. The CBA or selected items (i.e., goals) should be administered two to three times per year.

The following vignette offers an example of how the five linked processes (i.e., screening, assessment, goal development, intervention, and evaluation) function as a linked system.

José is a 1-year-old who lives in a home. His family has a history of domestic violence, which places him in a risk group that is monitored by the local child protection services agency. At his 12-month checkup, José's mother, Elaina, is asked to complete the ASQ:SE Questionnaire and the ESQ. Elaina speaks little English, so a staff member of child protection services assists her in completing the screening measures in Spanish. José's performance on the ASQ:SE is above the cut-off score, indicating the need for further assessment. In addition, the family's score on the ESQ indicates potential deficiencies or problems in the home. These findings require that José and his mother be referred to the local intervention program that serves young children at risk.

Staff of the home-visiting intervention program administer the Social Emotional Assessment/Evaluation Measure (SEAM): Infant to José's family with the help of José's mother. This assessment provides information on José's social emotional competence and the quality of his environment.

Based on the finding from the assessment, José and his mother qualify for services, and thus the next step is to formulate appropriate and functional social emotional goals for José.

Using information garnered from the SEAM, the interventionist and José's mother target five intervention goals. Once these goals are written, Elaina indicates the goals she considers most vital, thus guiding the intervention staff in the prioritizing of the selected goals. The majority of the intervention efforts will focus on the three goals that Elaina feels are most important:

1. *Remove or keep José from unsafe objects or home conditions.*

2. *Provide José at least three nutritious meals per day.*

3. *Encourage José to initiate and maintain interactions with familiar adults.*

Elaina and the interventionist agree to address the two remaining goals, which center on José's ability to display a range of emotions and interact with older peers, at a later time.

Based on the selected goals, the home visitor and Elaina develop an intervention plan. The plan focuses on assisting Elaina to find ways to make José's surroundings safer and to create a meal routine. In addition, the home visitor and Elaina discuss ways that the family's daily routines can be used to encourage social interactions with José. For example, the home visitor and Elaina talk about ways she can use diapering and meal times to promote José's social interactions.

After 3 months of intervention, the home visitor again completes the items on the SEAM that focus on the selected goals for José and Elaina. These results are compared with the initial assessment to ascertain if progress is being made. The findings indicate that José now lives in a home that is safe from dangerous objects and conditions and his social interactions with adults have increased. However, Elaina still has not been able to provide José with regularly scheduled, nutritious meals. Consequently, Goal 2 remains a target and requires some change in the home visitor's ap-

proach. In addition, the home visitor and Elaina add a new goal of assisting José to appropriately display a range of emotions. These findings emphasize the importance of ongoing evaluation in order to ensure that time and resources are being used effectively and wisely.

SUMMARY

This chapter has offered an overview of how to use the ABI:SE Approach. The approach's framework relies on a linked system in which the processes of screening, assessment, goal development, intervention, and evaluation are directly related. The content addressed by these five processes is provided by a set of key social emotional benchmarks that have been derived from the literature and research on social emotional development in young children.

The remaining chapters in this section provide detailed discussions of how each of these processes are implemented within the ABI:SE Approach.

5

Screening for
Social Emotional Problems

This chapter describes screening, the first process in the ABI:SE Approach. To begin, developmental screening and its outcomes are discussed. Next, the process of screening for social emotional problems is described, after which challenges related to screening and early identification are summarized. Standards for screening measures are then presented, and screening measures focused on determining the social emotional competence of young children and the quality of the child's environment are discussed. Environmental screening is addressed next. Finally, steps for screening using the ABI:SE Approach are presented.

DEVELOPMENTAL SCREENING
AND SCREENING OUTCOMES

Screening is a brief, formal evaluation of developmental skills intended to identify those children with potential problems who should be referred for a more in-depth assessment. Screening usually yields three child outcomes based on the child's performance score: 1) developmental status is typical, 2) developmental status is at risk, and 3) developmental status is questionable. On many social emotional measures that identify problem behaviors, children are classified as typical if their performance score is below the screening cutoff point. They are classified as at risk if their performance score is above the screening cutoff point. The screening process also may yield a questionable outcome for children whose performance scores fall into the range close to the cutoff point. For example, if the adaptive behavior area has a cutoff point of 32, children who score 31 and less may be considered *typical*, children who score 35 or above may be considered *at risk*, and children whose scores range from 30 to 34 may be considered

This chapter and the Environmental Screening Questionnaire (ESQ), Experimental Edition, were developed with the assistance of Hyeyoung Bae, Elizabeth Benedict, Jantina Clifford, Hollie Hix-Small, Mona Ivey-Soto, Karen Lawrence, Suzanne Bells McManus, Jin Ai No, Juli Pool, Deborah Russell, Helen Sharp, Hasnah Toran, and Jennifer Westover.

questionable and usually warrant careful follow-up monitoring. Screening does not yield a definitive diagnosis but rather should function as a first-level detection to indicate those children who need additional, more comprehensive assessment and evaluation (Nickel & Squires, 2000).

Empirical evidence supports the need for the ongoing developmental screening and early identification of children with general developmental delays (American Academy of Pediatrics Committee on Psychosocial Aspects of Child and Family Health, 2001; Bricker, 1989; Ramey & Ramey, 1998; Squires, Nickel, & Eisert, 1996). Through early identification and intervention, children's developmental trajectories can be improved (Filipek et al., 2000; Sameroff & Fiese, 2000), developmental outcomes maximized (Farran, 2000; Meisels & Fenichel, 1996), secondary conditions minimized (Dworkin, 2000; Liptak, 1996; Nickel & Desch, 2000), and parental support provided at a critical time (Kelly & Barnard, 2000; Turnbull, Turbiville, & Turnbull, 2000).

Recommendations for developmental screening include the use of formal screening tests with established validity and reliability (Glascoe, 1993; Nickel & Squires, 2000). Screening should be conducted at repeated intervals in order to identify problems as soon as they are apparent (American Academy of Pediatrics, 2006; American Academy of Pediatrics Committee on Psychosocial Aspects of Child and Family Health, 2001; Aylward, 1990; Filipek et al., 2000). In order to enhance the validity and reliability of the screening process, inclusion of parental input is recommended (American Academy of Pediatrics Committee on Psychosocial Aspects of Child and Family Health, 2001; Squires, Bricker, & Twombly, 2002; Squires, Potter, & Bricker, 1999). Other guidelines address the importance of cultural sensitivity of test items and cultural appropriateness of the screening process in general (American Psychological Association, 1985; Glascoe, 1991; Nickel & Squires, 2000).

Developmental screening has gained legitimacy since the 1970s and now is accepted as best practice, usually focusing on language, cognitive, motor, social, and adaptive areas. Until recently, little attention has been given to the area of social emotional development, however. The next section briefly discusses the advent of social emotional screening.

SOCIAL EMOTIONAL SCREENING

Since the mid-1990s, researchers and professionals in the fields of childhood mental health care and development have issued a call for early and ongoing screening for social emotional problems in addition to screening for general developmental delays (Shonkoff & Phillips, 2000; Zeanah, 2000). The importance of social emotional screening has been emphasized in part because of findings from brain imaging research that uses techniques such as magnetic resonance imaging (MRI) and positron emission tomography (PET). This work has shown effects of emotions on the developing brain and the consequent need for ongoing and systematic screening of social, emotional, and behavioral domains. For example, in a sample of mothers with depression, brain imaging research found that 40% of their children showed decreased brain activity, particularly in the areas of outwardly directed emotions such as joy, interest, and anger (Dawson, Frey, Panagiotides, Osterling, & Hessl, 1997). Brain imaging was also used to determine that mothers' substance abuse and smoking had an impact on the developing brains of their young children (Shore, 1997). Brain imaging research has allowed researchers to gather evidence that stresses the importance of a supportive and nurturing environment for optimal brain growth and development across the early childhood years (Cicchetti & Cohen, 2006; Shore, 1997).

Like developmental screening tools, acceptable social emotional screening tests use empirically derived cutoff scores to assist in decision making. For example, when scoring the ASQ:SE, problem behaviors such as tantrums and violent outbursts receive designated points, and all problem behavior scores are added together for a total score. High scores indicating accumulated problem behaviors on the ASQ:SE are indicative of potential social emotional difficulties.

Recommendations associated with screening in the social emotional area parallel those for general developmental areas, such as the systematic use of formal screening measures with established validity and reliability. Other requirements for effective screening include input from parents and other caregivers, cultural sensitivity, and behavior sampling across settings and adult caregivers (Squires et al., 2002). Because of the interdependence of behavioral and other developmental domains (Squires et al., 2002), the use of a developmental screening measure in addition to a social emotional measure is recommended. For example, a toddler may pinch her peers and/or pull their hair because she has poor expressive language skills and is therefore unable to make her needs known. Whereas a social emotional screening measure may identify her aggressive behaviors, a more comprehensive developmental screen may identify poor expressive communication skills. Information about children's performance across developmental areas is critical to designing appropriate follow-up evaluation.

Given the substantial need for social emotional screening, progress in this area has been slow. The next section addresses the challenges facing the development of accurate, reliable, and useful social emotional screening measures.

Early Screening Challenges

Screening for social emotional problems can be more challenging than screening for general developmental delays for four major reasons: 1) context, 2), individual tolerances and expectations, 3), difficulty in quantifying and measuring, and 4) the developmental nature of behaviors. Each is described in more detail next.

Context   First, social emotional problems are embedded in a context that defines their acceptability. For example, in a home in which regular schedules and quiet are emphasized, an infant who cries frequently may be perceived as fussy and irritable when, in fact, she may be responding appropriately to internal conditions (e.g., hunger, pain). A toddler who usually plays contentedly at home without peers may be forceful and loud in a home-based child care setting filled with other children making noise and competing for toys. Cultural variations such as views of child independence and of adaptive skills, including toileting and feeding, may also have a significant impact on the acceptability of certain social emotional skills.

Individual Tolerances and Expectations   In addition to the context, a second challenge to accurate screening and identification of problem social emotional behaviors is that individual tolerances and expectations often affect the acceptability of behaviors. One mother may appreciate the boisterous laughter and rough physical interactions between a toddler and his peers; another may find these behaviors troubling and in need of intervention. A child care provider may welcome a quiet and shy toddler who most often plays by herself in the block area; another child care provider might be concerned about the child's lack of emerging parallel play skills and inability to engage either adults or children in social interactions.

Difficulty in Quantifying and Measuring Social Emotional Behaviors   Third, quantifying and measuring social emotional behaviors in the assessment process can be challenging. For instance, how much is too much screaming? For a 15-month-old, how do you measure "appropriate responses to strangers"? The subjective nature of social emotional behavioral assessments together with the difficulties of pinpointing "how much is enough" and "how much is too much" contribute to the challenges of conducting accurate and sensitive social emotional assessment.

The Developmental Nature of Behaviors   Finally, the developmental nature of behaviors often makes it difficult to determine if behaviors are appropriate for one child at a certain age and not for another. If a 3-year-old child has a tantrum when denied chocolate ice cream, is this behavior appropriate or inappropriate? An 8-year-old with developmental disabilities may not be able to control his emotions, yet he still might be expected to remain calm and quiet in an inclusive classroom environment with peers who are typically developing. Intensity and duration are often the determinants of whether behaviors are considered acceptable or unacceptable, together with the developmental age of the child and the expectations of specific environments.

In addition to the complexities of assessing social emotional and behavioral difficulties, another challenge to effective social emotional screening exists. In large measure, both currently and historically, health care professionals such as physicians and nurses have not focused on early identification of developmental problems in very young children and in particular, they have overlooked social emotional problems (Jellinek, Patel, & Froehle, 2002). Medical practitioners have been found to seriously underidentify mental health disorders. Some studies report that physicians fail to recognize more than half of psychosocial or psychiatric problems in young children in their practice (Jellinek, 1998; National Alliance for the Mentally Ill, 2000; Stancin & Palermo, 1997; Wildman, Kizilbash, & Smucker, 1999). For children under the age of 5, the figure for underidentification of social emotional and behavioral problems is just as substantial (Stancin & Palermo, 1997; Wildman, Kinsman, Logue, Dickey, & Smucker, 1997). Lavigne and colleagues (1993) found that pediatricians identified 9% of children ages 2–5 as having an emotional or behavioral problem, whereas psychologists diagnosed 13%–15% of children in the same age group as having a problem.

Although medical practitioners are urged to use standardized formal assessments during well-child visits (Squires & Nickel, 2000), one survey found that only 57% used a developmental assessment for children age 10–35 months (Halfon, Regalado, Sareen, et al., 2004). In a second survey, two-thirds of physicians sampled did not routinely evaluate mental, emotional, or behavioral development in their young patients (National Alliance for the Mentally Ill, 2000). A lack of time to address problems, training, and, until recently, technically adequate, low-cost screening instruments all contribute to this under-identification. In addition, many practitioners working in managed care insurance systems are encouraged to avoid referring patients for mental health and other specialized services in order to minimize insurance company costs (Jellinek et al., 2002; Nickel & Squires, 2000).

Since the mid-1990s, the four challenges to early social emotional screening have been addressed in part by the developers of a variety of new screening measures.

Social Emotional Screening Instruments

Prior to the mid 1990s, few social emotional screening instruments existed for infants, toddlers, and preschool children. Increased awareness of the importance of early identification and intervention along with a growing public emphasis on infant mental health (c.f., Zeanah, 1997; 2000) has encouraged research and development of screening instruments targeting infants and young children. An additional impetus for developing screening measures came with the passage of IDEA '97 (PL 105-17). This act required the use of assessment procedures to address children's social emotional competence as well as developmental delays and disabilities. Finally, the Head Start standards mandate for screening in social emotional domains in both infant/toddler (Early Head Start) and preschool (Head Start) programs have provided an important precedent for the development of screening measures focused on early social emotional behavior. For the most part, measures have been developed to meet the quality standards that were previously established for developmental screening. These standards are described next.

Standards for Screening Measures

Screening standards require that test developers address five important areas: 1) accuracy, 2) reliability, 3) utility, 4) cost, and 5) parent input/cultural sensitivity.

Accuracy   In terms of accuracy, screening instruments are evaluated by their *sensitivity*, or the ability to detect children with true problems and delays, and by their *specificity*, or the ability to accurately label children without problems as typically developing. Sensitivity of at least 75%–80% and specificity of at least 85%–90% are recommended for screening tests (Nickel & Squires, 2000).

In addition, measures should have studies to support their *validity*, or accuracy, including their concurrent validity (i.e., agreement with the results of a more in-depth assessment), such as a clinical assessment using the Child Behavior Interview (Achenbach & Rescorla, 2000). The standardization sample of a measure should include at least 100 children per age level and be representative of the population where the test will be used (American Psychological Association, 1995). Often, U.S. Census data are used to determine if the test is representative of a region, area, or general U.S. population sample. For example, if a screening test is going to be used in rural Texas, psychometric data should reflect rural southern populations, with similar ethnic and economic backgrounds, in the normative studies.

Reliability   *Reliability* refers to the consistency of screening measures and should also be studied in screening measures for social emotional behaviors. Reliability between examiners (i.e., interobserver consistency) helps to ensure that different testers obtain similar results when testing the same child. A test should also yield similar results when given to the same child within a short time span. This reliability is called test–retest reliability. Both types of reliability, test–retest and interobserver, should have an agreement of 80% or greater (American Psychological Association, 1995).

Utility   Utility refers to the usefulness of a measure. Screening measures should be quick, easy to administer, attractive to children, and have clear instructions. Guidelines for discussing results with families should also be included (Glascoe, 1991).

Cost   Costs for screening measures must be economical in order for large numbers of children to be screened without undue expense (Glascoe, Foster, & Wolraich, 1997). One of the recommended strategies to enable programs to keep costs to a minimum and screen large numbers of children at suitable intervals is the use of parents and caregivers in the screening process (Chan & Taylor, 1998; Glascoe et al., 1997; Squires, 1996). Using parents and caregivers as responders is economical because parents usually are not reimbursed for completing questionnaires about their child's development. Expensive professional resources can then be targeted toward children with more complex needs or toward families in which parents are unable to complete questionnaires. Test kits and materials should also be affordable for programs.

Parent Input/Cultural Sensitivity   Parent input/cultural sensitivity refers to the requirement that screening measures should incorporate input from parents and be sensitive to different cultural and family practices. Enlisting parental assistance in screening may improve screening accuracy as well as encourage subsequent parental involvement in assessment and intervention phases as specified by IDEA (Lichtenstein & Ireton, 1984; Squires, 1996). In addition, parent-completed screening instruments may assist medical and other providers to make better decisions about referral and intervention for social emotional problems in young children (Merritt, Thompson, Keith, et al., 1993; Wildman et al., 1997). As with screening assessments in the developmental areas, parents and caregivers have been found to be accurate evaluators of their child's social emotional competence (Achenbach & Rescorla, 2000;

Bishop, Spence, & McDonald, 2003; Briggs-Gowan & Carter, 1998; Briggs-Gowan, Carter, Irwin, Wachtel, & Cicchetti, 2004; Carter, Little, Briggs-Gowan, & Kogan, 1999) when asked clearly worded questions about current behaviors (Squires et al., 2002). Also, when two or more caregivers in different settings complete a screening test on the same child, different perspectives on troubling or problem behaviors may be garnered. Because child care providers and other caregivers such as grandparents may see children responding to different demands and expectations from those observed in the home environment, these caregivers may provide information that assists in a comprehensive view of child functioning (Diamond & Squires, 1993).

Cultural expectations and variations may also be better integrated into screening results when parents and caregivers complete screening instruments. Such cultural factors are important to consider because they may affect a child's results, and thus, must be seen as part of the child's social emotional makeup.

Existing Social Emotional Screening Measures

As noted, a number of social emotional screening measures have been developed since 1995. Most of these measures meet at least some of the five standards just described. Selected social emotional screening instruments for preschool children are described in Appendix C at the end of this book. Psychometric properties as well as publication information are given.

Although parents can offer valuable information on child behaviors in home and community settings, there may be times that additional caregiver input is sought. In classroom situations and in some parent populations who have difficulty completing interviews (e.g., parents with limited cognitive capacities, foster parents who do not know a child well), practitioners such as early intervention practitioners and early childhood teachers can assist in early identification by completing social emotional screening tests. Practitioners can complete a screening interview designed for parents as long as they have adequate time with the child to observe his behaviors.

Some test developers have published separate versions of social emotional tests for practitioners—usually teachers—and most often for preschool children from age 3 and older who are in classroom settings. An example of a practitioner-completed screening tool is the Social Skills Rating Scale (SSRS), Ages 3–5 (Gresham & Elliott, 1990). The SSRS also has a parent form with questions about home behaviors such as helping with household tasks without being asked and using free time at home in an acceptable way. The SSRS teacher form asks about social skills in the classroom such as following directions, responding appropriately to teasing, and producing "correct" schoolwork. Another example is the Brief Infant–Toddler Social and Emotional Assessment (BITSEA; Briggs-Gowan & Carter, 2006), which has separate parent and child care provider forms. These forms ask about children's problem behaviors such as difficulties with falling asleep or staying awake, or in adjusting to change. Competence behaviors are also assessed on the BITSEA, including looking for a caregiver when upset and showing affection to loved ones.

ENVIRONMENTAL SCREENING

Clearly, it is essential to evaluate children's social emotional repertoires in order to determine if their behavior is typical. It is equally important to evaluate the environment(s) in which the child resides. An assessment of the environment in which the child lives is important to determine potential stresses on the child and caregiver, and whether additional family supports for providing a nurturing environment are needed.

Environmental Screening Instruments

Programs focused on young children often use instruments to assess the quality of the caregiving and home environment.

Home Observation for Measure of the Environment   The Home Observation for Measure of the Environment (HOME; Caldwell & Bradley, 1984, 2001) assesses several facets of the environment including the emotional and verbal responsivity of the caregiver and the caregiver's organization of the physical environment, such as providing appropriate play materials (e.g., books, push toy, stroller). The temporal environment is also targeted (e.g., child gets out of house at least four times a week, child is taken regularly to doctor's office or clinic), with questions relating to play and learning opportunities. Parent–child interactions are assessed with questions about caregiver's verbal responses to the child (e.g., mother spontaneously vocalizes to child at least twice during visit) and emotional affect (e.g., mother caresses or kisses child at least once during visit).

Although the HOME has been criticized for a lack of cultural sensitivity (Gottfried, 1984), it remains a widely used instrument in early childhood programs such as Head Start. The HOME Screening Questionnaire (HSQ) (Coons, Gay, Fandal, Ker, & Frankenburg, 1981; Pessanha & Bairrão, 2003) is a survey version of HOME that can be administered either in the home or in a center, and is parent-completed. Questions about the quality of cognitive stimulation and emotional support are included on the HSQ.

The Difficult Life Circumstances Assessment   The Difficult Life Circumstances (DLC; Barnard, 1994) is a second example of an environmental assessment. The DLC is an interview that asks whether a parent is experiencing problems at home related to life circumstances such as an abusive or absent partner, employment, and prolonged illness. The manual accompanying the DLC suggests guidelines to follow when families require intensive supports/services due to accumulated risks.

General Measures   General measures to rate the quality of a young child's environment include the Early Childhood Environment Rating Scale-Revised (ECERS-R; Harms, Cryer, & Clifford, 1997), designed to assess classroom environments that target children from 2½ to 5; and the Infant/Toddler Environment Rating Scale–Revised (ITERS-R; Harms, et al., 1997), which targets infants and toddlers up to 30 months. Both the ECERS-R and ITERS-R are designed for group care and preschool settings and evaluate the quality of home and classroom furnishings, health and safety, teacher–child interactions, and program structure. These rating scales may be used to determine whether the environment might be contributing to problem behaviors in young children.

Although each of the environmental measures described here can be helpful, they often have major drawbacks. First, many measures require a significant time commitment to complete, and thus do not qualify as screening procedures. Second, many of the measures do not include items thought to be significant risk or protective indicators (e.g., domestic violence, transportation needs). Consequently, the ABI:SE Approach includes an environmental questionnaire, the Environmental Screening Questionnaire (ESQ), Experimental Edition, which 1) can be completed quickly and 2) includes items that address most major risk/protective factors.

The Environmental Screening Questionnaire

The ESQ is designed to identify risk and protective factors in a child's environment that might affect a parent's or caregiver's ability to support his or her child's social emotional development. Items address risk factors that may make parenting more difficult, such as domestic violence, poor health, and drug or alcohol abuse. The ESQ also includes items that assess protective factors or supports that may assist a family in providing a supportive environment for their child's social emotional development. Supports include family and friends who help out, a regular job, and a high school education. A copy of the ESQ is contained in Appendix A of this book.

Caregivers may complete the ESQ independently or it can be completed through an interview format. For the latter, either a classroom teacher, home visitor, or other professional may conduct the interview with caregivers.

The ESQ is composed of six areas: 1) education, 2) housing, 3) health/behavior, 4) economic, 5) home, and 6) community. Each area has five questions to be answered by checking "Yes" or "No." Once completed, professional staff can score the ESQ by assigning either a 0 (*protective responses*) or a 10 (*risk factors*) on the accompanying Summary of Scores/Referral Form. The scores can then be added for each area. Scores of 30 and above in any area should be followed up with a more comprehensive assessment (e.g., an in-depth interview) and/or referral to an appropriate agency (e.g., child protection services).

The ESQ questions are of a personal nature by design. Experts in the field of children's mental health stress the importance of environmental risk and protective factors (Sameroff et al., 2000), a stance that argues strongly for program personnel to complete a formal or informal screening of young children's environments. If program personnel feel that the ESQ asks questions that are too personal, those items can be omitted or another environmental screening measure may be used. Caregivers or families in need of additional community services should be referred to an appropriate agency. IDEA eligibility definitions for infants/toddlers (Part C) and preschoolers (Part B) as well as community mental health resources will determine whether a child is eligible for state or federally funded psychological or behavioral services. If a child *is not* found to be eligible for services, the child/family can be considered for the ABI:SE Approach for social emotional prevention/intervention activities. These prevention activities are designed so that caregivers and service providers can target one or two problem areas for families and focus on preventing escalating problem behaviors that require more specialized intervention.

Children with scores *near* the screening cutoff points on screening instruments such as the ASQ:SE and/or the ESQ may also benefit from ABI:SE prevention/intervention activities. These children/families may be struggling with parent–child relationships or other issues and may benefit from targeted prevention/intervention activities directed at problem behaviors.

Although children with scores reflecting typical social emotional behaviors and few environmental risk factors may also benefit from prevention activities, most programs do not have the necessary resources to offer services to these children. However, all children should receive ongoing screening and monitoring to ensure that their behaviors remain within typical ranges. Family environmental risk factors should be periodically reassessed because family conditions may fluctuate due to changes in circumstances such as losing a job, being forced to move, or developing a serious medical condition.

ABI:SE SCREENING PROCESS

As noted earlier, screening is the first process in the ABI:SE Approach. The screening process associated with the ABI:SE Approach is displayed in Figure 5.1 for the two groups (i.e., children with disabilities and those at risk) targeted by the ABI:SE Approach. As indicated in Figure 5.1, the ASQ:SE and the ESQ are administered to both groups. Based on children's performance, their developmental status can be classified as *typical, at risk,* or *questionable.* Depending on the classification, children can be referred to one of three options: monitoring, referral for mental health assessment, or intervention. The monitoring option is appropriate for children who are classified as typical, and periodic follow-up screening is recommended. The mental health referral option is appropriate for children who are classified as at risk, and referral for a mental health evaluation is recommended. The intervention option is appropriate for children who are classified as questionable, and it is recommended that these children participate in the ABI:SE Approach. The steps in the screening process and the options are described next.

Screening, the initial phase in the ABI:SE system, includes administration of both a social emotional screening test and an environmental assessment. An environmental assessment such as the ESQ or the HOME (Caldwell & Bradley, 1984) can be used to determine if caregiver and environmental risk factors are sufficient to consider referral for eligibility determination and/or additional services regardless of social emotional screening outcomes. Social emotional

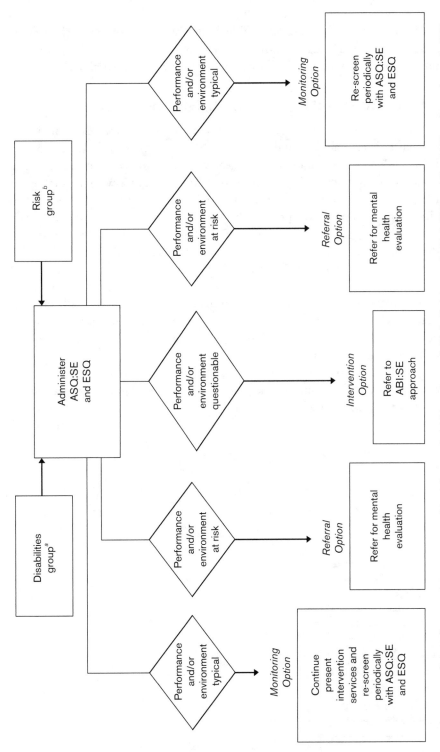

Figure 5.1. The ABI:SE Approach screening process. (Key: [a] Composed of children who are eligible for Early Intervention/Early Childhood Special Education services under IDEA; [b] Composed of children who have family risk factors [e.g., poverty, teen parents]).

screening assessments will have cutoff scores to suggest when a referral for an outside evaluation is warranted. If either the social emotional or environmental scale indicates the presence of problems or risk conditions, the child/family should be referred for an eligibility evaluation for IDEA (i.e., Early Intervention, Early Childhood Special Education) or community mental health services.

Step One: Completing the ASQ:SE and ESQ

As mentioned, screening is the first process in the ABI:SE Approach, and is conducted to determine if a child needs a more in-depth assessment. As shown in Figure 5.2, the screening process can lead to one of three options: a) repeat periodic screening/monitoring if scores on screening and environmental assessments are below cutoff points (i.e., typical), indicating typical behaviors and environmental supports are present; b) refer for more in-depth mental health evaluation (i.e., at risk); and c) begin the ABI:SE Approach if outcomes are near the cutoff score (i.e., questionable) and resources are available.

Parents or other appropriate caregivers should begin by identifying the appropriate ASQ:SE age interval. Before caregivers complete the ASQ:SE (or another screening test), the screening administrator should discuss with them the purpose of the screening, how the measure is scored, and how information will be shared. The *ASQ:SE User's Guide* (Squires et al., 2002) describes steps for ASQ:SE administration in detail.

In addition to completing the ASQ:SE, caregivers should be encouraged to complete the ESQ. Again, the purpose of the measure should be explained and caregiver questions answered.

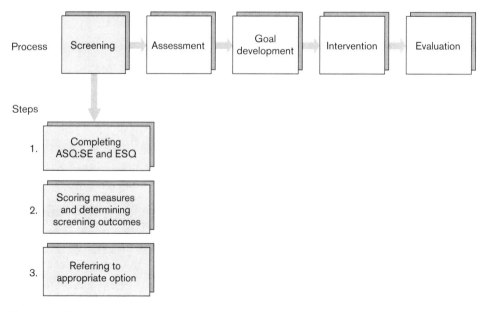

Figure 5.2.   Steps in the ABI:SE screening process.

Step Two: Scoring Measures and Determining Screening Outcomes

For the ASQ:SE, the screening cutoff score appears on a final, separate page following the assessment items. If a child's score is on or above the specified cutoff score, it is suggested that the child and family be referred for a further evaluation. If a child's score is below the cutoff score, it is suggested that the child's social emotional behaviors are within typical limits and do not warrant referral at present. For the ESQ, families who have scores over 30 on any of the ESQ areas (e.g., housing, education) should be considered for participation in the ABI:SE Approach as well as for referral for further evaluation by community agencies.

After social emotional and environmental screening tests have been administered and the scores tallied, a decision needs to be made based on the test manual guidelines and discussion with parents about whether the child appears to have typical social emotional competence or if further evaluation for possible problem behaviors is needed. Based on screening scores, three options are possible, and each is described next.

Step Three: Referring to Appropriate Option

Based on the outcome of the screening tests, one of three options is indicated: monitoring, referral, or intervention. Service providers should discuss these options with parents to ensure family support as well as to tailor the selection to individual family needs.

Monitoring Option   If scores are within the typical range on the social emotional and environmental screens, then no referral is necessary; continue periodic screening/monitoring.

If a child has a score within the typical range as specified by the measure's guidelines on both social emotional and environmental assessments, most likely the child will not need further referral and evaluation. The child can be monitored periodically through the administration of an appropriate screening test in 6–12 months. In cases in which parents or other caregivers/teachers are still concerned and request additional assessment, the child may be referred for further evaluation based on caregiver/teacher concerns alone and/or suggestions may be given to address their concerns. In most cases, however, a child with scores in the typical range will not be referred for further assessment or prevention activities.

Jamal is an active 18-month-old toddler. His mother, Angela, is concerned about his aggressive behaviors at home such as hitting his infant sister, throwing toys, and running in the house. Angela completed the 18-month interval of the ASQ:SE and helped tally Jamal's total score, which was 40. Angela also completed the ESQ and the score indicated several protective factors and no serious environmental risk factors. Because the cutoff score for the 18-month ASQ:SE is 55, Jamal's score was not in the at risk or problematic range, which indicated that further referral was unnec-

essary. Instead, Angela's home visitor gave her some suggestions for decreasing Jamal's aggressive behaviors such as spending individual time with Jamal and praising him when he plays appropriately with his sister and walks through the house instead of running. After Angela began to give Jamal 15 minutes of play time by himself each morning, these problem behaviors were greatly reduced. Jamal and Angela will not begin intervention activities at this time, and will be re-screened in 5–6 months.

Referral Option   If scores are above cutoff points on social emotional and/or environmental screening measures, then the child should be referred for a mental health examination.

If a young child has a score above the recommended cutoff point, or in the clinical range as indicated in the testing manual, he or she should be referred to community resources such as early intervention, early childhood special education, or early childhood mental health providers for further assessment.

Myle is the single parent of 9-month-old Drew. Myle and Drew attended a parenting group at Myle's neighborhood infant center. The group leader, Joan, asked each parent to complete an ASQ:SE as a first step in identifying and talking about competence and problem behaviors in their infants. Drew's score on the ASQ:SE was 65, well above the cutoff score of 48. In addition to the ASQ:SE, Myle completed the ESQ. Results from the ESQ indicated possible serious environmental risk factors associated with economics and housing. After talking with Myle, Joan arranged for a referral to the community mental health nurse, who then visited Myle and Drew in their apartment. The nurse evaluated Drew's feeding and sleeping behaviors. She gave Myle suggestions for encouraging Drew to make eye contact as well as a suggested feeding and eating schedule. The nurse also referred Myle to a home visitor program. The home visitor was able to help Myle clean up the apartment and prepare more balanced and nutritious meals for Drew. The nurse continued the home visits for 3 months and eventually referred Drew for an eligibility evaluation for Part C IDEA services.

Intervention Option   If scores are in neither the typical nor the at-risk point but fall somewhere near the cutoff point, in the questionable range, then begin the ABI:SE Approach.

If a child has a score near the cutoff points on either a social emotional assessment such as the ASQ:SE or an environmental screening assessment such as the ESQ, the child/family can be considered for ABI:SE prevention/intervention activities and family support. Children who are *not* found to be eligible for IDEA or mental health services under the referral option can also be considered for prevention/intervention activities.

The ABI:SE Approach is primarily preventative and not meant for children with serious mental health disorders or disturbances. For example, in all likelihood, a child who is repeatedly injuring himself or others will be identified by a screening test as needing further assessment. Such a child may be in need of professional psychological and/or mental health services, and prevention activities would not be appropriate because of the severity of his problems and the need for specialists to devise an individualized intervention plan.

Trista is 4 years old and attends an all-day preschool classroom in her neighborhood. Trista's classroom teacher and mother completed a 48-month ASQ:SE screening assessment. Trista scored a 65 on the parent-completed ASQ:SE and she scored a 60 on the teacher-completed ASQ:SE; both were below the cutoff of 70. On both Parent and Teacher ASQ:SE Questionnaires, however, problem behaviors such as not calming down, not sharing toys, and demonstrating few play skills with peers were evident in both home and preschool settings. Trista's mother completed the ESQ, and results suggested no serious environmental risk factors. After meeting with the classroom teacher and parent, the preschool administrator decided to have Trista's mother and teacher work at home and in the classroom on specific ABI:SE activities. These activities were focused on increasing her play skills, lengthening the time she can sit and play, and improving her relationships with peers.

After screening outcomes have been determined, those children and families deemed appropriate for the intervention option and those deemed appropriate for the referral option but who subsequently are *not* found to be eligible for additional services and who may benefit from prevention activities should move to the next ABI:SE process, assessment. In the ABI:SE linked system, children and caregivers are then assessed on key social emotional benchmarks using the Social Emotional Assessment/Evaluation Measure (SEAM), Experimental Edition. The assessment process is described in Chapter 6, and goal development is addressed in Chapter 7.

SUMMARY

The first process in the linked ABI:SE Approach—screening—has been described in this chapter. Screening is a brief assessment designed to identify children in need of further evaluation for potential developmental difficulties. Two types of screening measures were recommended: one to determine a child's social emotional competence and one to assess environmental risk and protective factors.

Once a screening test is administered, outcomes are determined based on screening cutoff scores. If a child has scores that are above the cutoff scores, indicating problem behaviors, the child/family should be referred for an eligibility or diagnostic assessment. If the child appears to be developing typically, no further referral is warranted; however, continued monitoring with the ASQ:SE or another screening test is recommended. For children with scores near the cutoff points on either the environmental rating scale or the social emotional screening assessment, the child/family can begin the ABI:SE assessment process using the SEAM.

6

Assessment to Determine Social Emotional Goals and Intervention Content

As noted in Chapter 4, the ABI:SE Approach is composed of five critical processes: screening, assessment, goal development, intervention, and evaluation. Moving forward from the screening process described in Chapter 5, this chapter addresses the more detailed and comprehensive assessment of young children who are identified during screening as *potentially* having social emotional problems. Infants, toddlers, and preschool children whose performance on a screening measure such as the ASQ:SE is above cutoff scores should be referred for early intervention or mental health assessments to determine if problems exist. If so, early childhood professionals can then determine program eligibility and intervention goals. Caregivers and children whose scores do not indicate that they have significant problems may begin the ABI:SE assessment process.

The assessment process associated with the ABI:SE Approach is not designed to determine eligibility for services or the etiology of a problem. Rather, the purpose of the assessment process described in this chapter is to produce outcomes that are directly applicable to the development of intervention goals and content for children and caregivers who show signs of problems or potential problems in the social emotional area. Attaining this purpose requires the use of a specific type of criterion-referenced measure often referred to as *curriculum-based* or *curriculum-embedded assessment.* Curriculum-based measures are composed of items that have associated a) criteria or examples and b) curriculum or intervention activities. In addition, most curriculum-based measures contain items that are functional (i.e., target behavior and information that enhances children's daily living skills and independence).

This chapter and the Social Emotional Assessment/Evaluation Measure (SEAM), Experimental Edition were developed with the assistance of Hyeyoung Bae, Elizabeth Benedict, Jantina Clifford, Hollie Hix-Small, Mona Ivey-Soto, Karen Lawrence, Suzanne Bells McManus, Jin Ai No, Juli Pool, Deborah Russell, Helen Sharp, Krista Swanson, Hasnah Toran, and Jennifer Westover.

This chapter begins with an overview of the assessment process associated with the ABI:SE Approach. Following the overview, a description of the assessment process is offered. Next, a description of the Social Emotional Assessment/ Evaluation Measure (SEAM), Experimental Edition is presented. The SEAM for three different age groups (infant, toddler, and preschool-age) is included in Appendix B. This measure is designed to provide outcomes or information that is directly relevant to the development of high-quality, functional goals and intervention content. The SEAM is the assessment component of the approach. General recommendations for the curriculum component are included in this chapter; an in-depth curriculum will subsequently be developed The chapter ends with a case study presented to illustrate the ABI:SE assessment process.

OVERVIEW OF THE ABI:SE ASSESSMENT PROCESS

At the outset, it is important to re-emphasize the purpose of the ABI:SE assessment process. The assessment process is designed to gather information about a) children's behavioral repertoires, with a particular focus on the social emotional area of development; and b) the environmental context that affects children's behavior including the nature of their daily interactions with caregivers, siblings and peers. We believe that having comprehensive and reliable information about children's social emotional behavior as well as information about how their social and physical environment responds is essential to the development of high-quality goals and intervention content.

Comprehensive, reliable, developmentally appropriate, and functional assessment outcomes are necessary for the creation of goals that provide a sound basis for subsequent intervention efforts. If intervention efforts are to be effective, they must be guided by high-quality goals. We define high-quality goals as those that target behaviors meeting the following criteria: functional, meaningful, measurable, and able to be integrated into daily activities and routines (Pretti-Frontczak & Bricker, 2004). Each is described in more detail next.

- *Functional* refers to goals that enhance the lives of children and their caregivers. For example, learning to communicate one's needs is clearly functional for young children.

- *Meaningful* refers to goals that address children's critical needs such as mobility and empathy for others. Goals that target irrelevant or unimportant behavior will likely result in wasted intervention efforts.

- *Measurable* refers to goals that can be operationalized and observed reliably. For example, a caregiver's responses to a child's emotional outbursts can be seen and noted.

- *Embedded* refers to goals that can be addressed throughout children's daily activities. For example, learning to respond to requests and demands can be addressed repeatedly throughout the day and across many activities.

In addition to having comprehensive information on children's social emotional behavioral repertoires, it is also essential to understand and take into account, to the extent possible, the risk and protective factors that affect children's lives. Therefore, an assessment of the basic conditions within which children live and the nature of their interactions with caregivers and other children is essential to the development of appropriate and high-quality goals, as illustrated in the following case study.

Two-year-old Amy, who spoke little for her age, was referred for evaluation by her family physician. Personnel in the evaluation agency administered a standardized developmental test and interviewed her mother, who was a single mother and her primary caregiver. Amy was noted to be a quiet child, and her performance on the standardized test suggested that Amy's language and adaptive behaviors were delayed by several months. During the interview, Amy's mother indicated that her only concern was Amy's "incessant" demands on her time. Based on this information, the following preliminary educational goals were developed:

- *Amy will increase her vocabulary through daily book reading activities with her mother.*

- *Amy will learn to self-feed using a spoon.*

Two visits by the home visitor revealed that Amy routinely entertained herself by engaging in somewhat repetitive activities and rarely initiated contact with her mother or the few other adults who visited her home. Amy had little to no opportunity to interact with other children because she had no siblings and her mother rarely took her out of the house. She displayed flat affect, rarely laughing, crying, or showing other emotions. The home visitor's subsequent assessment revealed that little progress was being made toward the selected goals. In addition, the home visitor noted the following behaviors:

- *Amy did not make eye contact with adults.*

- *Amy did not initiate social contact with adults.*

- *Amy's mother showed signs of depression, including withdrawal, an inability to meet daily demands, and an inability to address the needs of her child.*

With further assessment using the SEAM: Toddler, which specifically focuses on the social emotional area, new goals were developed. These goals included supports for Amy and her mother that would foster improvements in the 2-year-old's social emotional competence. The ABI:SE items from the Toddler interval that were chosen as goals for Amy included

- *Amy will initiate and respond to communicative interactions with her mother and other adults. (C-1.3)*

- *Amy will identify her own emotions with help. (C-2.3)*

- *Amy will play alongside other children. (C-5.4)*

At the mother's request, the home visitor modeled how to react more contingently to Amy's bids for attention. She also assisted Amy's mother in finding a support group to address her depression and a play group for Amy that met three times per week.

The home visitor and Amy's mother began to work on the three SEAM goals during home visits. Within 6 weeks, the home visitor's evaluation found that this new intervention focus and adjustments made to the home environment were producing changes in Amy's behavior. Amy's mother also felt that she was getting some needed support and that she had some concrete steps to help her improve Amy's social emotional competence.

THE ABI:SE ASSESSMENT PROCESS

The ABI:SE assessment process requires collection of two important types of information: a) measures of children's social and emotional competence, and b) measures of caregivers' ability to provide safe, supportive, and interesting environments for their children and their interactions with their children. The SEAM provides information on children's social emotional competence and some important aspects of caregivers' competence. This instrument produces information that can be used to develop high-quality goals and intervention activities to support these goals. Another important information requirement is to assess the associated risk and protective factors that surround children. Use of the ESQ, discussed in Chapter 5, during the screening process addresses this requirement.

Once the screening using the ASQ:SE and the ESQ has been completed, the ABI:SE assessment process can begin. The ABI:SE assessment process is composed of three steps, as shown in Figure 6.1:

Step One: Preparing with the caregiver(s) for the assessment process.

Step Two: Completing the SEAM assessment.

Step Three: Reviewing the results with the caregiver.

Each of these steps is discussed next.

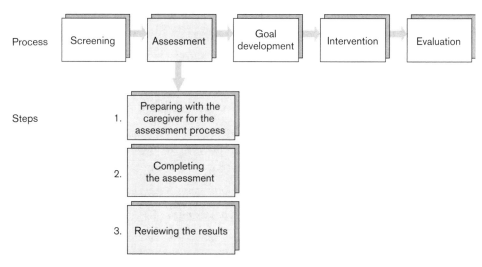

Figure 6.1. Steps in the assessment process.

Step One: Preparing with the Caregiver(s) for the Assessment Process

Before beginning the assessment, it is ideal to have time to build a relationship with a caregiver and to establish a base of mutual trust and understanding. It may take two or three visits or more before the caregiver will feel comfortable sharing problems and concerns related to her child and her own issues and concerns. Cultural values, family demands, child-rearing practices, and personal characteristics such as reading ability may also affect how caregivers answer the assessment questions. Although not always possible, it is recommended that early childhood professionals make several home visits or classroom contacts at a minimum in order to build mutual trust before they ask caregivers to help complete the SEAM.

As indicated, the first step is focused on explaining to the caregivers the purpose and procedures of the assessment process. This may require answering many questions to ensure that the caregiver is comfortable with and understands why collecting a range of information is essential to the development of effective intervention efforts.

Caregivers should become partners in the process and participate in the assessment to the extent possible. It is, however, important to remember that caregivers' needs and values may vary widely, leading to equally wide variations in how each caregiver may choose to participate in the assessment process. Whenever possible, professionals should tailor caregiver participation to match the caregiver's individual needs and desires.

Caregivers should also understand that each of the three developmental intervals of the SEAM (i.e., Infant, Toddler, Preschool-Age) covers a wide range of behaviors and that their particular child is not expected to do all of the behaviors on the assessment. For example, the preschool-age assessment interval covers the developmental range of 36–63 months (approximately 3–5 years). A 36-month-old or 3-year-old may not be using words to describe the emotions of others, whereas most 5-year-olds are using descriptive words very capably. Questions can be omitted that do not seem relevant to the child at the time. Caregivers should be reminded of the wide developmental range and individual variability existing among children before beginning the assessment. Cultural variations and family values will also affect the relevance of some of the items with a particular family and child. Again, questions that do not seem pertinent to a child or family can be omitted.

Step Two: Completing the Assessment

The second step in the process is completing the SEAM and the ESQ, if it was not completed during the screening process. (A copy of the ESQ screening measure is contained in Appendix A.) Both the ESQ and SEAM measures can be completed independently by a caregiver or by using an interview format in which a professional can ask the caregiver about each item and then note the caregiver's responses. Some caregivers may wish to bring a friend or family member when providing the information. Reasonable variations suggested by caregivers should be accommodated if possible. For some families, a professional may have to observe the home and child–caregiver interactions in order to assist the caregiver in completing the measures reliably. When possible, the accuracy of the assessment, regardless of the strategy used, should be verified through subsequent observation. Caregivers and professionals must partner together in order to develop accurate and relevant goals that can form a sound basis of subsequent intervention activities.

Step Three: Reviewing the Results

The third and final step of the assessment process addresses the need to review the information gleaned from the completed measures. The professional should review the information in concert with the caregiver. If the professional notes any discrepancies between his perceptions and those of the caregiver, the professional should attempt to clarify them with the parent. For example, if the home visitor notes that a child has difficulty regulating her emotional responses but her mother does not indicate this as a problem area, a discussion should ensue to help both parties understand this difference in perception of the child's behavior.

The assessment information should be summarized in such a way that it can be used directly during the goal-developing process. A Goal Development and Intervention Plan, described in Chapter 7, can be used for summarizing the areas of child and environmental concern as well as child and caregiver strengths. During the goal developing process, also described in the following chapter, the caregiver and professional can select the goals to be targeted from the list of concerns.

THE SOCIAL EMOTIONAL ASSESSMENT/EVALUATION MEASURE (SEAM)

As stated earlier, a functional assessment that yields information necessary to create high-quality goals and intervention content requires the use of a curriculum-based measure. The SEAM was specifically developed to provide a comprehensive picture of a child's social emotional repertoire. The outcomes from this measure lead directly to the development of quality goals and linked intervention activities.

The SEAM is composed of three different age interval forms:

1. *Infant,* with a developmental range of 3–18 months

2. *Toddler,* with a developmental range of 18–36 months

3. *Preschool-age,* with a developmental range of 36–63 months

Although these divisions are somewhat arbitrary, research indicates that some important developmental shifts or reorganizations occur within these time intervals (Cicchetti & Cohen, 1995; Sroufe, 1996;). It is important to emphasize that these intervals refer to developmental ages and not chronological ages. For children with disabilities, the interval that most reflects their current skill level should be used rather than the one matching their chronological age range. For example, a 40-month-old boy (a little older than 3 years) with significant cognitive and language delays may have skills closer to those of a toddler who is typically developing; in this case, the toddler assessment interval may be the appropriate interval to use.

The content for the SEAM items was derived from a series of child and caregiver/adult benchmarks (see Chapter 4 for an expanded description of the benchmarks). As discussed previously, benchmarks represent critical areas for social emotional competence in young children and their caregivers. A list of the benchmarks for the infant, toddler, and preschool intervals and their corresponding assessment items from the SEAM are contained in Tables 6.1, 6.2, and 6.3.

Table 6.1.   Benchmarks and assessment items for the Social Emotional Assessment Measure (SEAM): Infant interval

Child benchmarks		Assessment items
C-1.0	Baby participates in healthy interactions.	1.1 Baby shows interest in you and other familiar caregivers. 1.2 Baby responds to you and other familiar caregivers. 1.3 Baby initiates and responds to communications. 1.4 Baby lets you know if she needs help or comfort.
C-2.0	Baby expresses a range of emotions.	2.1 Baby smiles at you. 2.2 Baby smiles at familiar adults. 2.3 Baby smiles and laughs at sights and sounds.
C-3.0	Baby regulates his social emotional responses, with caregiver support.	3.1 Baby responds to your soothing when upset. 3.2 Baby calms down after exciting activity. 3.3 Baby soothes himself when distressed.
C-4.0	Baby begins to show empathy for others.	4.1 Baby mimics your facial expressions. 4.2 Baby looks at and notices you and other familiar caregivers. 4.3 Baby looks at and notices others' emotional responses. 4.4 Baby responds to another's distress, seeking comfort for self.
C-5.0	Baby attends to and engages with others.	5.1 Baby makes eye contact with you and others. 5.2 Baby looks at or toward sounds and visual events. 5.3 Baby focuses on events shown by you and others. 5.4 Baby shares attention and events with you.
C-6.0	Baby explores hands and feet and surroundings.	6.1 Baby explores his hands and feet. 6.2 Baby explores toys and materials. 6.3 Baby explores his surroundings. 6.4 Baby crawls or walks a short distance away from you.
C-7.0	Baby displays a positive self-image.	7.1 Baby laughs at, or smiles at, her image or picture of self. 7.2 Baby recognizes his name. 7.3 Baby calls attention to herself.
C-8.0	Baby regulates activity level.	8.1 Baby participates in simple routines and games with you. 8.2 Baby looks at books or pictures for several minutes or longer. 8.3 Baby engages in motor activities for several minutes or longer.
C-9.0	Baby cooperates with daily routines and requests.	9.1 Baby opens her mouth for food. 9.2 Baby follows simple routines, with your help. 9.3 Baby cooperates with diaper and clothing changes.

(continued)

Table 6.1.   *(continued)*

Child benchmarks	Assessment items
C-10.0 Baby shows a range of adaptive skills.	10.1 Baby eats and gains weight on schedule. 10.2 Baby eats a variety of age-appropriate foods. 10.3 Baby sleeps with few problems. 10.4 Baby eliminates (pees and poops) on regular schedule.

Adult/caregiver benchmarks	Assessment items
A-1.0 Caregiver responds positively to baby.	1.1 Caregiver responds to baby's nonverbal communication appropriately. 1.2 Caregiver responds to baby's verbal communication appropriately. 1.3 Caregiver helps baby to calm down.
A-2.0 Caregiver provides the developmentally appropriate type and level of activity for baby.	2.1 Caregiver offers age-appropriate books, toys, and playthings for baby. 2.2 Caregiver plays with baby using age-appropriate games.
A-3.0 Caregiver provides baby with predictable schedules/routines and appropriate environment.	3.1 Caregiver creates and follows routines for baby's eating and sleeping. 3.2 Caregiver provides a nap and sleeping schedule for baby that is predictable and appropriate for her age. 3.3 Caregiver provides times each day to play with baby. 3.4 Caregiver helps baby regulate his emotional responses.
A-4.0 Caregiver provides baby with a safe home and play environment.	4.1 Caregiver checks the home for things that may be dangerous to baby. 4.2 Caregiver transports baby safely. 4.3 Caregiver supervises baby or provides a way for baby to be safe. 4.4 Caregiver has trusted person who can provide child care. 4.5 Caregiver obtains regular medical care for baby. 4.6 Caregiver manages feelings of anger or frustration that may occur while with baby.

Table 6.2.   Benchmarks and assessment items for the Social Emotional Assessment Measure (SEAM): Toddler interval

Child benchmarks	Assessment items
C-1.0 Toddler participates in healthy interactions.	1.1 Toddler talks and plays with adults whom she knows well. 1.2 Toddler responds when you show him affection. 1.3 Toddler initiates and responds when you communicate with her. 1.4 Toddler lets you know if he needs help, attention, or comfort.
C-2.0 Toddler expresses a range of emotions.	2.1 Toddler smiles and laughs. 2.2 Toddler expresses a range of emotions using a variety of strategies. 2.3 Toddler identifies her emotions, with your help. 2.4 Toddler identifies his own emotions.
C-3.0 Toddler regulates her social emotional responses.	3.1 Toddler responds to soothing when upset. 3.2 Toddler can settle herself down after periods of exciting activity. 3.3 Toddler can calm self when upset.
C-4.0 Toddler begins to show empathy for others.	4.1 Toddler matches his response to other's emotional responses. 4.2 Toddler tries to comfort others when they are upset. 4.3 Toddler uses words to talk about another child's emotions.

Table 6.2.   *(continued)*

Child benchmarks		Assessment items	
C-5.0	Toddler shares attention and engages with others.	5.1	Toddler makes eye contact with you and other caregivers and peers.
		5.2	Toddler focuses on events that you show him.
		5.3	Toddler greets you and other familiar adults.
		5.4	Toddler plays alongside other children.
		5.5	Toddler shares in daily activities.
C-6.0	Toddler begins to demonstrates independence.	6.1	Toddler explores new environments, while maintaining some contact.
		6.2	Toddler can separate from you in familiar environment with minimal distress.
		6.3	Toddler tries new tasks before seeking help.
C-7.0	Toddler displays a positive self-image.	7.1	Toddler points to self in picture.
		7.2	Toddler knows personal information.
		7.3	Toddler tells caregiver what he did or accomplished.
C-8.0	Toddler regulates attention and activity level.	8.1	Toddler stays with motor activities for 5 minutes or longer.
		8.2	Toddler looks at book or listens to a story for 5 minutes or longer.
		8.3	Toddler moves from one activity to another without problems.
		8.4	Toddler participates in simple games.
C-9.0	Toddler cooperates with daily routines and requests.	9.1	Toddler follows routines.
		9.2	Toddler cooperates with simple requests.
C-10.0	Toddler shows a range of adaptive skills.	10.1	Toddler eats and feeds self a variety of foods without problems.
		10.2	Toddler falls and remains asleep with few problems.
		10.3	Toddler accepts changes in routines and settings.
		10.4	Toddler shows an interest in using the toilet.
Adult/caregiver benchmarks		**Assessment items**	
A-1.0	Caregiver responds positively to toddler.	1.1	Caregiver responds to toddler's nonverbal communication appropriately.
		1.2	Caregiver responds to toddler's verbal communication appropriately.
		1.3	Caregiver supports toddler's emotional needs.
		1.4	Caregiver uses positive comments and language with child.
		1.5	Caregiver successfully redirects child's inappropriate behaviors.
		1.6	Caregiver can recognize the function of a child's (negative) behaviors and, with assistance, can modify environment.
A-2.0	Caregiver provides the developmentally appropriate type and level of activity.	2.1	Caregiver offers age-appropriate books, toys, and playthings for toddler.
		2.2	Caregiver plays with toddler and has ideas for age-appropriate games.
A-3.0	Caregiver provides toddler with predictable schedule/ routines and appropriate environment.	3.1	Caregiver provides a mealtime routine for toddler that is predictable and appropriate for his age.
		3.2	Caregiver provides a rest and sleeping schedule for toddler that is predictable and appropriate for his age.
		3.3	Caregiver provides toddler with predictable limits and discipline.
		3.4	Caregiver provides time each day to play with toddler.
A-4.0	Caregiver provides toddler with a safe home and play environment.	4.1	Caregiver checks the home for things that can be dangerous to toddler.
		4.2	Caregiver is able to provide safe travel arrangements for toddler.
		4.3	Caregiver supervises toddler or provides a way for toddler to be safe.
		4.4	Caregiver obtains regular medical and dental care for toddler.
		4.5	Caregiver manages feelings of anger or frustration that may come up while with toddler.

Table 6.3.   Benchmarks and assessment items for the Social Emotional Assessment Measure (SEAM):
Preschool-Age interval

Child benchmarks		Assessment items
C-1.0	Preschool-age child demonstrates healthy interactions with others.	1.1 Child shows affection toward you and other familiar adults and children.
		1.2 Child talks and plays with you and adults he knows.
		1.3 Child uses words to let you know if she needs help, attention, or comfort.
		1.4 Child shares and takes turns with other children.
		1.5 Child plays with other children.
C-2.0	Preschool-age child expresses a range of emotions.	2.1 Child smiles and laughs.
		2.2 Child expresses a range of emotions using a variety of strategies.
		2.3 Child describes emotions of others.
		2.4 Child identifies own emotions.
C-3.0	Preschool-age child regulates social emotional responses.	3.1 Child responds to peer's or caregiver's soothing when upset.
		3.2 Child can calm self when upset within 5 minutes.
		3.3 Child can calm self after periods of exciting activity.
		3.4 Child remains calm in disappointing situations.
C-4.0	Preschool-age child shows empathy for others.	4.1 Child responds appropriately to others' emotional responses.
		4.2 Child tries to comfort others when they are upset.
C-5.0	Preschool-age child shares and engages with others.	5.1 Child focuses on event indicated by another.
		5.2 Child greets adults and peers.
		5.3 Child cooperates in play or when completing a task.
		5.4 Child participates appropriately in group activities.
C-6.0	Preschool-age child demonstrates independence.	6.1 Child explores new materials and settings.
		6.2 Child tries new task before seeking help.
		6.3 Child stays with or returns to challenging activities.
		6.4 Child can leave caregiver without distress.
C-7.0	Preschool-age child displays a positive self-image.	7.1 Child knows personal information.
		7.2 Child shows off work, takes pride in accomplishments.
		7.3 Child makes positive statements about self.
C-8.0	Preschool-age child regulates attention and activity level.	8.1 Child stays with motor activity for 10 minutes or longer.
		8.2 Child participates in early literacy activities.
		8.3 Child moves from one activity to another without problems.
		8.4 Child participates in games with others.
		8.5 Child regulates his activity level to match setting.
C-9.0	Preschool-age child cooperates with daily routines and requests.	9.1 Child follows routines and rules.
		9.2 Child does what he is asked to do.
		9.3 Child responds appropriately when corrected by adults.
C-10.0	Preschool-age child shows a range of adaptive skills.	10.1 Child feeds self and eats a variety of foods without a problem.
		10.2 Child dresses self.
		10.3 Child goes to bed and falls asleep without a problem.
		10.4 Child uses the toilet appropriately.
		10.5 Child manages changes in settings and conditions.
		10.6 Child keeps himself safe in potentially dangerous conditions.
		10.7 Child solves problems to meet her needs.

Adult/caregiver benchmarks		Assessment items
A-1.0	Caregiver responds positively to preschool-age child.	1.1 Caregiver responds to child's nonverbal communication appropriately.
		1.2 Caregiver responds to child's verbal communication appropriately.
		1.3 Caregiver supports child's emotional needs.
		1.4 Caregiver uses positive comments and language with child.

Table 6.3.   *(continued)*

Adult/caregiver benchmarks		Assessment items	
		1.5	Caregiver successfully redirects child's inappropriate behaviors.
		1.6	Caregiver can recognize function of child's behaviors and, with assistance, can modify environment.
A-2.0	Caregiver provides developmentally appropriate type and level of activity.	2.1	Caregiver offers age-appropriate books, toys, and playthings for child.
		2.2	Caregiver plays with child and has ideas for age-appropriate games.
A-3.0	Caregiver provides preschool-age child with predictable schedule/routines.	3.1	Caregiver provides a mealtime routine for child that is predictable and appropriate for his age.
		3.2	Caregiver provides a rest and sleeping routine for child that is predictable and appropriate for his age.
		3.3	Caregiver provides child with predictable limits and discipline.
		3.4	Caregiver provides time each day to play with child.
A-4.0	Caregiver provides preschool-age child with a safe home and play environment.	4.1	Caregiver checks the home for things that can be dangerous to child.
		4.2	Caregiver is able to provide safe travel arrangements for child.
		4.3	Caregiver supervises child.
		4.4	Caregiver takes child for regular medical and dental care.

The key child and adult/caregiver benchmarks listed in Tables 6.1, 6.2, and 6.3 provide the content focus for the assessment/evaluation measure and linked intervention activities that are described in Chapter 8. Like the goals for targeted interventions, a set of specific criteria were used to formulate the assessment items. Specifically, each item

- Must be functional

- Must be meaningful

- Must be observable and measurable

- Can be easily embedded into daily activities

- Must be written in jargon-free language

- Could serve as an intervention goal

These six criteria resulted in the elimination of many items that frequently appear on diagnostic measures such as *Child clings to parent*; *Child hits and bites other children*; or *Child shows anger and distress*. We believe that targeting such negative responses as intervention goals is not appropriate; rather, the reciprocal positive response should be the intervention target. On a measure such as the SEAM, which garners results that can be used for goal selection and intervention activities, items should focus on what to encourage and teach rather than on what to eliminate. For example, the common item on many social emotional assessments, *Child clings to adult*, was changed on the SEAM to *[Child] explores new environments, while maintaining some contact* (e.g., Toddler SEAM 6.1). Rather than *Child hits or bites*, the item was changed on the SEAM to *[Child] cooperates in play or when completing a task* (e.g., Preschool-Age SEAM 5.3). Rather than assessing anger and distress, the focus is on the child's acquisition of positive affective responses. The same strategy was applied to items for caregivers so that each item can serve as a potential intervention goal. As mentioned, the SEAM for the infant, toddler, and preschool-age intervals is contained in Appendix B.

Each item is followed by three response options: "Most of the time," "Sometimes," and "Rarely or never." These boxes can be used to record whether the child (or caregiver) engages in the behavior on a regular basis (i.e., most of the time), occasionally or inconsistently (i.e., sometimes), or rarely or never if the child or caregiver does not exhibit the behavior or engages in the behavior very infrequently.

The "Is a concern" column, designated with circles for each item, can be used to indicate if the caregiver and/or professional see the behavior or condition as a potentially problematic area. For example, if an infant responds to the caregiver's physical actions sometimes but does so in a way that is unsatisfying to the caregiver, the "concern" item could be checked. The "Intervention goal" column, designated with triangles for each item, can be used to indicate those items that will be targeted for intervention plans. For example, the caregiver might choose to consider helping the infant modify his response to familiar caregivers and would, therefore, check the intervention goal column for SEAM: Infant C-1.1.

The use of the SEAM is critical to the development of high-quality goals. Without the use of such a tool, selected or developed goals may not be of high quality (i.e., functional, meaningful, measurable, and addressable during daily activities), and thus, intervention efforts may not be relevant or effective in terms of enhancing children's and caregivers' social emotional competence.

The Infant, Toddler, and Preschool-Age assessment interval forms follow a consistent format. As shown in Figure 6.2, the cover sheet has space for identifying information including the child's name, child's date of birth, family's name, name of person completing the form, and the administration date. The remainder of the cover sheet for each assessment interval provides instructions for completion of the form.

In addition, the SEAM can be used as a progress monitoring and evaluation tool. A discussion of these processes associated with the ABI:SE Approach is continued in Chapter 9.

The pages following the cover sheet contain the benchmark and assessment items. The assessment format for each assessment interval is the same. Each child benchmark is designated with a *C*, whereas each caregiver/adult benchmark is designated with an *A*. Child benchmarks and their associated assessment items appear first on the SEAM followed by the adult benchmarks and their associated assessment items.

Each benchmark has two or more associated items that are behavioral indicators for the benchmark. These items can serve as intervention goals when a child does not demonstrate the behavioral indicators. For example, if a child fails to demonstrate item C-10.0, (i.e., *[Child] shows a range of adaptive skills*), this item may be selected as an intervention goal. Caregivers and service

Social Emotional
Assessment/Evaluation Measure

INFANT

(for developmental range 3–18 months)

Child Benchmarks
and Assessment Items

Child's name: _____

Child's date of birth: _____

Family's name: _____

Name of person completing form: _____

Date of administration: _____

Instructions

Please read each benchmark and item carefully before selecting an answer. Each item is accompanied by several examples. Children may be able to successfully meet the item criterion in a variety of ways. Some items may be too difficult for the child; for example, a 4-month-old may not yet be able to imitate a parent's sounds. Professionals should ensure that caregivers understand that the SEAM may contain items that are developmentally too advanced for their child. Age norms should not be used with children with delays or developmental disabilities.

The three scoring options listed in the first three columns of the SEAM include "Most of the time," "Sometimes," and "Rarely or never" to indicate the frequency or likelihood of a child's behavior. For example, if an infant shows an interest in adults whom he knows well consistently over time, a check should be placed in the box under "Most of the time" for item C-1.1. Items marked "Most of the time" are generally considered strengths. If the infant shows interest in familiar adults inconsistently, the box under "Sometimes" should be checked. If the infant seldom shows an interest in familiar adults, the box under "Rarely or never" should be checked. The latter two columns allow participants to indicate whether a particular behavior is of concern and whether it should become an intervention goal, respectively. After you are finished with this SEAM and the corresponding Adult/Caregiver SEAM, record answers on the accompanying Summary Form.

Figure 6.2.   Cover page of the SEAM™: Infant, Experimental Edition.

providers can then develop activities to address this selected goal. In actuality, each assessment item on the SEAM can become an intervention goal. Examples of child benchmarks and associated items appear in Figure 6.3.

As shown in Figure 6.3, each benchmark 1.1 through C-1.4 has an associated set of items that are noted by corresponding numbers (e.g., C-1.0). Each item has one to two illustrative examples.

Each SEAM assessment interval has a final page that contains a summary form that has space to record scores and other information. This summary form permits monitoring child and caregiver change over time. As shown in Figure 6.4, the summary form has space to enter the administration date, whether the item is a strength or a concern, and whether the item was chosen as an intervention goal for three different administrations (e.g., quarterly). Evaluation can focus on selected goals or on all items (e.g., goals) depending on program goals and resources.

To assist in understanding the assessment process, the following section offers a case study.

A CASE STUDY OF THE ABI:SE ASSESSMENT PROCESS

LeBron and his mother, Shawna, participate in the WIC program. At LeBron's 19-month well-baby checkup, Shawna completed the ESQ and the ASQ:SE. Going over the results of the environmental screen with Shawna revealed several risk factors including teen mother, poverty, and limited support network. In addition, LeBron's performance on the ASQ:SE was above the cutoff score, suggesting some potential social emotional difficulties. These findings were sufficient for the WIC personnel to refer Shawna and LeBron to a home visitor program for high-risk toddlers.

The referral was evaluated and found to be appropriate for the local community home visitor program. Shawna and LeBron were asked to visit the center for an initial interview. During this interview, the intake coordinator explained in detail the purpose of the home visiting program and its procedures. She answered Shawna's questions and observed LeBron as he played on the floor. The coordinator noted that the toddler appeared to have a very short attention span and few functional play skills. She also noted that he produced no intelligible words but rather, fretted and cried when he seemed to want something. The coordinator explained to Shawna that a home visitor would come to her home the following week and would bring a special toy for LeBron. Shawna expressed her pleasure in receiving a new toy for her baby.

At the appointed time, Cari, the home visitor, arrived at Shawna's home. Cari sat down in the kitchen to explain the assessment process, to answer questions, and to observe LeBron playing with the toy she had brought him. While she described the purpose and procedures associated with the assessment, Cari answered Shawna's questions and observed the following:

- *LeBron's interest in the new toy was brief.*

- *LeBron's environment contained many dangers (e.g., electrical outlets uncovered, stairs with no protective gate).*

Child Benchmarks and Assessment Items
Infant

Please read each question carefully and
1. Check the box ■ that best describes your child's behavior.
2. Check the circle ● if this behavior is a concern.
3. Check the triangle ▲ if this will be an intervention goal.

	Most of the time	Sometimes	Rarely or never	Is a concern	Interven-tion goal
C-1.0 Baby participates in healthy interactions.					
1.1 Baby shows interest in you and other familiar caregivers.	■	■	■	●	▲
Follows you with his eyes *Quiets when talked to* *Looks at you when touched* *Shows pleasure when you return*					
1.2 Baby responds to you and other familiar caregivers.	■	■	■	●	▲
Reaches for you *Raises arms to be picked up* *Responds to her name* *Waves "bye-bye"* *Gives hugs*					
1.3 Baby initiates and responds to communications.	■	■	■	●	▲
Coos, chuckles, smiles, or laughs *at you* *Coos or vocalizes when you talk* *to him* *Laughs aloud* *Imitates your coos and babbles*					
1.4 Baby lets you know if she needs help or comfort.	■	■	■	●	▲
Lets you know when wet or hungry *Expresses emotions such as fear of* *loud sounds or new people, shyness,* *and surprise*					
C-2.0 Baby expresses a range of emotions.					
2.1 Baby smiles at you.	■	■	■	●	▲
Smiles when you smile at her *Smiles when you talk to him*					

Figure 6.3.   Sample child (C) benchmarks and associated assessment items from the SEAM: Infant, Experimental Edition.

	Admin date	Strength	Concern/continue monitoring	Identified as goal	Admin date	Strength	Concern/continue monitoring	Identified as goal	Admin date	Strength	Concern/continue monitoring	Identified as goal
CHILD												
Benchmark C-1.0												
Item 1.1												
Item 1.2												
Item 1.3												
Item 1.4												
Benchmark C-2.0												
Item 2.1												
Item 2.2												
Item 2.3												
Benchmark C-3.0												
Item 3.1												
Item 3.2												
Item 3.3												
Benchmark C-4.0												
Item 4.1												
Item 4.2												
Item 4.3												
Item 4.4												
Benchmark C-5.0												
Item 5.1												
Item 5.2												
Item 5.3												
Item 5.4												
Benchmark C-6.0												
Item 6.1												
Item 6.2												
Item 6.3												
Item 6.4												
Benchmark C-7.0												
Item 7.1												
Item 7.2												
Item 7.3												
Benchmark C-8.0												
Item 8.1												
Item 8.2												
Item 8.3												

Figure 6.4.　A sample page from the SEAM: Infant, Experimental Edition, Summary Form.

- *Little positive physical contact occurred between Shawna and LeBron.*

- *Communication between Shawna and LeBron consisted primarily of Shawna saying no to her son.*

At the end of the visit, Cari scheduled a second appointment when she and Shawna could complete the SEAM: Toddler.

At the second visit, Cari showed Shawna the assessment measure and asked if Shawna would prefer that Cari read the items to her. They discussed each item and agreed on the response to check that was most descriptive of the frequency of LeBron's behaviors (i.e., "Most of the time," "Sometimes," or "Rarely or never"). Cari also encouraged Shawna to indicate which items were of concern to her and which items might be good intervention goals. After they completed the assessment, Cari set a time for her next visit.

Cari will discuss Shawna's completed measure with her supervisor before her next home visit with Shawna. On this next visit, Cari and Shawna will discuss which goals to target based on the responses on the SEAM.

SUMMARY

This chapter emphasizes the importance of using an appropriate measure in order to ensure that the usefulness of the assessment process is optimized and produces information that can be used directly to formulate high-quality goals and intervention content. The SEAM was developed to meet this requirement.

In addition, in order for a measure to be functional, it is essential to have a process that is comprehensive and respectful of caregivers' values, desires, and needs. This second requirement helps to ensure that caregivers become participating members of the assessment and intervention team. The following chapter addresses in detail the process for using assessment outcomes to formulate high-quality goals.

7

Developing Intervention Goals

The previous chapters have described the ABI:SE Approach, with an emphasis on the first two processes: screening and assessment. The screening process is intended to evaluate the child's social emotional responses and critical variables in the child's environment that might affect his or her social emotional development. This screening process allows potential serious problems to be identified so that children and caregivers can be referred for specialized intervention with community specialists when needed.

For caregivers and children who do not appear to have significant problems, the ABI:SE Approach can assist service providers in partnering with caregivers and focusing on areas of identified concern. Children's problem behaviors can be identified as well as potential activities and supports for caregivers that may enhance children's social emotional skills.

Chapter 6 introduced the Social Emotional Assessment/Evaluation Measure (SEAM), Experimental Edition. To reiterate in brief: the SEAM is a curriculum-based assessment targeting important benchmarks and associated goals that form the building blocks of healthy social emotional development. Items focus on two main areas: 1) key child social emotional behaviors and 2) the caregiver's behaviors that affect a child's social emotional competence. In addition, SEAM items target important functional behaviors that can be operationalized and reliably observed throughout the child's daily activities. This chapter describes steps for developing goals from SEAM results.

As noted in Chapter 6, Shawna and LeBron completed the SEAM during a second home visit. Together, the home visitor, Cari, and LeBron's mother, Shawna, discussed each of the items on which Shawna indicated whether LeBron demonstrated the behavior most of the time, some of the time, or rarely or never. Shawna also indicated which items were of concern to her and which items might be appropriate intervention goals for LeBron. After completing the SEAM: Infant with Shawna, Cari returned to her office and discussed the results with her intervention team. In addition

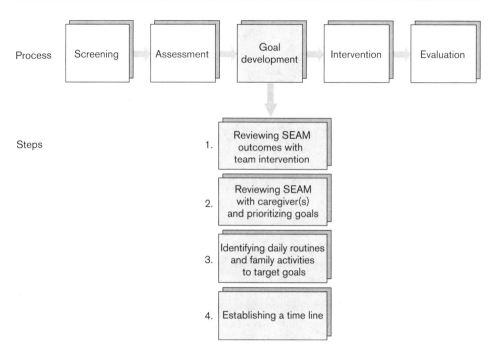

Figure 7.1.   Steps in the goal development process.

to the items that Shawna indicated were of concern to her, her team suggested that Cari talk with Shawna about adding one additional goal—"The child's living areas should be free of overt dangers." The team added this goal in response to Cari's observation that there were dangers in the home that could be addressed, such as uncovered electrical sockets and steep stairs without a child safety gate.

GOAL DEVELOPMENT

Following screening and assessment, goal development is the next process in the ABI:SE Approach. Results from the SEAM or a similar CBA should be used to develop one to three social emotional goals. The goal development process is composed of four steps, as shown in Figure 7.1:

1. *Review parent-completed SEAM or other CBA.* The first step is to review the parent-completed SEAM or other CBA, as well as other information that may have been gathered during the screening or assessing process (e.g., information from the ESQ) with team members to determine whether the ABI:SE Approach is appropriate for the family's situation or whether the family has more intensive needs in the social emotional area that may need to be referred to community mental health providers.

2. *Review SEAM with caregiver(s) and prioritize goals.* For families deemed appropriate for the ABI:SE Approach, complete the SEAM Goal Development and Intervention Plan form. This form has been designed to assist in completing this and subsequent steps in the goal development process and

is provided as Figure 7.2.) This form is not required, but it is important to gather the information targeted on the form.

   To begin, review with the caregiver her strengths and the child's strengths as well as the items that have been marked as concerns and those checked as intervention goals. Next, ask the caregiver to rank order the items checked as possible intervention goals. The caregiver should rank the checked items from 1 to 3, with 1 designating *most important* and so forth, and then select one to three priority goals as intervention targets.

3. *Identify daily routines and activities.* Once the intervention goals have been identified, assist the caregiver in identifying the daily routines and family activities (e.g., mealtimes, playtimes, bathtimes) that may provide opportunities for practicing the targeted goals throughout the child's day. These potentially useful routines and activities should be noted on the Goal Development and Intervention Plan.

Goal Development and Intervention Plan

1. **Child Strengths**
   Summarize the child's strengths. Child goals on the SEAM can serve as a guide.

2 **Caregiver Strengths**
   Summarize the strengths of the caregiver(s)/adult(s). Adult goals on the SEAM can serve as a guide.

3. **Goals**
   Write down intervention goals on the table below. Goals targeted by caregivers are marked in the Intervention Goal column on the SEAM. List by number (e.g., C-2.1, C-2.3) as well as key words.

Goal Number (e.g., C-2.1, A-3.2)	Key words (e.g., *eye contact, safe home*)	Priority (1 = highest)	Suggested activities to target goals	Time line	
				Begin	End

Figure 7.2. Blank Goal Development and Intervention Plan.

4. *Develop a time line for addressing each goal with caregivers.* The estimated start and ending dates for each goal can be noted in the "Time line" column on the Goal Development and Intervention Plan.

Details for the implementation of the four steps in the goal developing process are discussed next.

Step One: Reviewing SEAM Outcomes with the Intervention Team

After meeting with the caregiver and completing the SEAM or another appropriate CBA, the first step in the goal development process is to identify and prioritize goals that have been selected by the caregiver as important behaviors and potential intervention goals. Before finalizing goals to be targeted, meet with the intervention team to review the results obtained from any previous screens and assessments, obtain feedback about the family's needs, and review any additional resources or referrals that the family might need. After discussing screening and assessment with the team, arrange to have a meeting with the caregiver to finalize goal selection.

Some agencies or programs may not require team members to discuss screening and assessment before targeting goals with caregivers. However, this first step is suggested as a means of confirming a family's appropriateness for the ABI:SE Approach and to discuss needed resources and strategies for meeting the families' targeted needs and concerns. Families that have intensive needs, such as those in which signs of child neglect, domestic violence, or prolonged depression have been detected, may need to be referred to an agency that specializes in mental health services. Even for those families who require more intensive services, however, the ABI:SE Approach may be helpful in identifying areas of concern and possible referral sources and in beginning the process of providing supports and assistance while the family is waiting for a referral for specialized services.

Jon, a single parent of 24-month-old Eduardo, completed the SEAM: Toddler with the assistance of his Healthy Start home visitor, Ana. Ana and Troy, the Healthy Start social worker, returned to Jon's apartment to review the completed SEAM and to discuss concerns that Jon had brought up during the previous home visit, such as Eduardo's sleep difficulties. Ana began the visit by asking Jon how his week had gone and if Eduardo had been able to get to sleep more easily. Second, they began the review of Jon's completed SEAM. Ana will start the discussion by highlighting Eduardo's strengths (indicated by items checked as "Most of the time") and then discuss skills of concern for Jon.

Step Two: Reviewing SEAM with Caregivers and Prioritizing Goals

The second step is to review the completed SEAM with the caregiver by highlighting the child's and caregiver's strengths (as noted in the "Most of the time" columns for each) that reflect social emotional competence. Next, the goals that the caregiver indicated based on main concerns and those identified as potential intervention targets should be discussed.

The Goal Development and Intervention Plan, shown in Figure 7.2, can be used to summarize strengths and concerns and can serve as a basis for the review of SEAM results. This summary information can also be entered on the SEAM form itself. However, this will require additional writing space on the SEAM form for step three, identifying routines and activities, and step four, establishing a time line.

The Goal Development and Intervention Plan is composed of three sections. The first two consist of spaces to enter the child's and caregiver's strengths. The third section is composed of columns in which to enter 1) key words associated with the goal (in lieu of writing out the entire goal); 2) the priority number assigned to the goal; 3) possible activities to target the goal; and 4) the time line (i.e., beginning and ending dates) associated with the goal.

After strengths and needs have been discussed, select one to three SEAM goals for intervention. Concentrating on more than a few goals may be overwhelming for the caregiver as well as the interventionist. The Goal Development and Intervention Plan can assist in prioritizing goals and deciding which behaviors are most important to target. It is critical that caregivers identify behaviors of greatest concern and assist in devising a plan for working on these important goals.

An example of step two is illustrated in the following vignette.

Ari is a preschool classroom teacher who works with a group of 3- and 4-year-old children. The mission of his center, Children First, is to provide social and emotional support to families and to assist children in gaining pre-academic skills for success in school. Ari conducted home visits with families during the first 2 months of school to meet caregivers and siblings and to complete the SEAM: Preschool with caregivers for each child in his class. Based on ASQ:SE and ESQ screening results and parent concerns noted on the SEAM completed by Brigid and Frank, the parents of 4-year-old Silvia. Ari conducted a second home visit with them. Brigid and Frank scored Silvia in the "Rarely or never" column for three out of four items under the first three benchmarks for preschool children including demonstrates healthy interactions with others (C-1.0), expresses a range of emotions (C-2.0), *and* regulates social emotional responses (C-3.0). *During the home visit, Silvia's parents voiced concerns about their daughter's social interactions.*

During the second home visit, Ari reviewed the SEAM outcomes with Brigid and Frank (step two in the goal development process). Ari already had shared the SEAM results with his program team, and they suggested that Ari discuss with Silvia's parents the possibility of focusing on goals under C-1.0 (demonstrates healthy interactions) *and C-2.0* (expresses a range of emotions) *because these goals could be addressed in the classroom environment. His supervisor gave Ari a list of community mental health agencies in the event that Brigid and Frank requested additional resources.*

Goal Development and Intervention Plan

1. **Child Strengths**
   Summarize the child's strengths. Child goals on the SEAM can serve as a guide.
   - Follows home and classroom rules
   - Gets ready for school independently in mornings
   - Is learning English very quickly

2. **Caregiver Strengths**
   Summarize the strengths of the caregiver(s)/adult(s). Adult goals on the SEAM can serve as a guide.
   - Provides nurturing, safe home environment
   - Follows predictable routines
   - Lots of toys, books at home for Silvia

3. **Goals**
   Write down intervention goals on the table below. Goals targeted by caregivers will be marked in the Intervention Goal column on the SEAM. List by number (e.g., C-2.1, C-2.3) as well as key words.

Goal number	Key words	Priority (1 = highest)	Suggested activities to target goals	Time line Begin	End
C-1.1	Shows affection	4			
C-1.4	Shares, takes turns	2	Outdoor games, snack time	11/3	2/1
C-1.5	Plays with other children	1	Soccer games, church school	9/1	12/15
C-3.0	Responds to soothing	3			
C-3.2	Calms self	5			

Figure 7.3. Example of a Goal Development and Intervention Plan for Silvia and her parents.

Ari began the second home visit by asking Brigid and Frank if they had questions about the SEAM outcomes. With the parents' input, Ari completed the Goal Development and Intervention Plan as they talked. They first discussed Silvia's strengths and entered this information under the Child Strengths section of the Goal Development and Intervention Plan (see Figure 7.3). They next talked about caregiver strengths. Brigid and Frank indicated how difficult it was for them to leave family and friends in their country of origin to emigrate to the United States. Brigid said that she felt depressed, isolated, and without friends, and was worried that her depression was affecting Silvia's happiness. On the positive side, Brigid and Frank were found to have many parenting strengths, such as providing a positive and nurturing home environment (A-1.0) and following predictable schedules/routines (A-3.0). Ari offered Brigid and Frank a list of community resources including information about immigrant support groups.

A second example of reviewing child strengths and prioritizing goals is presented in the story of Shawna and her son LeBron, and their home visitor, Cari.

Cari and Shawna reviewed the SEAM: Infant that Shawna had completed previously. Cari asked Shawna to talk about LeBron's strengths in terms of his social emo-

tional skills. Shawna identified LeBron's engaging smile as a strength (Infant SEAM C-2.1, C-2.2, and C-2.3), and Cari noted that LeBron appeared to be interested in new surroundings (C-6.1, C-6.2, and C-6.3). These strengths were listed under the heading "Child strengths" on the SEAM Goal Development and Intervention Plan as shown in Figure 7.4. Under the next heading, "Caregiver strengths," Shawna appeared inhibited by the assessment process and could not at first identify any of her own strengths related to caring for LeBron. Cari helped by noticing that Shawna takes good care of LeBron's needs such as diapering him and washing his bottles (A-3.1) and taking him regularly to the clinic for his well-baby checkups (A-4.5), and makes sure he spends time around his cousins. Shawna agreed that these are some of her strengths.

Cari and Shawna then discussed her concerns about LeBron, reviewing all items that Shawna had marked "Rarely or never," as well as those items checked as concerns and intervention goals. Figure 7.5 contains sample items from one page of LeBron's

Goal Development and Intervention Plan

1. **Child Strengths**
   Summarize the child's strengths. Child goals on the SEAM can serve as a guide.
   - Great smile
   - Looks at you—makes eye contact
   - Interested in things around him; explores surroundings

2. **Caregiver Strengths**
   Summarize the strengths of the caregiver(s)/adult(s). Adult goals on the SEAM can serve as a guide.
   - Takes good care of LeBron's physical needs
   - Always takes LeBron to doctor when he is sick or needs check-up; immunizations are up to date
   - Provides lots of toys, books at home for LeBron

3. **Goals**
   Write down intervention goals on the table below. Goals targeted by caregivers will be marked in the Intervention Goal column on the SEAM. List by number (e.g., C-2.1, C-2.3) as well as key words.

Goal number	Key words	Priority (1 = highest)	Suggested activities to target goals	Time line Begin	Time line End
C-1.3	Responds to caregiver	3			
C-1.4	Lets caregiver know needs	2*	Bath time, mealtime, bedtime	5/20	7/20
C-8.0	Follows routines	5			
C-8.2	Looks at books and pictures	4			
C-8.3	Stays with motor activities	1*	Bath time, playtime with toy cars	5/20	7/20
A-4.1	Keeps areas free of danger		Go through house on hands and knees to identify danger		

Figure 7.4. Example of Goal Development and Intervention Plan for LeBron and Shawna. The highest priorities are marked with an asterisk.

	Most of the time	Sometimes	Rarely or never	Is a concern	Intervention goal
C-6.0 Baby explores hands and feet and surroundings.					
6.1 Baby explores his hands and feet.	☐	✓	☐	○	△
Grabs foot when on back Grasps hands together and wiggles fingers Bangs objects together with both hands Kicks or pushes a mobile to make it move					
6.2 Baby explores toys and materials.	✓	☐	☐	○	△
Looks at object Grabs objects or people within reach Holds and explores toys Crawls to his favorite toys or caregiver Tries different actions with toys and objects					
6.3 Baby explores surroundings.	✓	☐	☐	○	△
Rolls onto back Turns head to see behind her Crawls to look at and touch objects on floor Moves to look behind doors and furniture Begins to run, climb, and jump					
6.4 Baby crawls or walks a short distance away from you.	✓	☐	☐	○	△
Crawls 10–20 feet away from you, looking back at you Leaves your side to explore new toy, object or person and remains at a distance for a few minutes Crawls or walks around living areas exploring people, locations, and objects					
C-7.0 Baby displays a positive self-image.					
7.1 Baby laughs at, or smiles at, her image or picture of self.	✓	☐	☐	○	△
Smiles at reflection in a mirror Laughs at self reflected in store window Points to self in mirror or picture Points to a picture of self	(Bring mirror next time.)				

Figure 7.5. Sample items from one page of LeBron's completed SEAM.

completed SEAM. Goals that Shawna indicated as intervention targets on the SEAM were written on the Goal Development and Intervention Plan (Figure 7.4).

Cari's next task was to assist Shawna in rank ordering the identified goals in order of importance, beginning with the most important. Shawna wanted to start with the first two goals: Lets caregiver know needs (C-1.4) *and* stays with motor activities (C-8.3). *Cari suggested that they also add one adult goal,* Keeps areas free of danger (A-4.1), *so that LeBron's environment would be safe and no one would have to worry needlessly about him getting hurt or injured. Shawna seemed puzzled at first about this additional goal that focused on overt dangers in the home environment. However, when Cari pointed out potential dangers in LeBron's home such as uncovered electrical sockets and stairs without a safety gate, Shawna agreed that there were some things that she could do immediately to make the home safer for LeBron, especially because it wouldn't be long before he would be able to reach both the sockets and the stairs. She readily agreed to include this goal.*

Step Three: Identifying Daily Routines and Family Activities to Target Goals

During step three, the focus is on having caregivers identify daily activities, routines, and family events during which the prioritized goal can be addressed. These activities and routines can be listed on the Goal Development and Intervention Plan under the column headed "Suggested activities to target goals." For example, if a child has difficulty moving easily from one activity to the next, free play time in the toddler classroom may be a good time to work on transitions, as well as at home after nap, snack, and bedtimes.

An example of the third step in the goal development process is illustrated with LeBron and Shawna.

After LeBron's goals were prioritized, Cari asked Shawna if there were home routines and family activities that might provide opportunities for her and LeBron to practice developing the behaviors targeted in these goals. Such routines and activities for LeBron included bath time, mealtimes, and bedtimes, and were listed under "Suggested activities to target goals" on the Goal Development and Intervention Plan presented in Figure 7.4. At the next home visit, Cari will begin intervention activities with Shawna and LeBron based on Shawna's suggested activities.

Step Four: Establishing a Time Line

A time line should be established for the child/caregiver to attain the priority goals. This time line will vary depending on the type of goal, opportunities for practicing the targeted skills, and the child and caregiver's current behavioral repertoire. Some SEAM goals such as *Checks the home for things that can be dangerous* (SEAM: Preschool-Age A-4.1) can be completed quickly, while other goals such as *Calms self when upset within 5 minute*s (SEAM: Preschool-Age, C-3.2) may take several months or longer. The time line can be modified as needed once intervention has begun and progress is monitored.

After prioritizing goals on the Goal Development and Intervention Plan shown in Figure 7.3, Ari asked Frank and Brigid if there were activities at home or in the pre-school classroom that might provide opportunities for Silvia to develop friendships (i.e., C-1.0: Demonstrates healthy interactions with others*). Frank and Brigid said that they did not know other families in the area as yet but that they were plan-ning to attend a nearby church, where they might meet other families with young children. Ari suggested that outdoor play time might provide good activities to target because Silvia excels at ball skills and he could introduce Silvia to simple soccer games with one or two other girls her age. They set a time line of 3 months for a next meet-ing to discuss Silvia's progress toward her goal of developing healthy peer interactions.*

SUMMARY

This chapter describes the process of developing goals for young children's so-cial emotional development. After children have undergone a screening process, early childhood professionals can use an assessment process using the SEAM or other appropriate CBAs to assist in targeting goals with families and in identi-fying daily activities for practicing these goals.

Four recommended steps for developing high-quality goals with families are presented. After reviewing the SEAM with the intervention team, targeted goals can be reviewed and prioritized with caregivers. A strengths-based ap-proach in which child and family competence are emphasized as well as partner-ships with families are essential for developing quality goals. A list of routines and activities, together with estimated time lines, can be developed with the family in preparation for the intervention process. Cultural and individual fam-ily values relevant in the daily lives of children and families need to be embed-ded in all aspects of developing goals and intervention activities.

The next process after developing goals is intervention. The intervention process is described in the following chapter.

8

The Intervention Process

After goals have been identified and an intervention plan written using the Goal Development and Intervention Plan form, the next process in the ABI:SE Approach is the intervention itself. Intervention refers to carrying out actions designed to assist children in acquiring and using targeted social emotional skills. Interventionists and caregivers should work cooperatively to develop these interventions.

The intervention process is guided by the SEAM goals that were identified during the assessment process and that were prioritized and written during the goal development process. Examples of goals derived from the SEAM were shown in Figures 7.3 and 7.4 in the previous chapter. Caregiver and child strengths and goals listed on the Goal Development and Intervention Plan serve to guide intervention activities. Intervention in the ABI:SE Approach is based on the elements that compose activity-based intervention, which primarily relies on child-directed, planned, and routine activities that are not predetermined but rather instigated by children as they negotiate their daily environments (Pretti-Frontczak & Bricker, 2004).

INTERVENTION IN A LINKED SYSTEMS APPROACH

As described in previous chapters, three processes—screening, assessment, and goal development—precede intervention (see Figure 8.1). In the screening process, children's social emotional skills are assessed using the ASQ:SE, the ESQ, or other social emotional screening measures.

Once goals for improving a child's social emotional development have been selected following screening and assessment, intervention is the fourth process in the ABI:SE Approach. Intervention consists primarily of embedding learning or practice opportunities into the everyday authentic (i.e., meaningful) activities of children and families, such as family trips to the grocery store and free-play time in a child care center. *Embedding* refers to addressing the targeted social emotional goals during daily activities, routines, and events in a manner that provides multiple and varied learning opportunities for children and caregivers (Pretti-Frontczak & Bricker, 2004). For example, snack and circle times

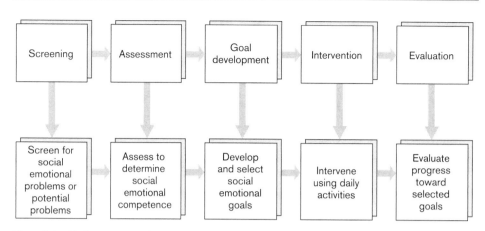

Figure 8.1.   The five processes of the linked system framework with associated activities.

in a preschool classroom might provide multiple opportunities for addressing SEAM goals related to sharing and engagement (SEAM: Preschool-Age C-5.0). To provide opportunities to focus attention on another person (C-5.1: *Child focuses on event indicated by another*), a child can identify and ask for a favorite snack food passed out by a peer. Suggesting and singing a variation of a familiar song, leading a finger play game at circle time, and playing Duck Duck Goose with a favorite puppet are additional examples of opportunities adults can address attention and engagement goals in the classroom.

The home environment also can provide multiple authentic opportunities for intervention activities in which SEAM goals can be embedded in a family's everyday routines and activities. For intervention with a toddler with established goals in the area of expressing a range of emotions, for example, a mother may model and label the emotion of "being sad" when a child has broken a favorite toy, and provide an opportunity for the toddler to identify his own emotions. During a trip to the park, this mother can ask her toddler, "How do you feel now?" after the toddler has mustered his courage to slide down the long, twisting, slippery slide. Afterward, she can provide the opportunity for her toddler to identify his own emotions when they have to leave the park for home.

After intervention, the final process in the linked system is *evaluation*. In the ABI:SE Approach, evaluating refers to documenting children's performance on targeted SEAM goals and comparing their previous performance with their current one. In a curriculum-based assessment (CBA), SEAM goals (i.e., items) are designed to serve as intervention as well as evaluation targets. That is, an item selected as a goal for the toddler mentioned in the previous paragraph such as *Child identifies own emotions* (SEAM: Preschool-Age C-2.4) can serve to guide intervention activities as well as to help the user evaluate whether the toddler has acquired the skill. The evaluating process is described in the following chapter.

Let's look again at the example of Silvia and her preschool teacher, Ari, and see how he plans classroom intervention activities for her.

Ari has conducted two home visits and completed the Goal Development and Intervention Plan with Silvia's parents, Frank and Brigid. Following Frank and Brigid's suggestions, Ari will embed opportunities for Silvia to play with other children (SEAM: Preschool-Age Goal C-1.5) and share and take turns with other children (C-1.4) during outdoor kickball games. Ari will plan "partner" kick ball games so that Silvia will first be able to practice kicking a ball back and forth with one other girl for 3 or 4 minutes, then gradually increase the time and number of players. All children will earn additional outdoor kickball playtime when they play cooperatively (i.e., without physical or verbal aggression) during the allotted outdoor playtimes. The natural consequence of engaging in a favorite activity for increasingly longer time periods may provide adequate reinforcement for Silvia to improve her play skills with other children.

COMPONENTS OF ACTIVITY-BASED INTERVENTION: SOCIAL EMOTIONAL

Activity-based intervention (ABI) involves focusing on targeted goals within daily activities and events and uses these activities and events to embed practice or learning opportunities for individual children or groups of children (Bricker & Cripe, 1992; Pretti-Frontczak & Bricker, 2004). The paramount advantages of this intervention approach are that it permits using meaningful daily routines and activities as training vehicles and also offers multiple opportunities to address targeted goals. The foundation of activity-based intervention is the daily transactions that occur between infants, toddlers, and preschool children and their physical and social environments. Within an ABI:SE Approach, learning opportunities that address children's social emotional goals are specifically embedded into authentic child-directed, routine, and planned activities. These authentic, meaningful activities provide a range of practice opportunities for young children and caregivers. The back-and-forth nature of relationships allows children and caregivers to experience exchanges with one another and to learn through these ongoing give-and-take interactions.

Activity-based intervention is composed of four major elements: 1) functional and generative goals developed from the SEAM or other CBA; 2) child-directed, routine, and planned activities; 3) multiple and varied learning opportunities offered throughout the day; and 4) timely and integral feedback and consequences (Pretti-Frontczak & Bricker, 2004).

Functional and Generative SEAM Goals

The first element, *functional and generative SEAM goals,* targets behaviors that will enhance the lives of children and their caregivers in a variety of settings. All SEAM goals target important, measurable behaviors that are critical for quality interactions between children and their environment.

Child-Directed, Routine, and Planned Activities

The second element in activity-based intervention, is *child-directed, routine, and planned activities.* These three types of activities are used as the context for intervention. Child-directed activities refer to those that are initiated or guided by the child. Examples of child-directed activities include play activities that children engage in without prompting, such as building with blocks and dressing and feeding a favorite doll. Because child-directed activities are often of high interest and motivating to children, they provide excellent opportunities to learn or practice targeted goals.

One example of a child-directed activity for SEAM: Toddler Goal C-1.4, *Toddler lets you know if he needs help, attention, or comfort,* is building a car with snap-together blocks. A caregiver can wait until his child asks for help before offering assistance. The caregiver can also engineer opportunities for practicing goals, such as putting several block pieces out of reach so that the child needs to request help to get the remaining pieces.

Routine activities are those daily, regular, and necessary events such as eating, bathing, dressing, and traveling. These routine activities can be used to embed learning opportunities to practice SEAM goals. Cooperation skills (e.g., SEAM: Toddler Goal C-9.0: *Toddler cooperates with daily routines and requests*) and adaptive skills (e.g., SEAM: Toddler Goal C-10: *Toddler shows a range of adaptive skills*) may be easily embedded during routine activities. A compliance goal, *Toddler cooperates with simple requests* (SEAM: Toddler Goal C-9.2) may be practiced by making simple requests of a toddler during dressing in the morning, such as lifting his arm to help put on his shirt and helping to zip up the last few inches of his coat zipper. *Child eats and feeds self a variety of foods* (SEAM: Toddler Goal C-10.1) may be practiced at dinner time by placing one or two age-appropriate new foods of varying textures and colors on a toddler's highchair tray and letting her touch and taste these different foods. Using routine activities allows children and caregivers to practice goals during events that reflect the family's values, culture, and experiences.

Planned Activities

The third type of activity—planned activities—are those events that occur with adult guidance, such as preparing food, taking a bath, or conducting a science experiment. Planned activities most often occur in classroom and child care settings but may also occur in the home; for example, when stormy weather requires caregivers to set up indoor playtime activities such as making a pretend fort with blankets or dressing up in old Halloween clothes. Planned activities provide increased learning opportunities for children when they are carefully constructed around children's goals, are based on children's interests, and use fun and motivating materials. Examples of child-directed, routine, and planned activities for providing opportunities to practice SEAM goals are described in Table 8.1.

Table 8.1. Examples of child-directed, routine and planned activities for practicing SEAM goals.

Goal	Child-directed	Routine activities	Planned activities	Settings
C-1.3. Baby initiates and responds to communications (Infant interval)	Baby asks caregiver to reach balloon by pointing hands up and saying "Mamma"	When dressing, caregiver responds to infant vocalizations with verbal responses	Caregiver signs for juice at snack time and gives juice after gestured request from infant	Home, park, library, child care center, in car/bus when traveling
C-4.2. Toddler tries to comfort others when they are upset. (Toddler interval)	Toddler returns favorite blanket to crying peer	During storytime before bed, toddler kisses picture of crying girl	During puppet play, toddler responds to peer's puppet by giving it a hug	Family child care setting, home, preschool classroom
C-8.5. Child regulates her activity level to match setting (Preschool-Age interval)	Child fills and pours beans into containers at science/math table	Child hangs up coat, puts away lunch, and joins puzzle table in classroom	Child and peers participate in singing activity with karaoke microphone	Preschool classroom, home child care setting, home

Multiple and Varied Learning Opportunities

The third element of the ABI:SE Approach is to provide multiple and varied learning opportunities. Children and caregivers must be able to practice new social emotional skills across a range of settings and conditions. Learning opportunities need to be relevant and meaningful, match the child's current developmental level, and be tailored to the child's interests and motivation. Table 8.1 also includes examples of multiple settings in which SEAM goals can be practiced. In addition, environmental arrangements, such as placing toys on a low shelf so that preschool children can have access to them and put them away, can add to the numbers of opportunities children have for practicing SEAM goals.

Timely and Appropriate Feedback and Consequences

The fourth and final element of activity-based intervention is to provide children with timely and appropriate feedback and consequences. The feedback/consequences must be immediate so that a child can discern the relationship between his response and the subsequent consequences, as in the following example.

Rashud and Shen are playing fort. In a fit of temper, Rashud kicks over the fort wall. His mother prompts him to apologize. When Rashud does apologize for his actions after this prompting, immediate feedback such as praise (e.g., "I think Shen feels better now that you apologized to him") should follow the apology. Positive, natural outcomes generally provide the most effective feedback and consequences. The most effective consequence to encourage Rashud's appropriate social behavior may then be to have him help to rebuild the fort wall with Shen or another peer.

Table 8.2. Examples of integrated, timely feedback and consequences during ABI:SE Intervention

Functional SEAM goals	Child-directed, routine, and planned activities	Multiple and varied opportunities	Timely and logical feedback/ consequences
Baby smiles at you (C-2.1)	Feeding times, trips to grocery store, storytime	Throughout day, opportunities provided for one-to-one relaxed time	Caregiver smiles back, lightly touches and tickles infant
Toddler greets you and other familiar adults (C-5.3)	In classroom, at park, before bedtime at home	During morning arrival times, at home when neighbors visit	Children and adults say greeting back. Adults make physical contact
Child can calm self within 5–10 minutes (C-3.2)	After favorite gross motor activities at home and in classroom setting	Outdoor free play time, transitions back into classroom, at home before bedtime stories	Social praise, choice of favorite quiet activity

Examples of multiple and varied practice opportunities and timely and integrated feedback and consequences are described in Table 8.2.

Environmental arrangements also can assist with providing timely and natural feedback and consequences. For example, access to a drinking fountain can provide immediate positive consequences to children who are thirsty, whereas access to a toy box can provide ways for children to remain engaged in productive activities.

Timely and meaningful, naturally and logically occurring consequences will enhance learning in children. Individually tailored, culturally appropriate learning situations can be provided through an activity-based approach. (See Pretti-Frontczak & Bricker, 2004, for a detailed description of activity-based intervention as well as intervention guidelines, data collection forms, and descriptions of conceptual and research foundations of ABI.)

As noted in Chapter 4, the ABI:SE Approach is most successful when implemented within a linked system framework (Bricker, 2002). Intervention in the ABI:SE Approach is based on SEAM goals targeted by caregivers during the goal development process. Children's strengths and interests are used as well as the arrangement of the physical environment to provide guidance and practice opportunities for children to learn targeted social emotional skills. All targeted activities should be guided by family values and routines as well as preferred child interests, toys, and activities. Ongoing evaluation, described in Chapter 9, is critical for effective and efficient intervention.

Shawna and her son LeBron, described in Chapters 6 and 7, have completed the Goal Development and Intervention Plan with their home visitor, Cari. The next steps that they will take in the intervention process are described here.

Shawna, LeBron's mother, wanted to target two goals for LeBron. First, Shawna wanted LeBron to practice letting her know of his needs (SEAM: Infant Goal C-1.4).

With Cari's help, Shawna identified bath, bed, and mealtimes as good times for providing LeBron with opportunities to practice this goal. She also identified bath and play times as activities for practicing the second goal, Baby engages in motor activities for several minutes or longer *(C-8.3).*

On her next home visit, Cari brought the Goal Development and Intervention Plan (displayed previously in Figure 7.3), which she will review with Shawna. Cari first modeled how to embed learning opportunities into the activities that Shawna suggested. In order to encourage LeBron to express his needs, during snack time Cari modeled putting out small bits of crackers initially and waited until Le-Bron vocalized or approximated saying "More." Shawna provided immediate and meaningful feedback by giving LeBron "more" crackers. Cari and Shawna then followed a similar process during snack time of waiting for LeBron's gestures or vocalizations for juice, then giving LeBron small sips of juice from a sippy cup.

For the second goal regarding staying with motor activities, Shawna identified bath time and playtime with cars for providing intervention opportunities. Cari modeled short child-directed play sessions with LeBron, which she suggested should be gradually increased as LeBron is able to play for longer periods. Because Shawna said she rarely sits on the floor to play with LeBron, Cari also modeled sitting on the floor, putting LeBron across from her so she could have eye-to-eye contact with him and putting his back against the couch for support. She modeled sharing a short playtime with LeBron using two or three of his favorite toys on the floor in which LeBron was allowed to choose one or more of the toys to play with. Cari modeled two or three ways to follow and expand on LeBron's play, thus increasing his playtime with his cars and other toys, as shown in Table 8.3. As Cari modeled appropriate interactions with LeBron, she encouraged Shawna to join in on the floor so that Shawna was a part of the activity. Shawna practiced expanding on her son's play and interests, engaging in reciprocal back-and-forth interactions when possible and matching her responses to those he initiated.

STEPS IN THE INTERVENTION PROCESS

The intervention process has four steps, as shown in Figure 8.2.

Table 8.3. Examples of expanding play and lengthening attention span

Child's (LeBron) action	Mother (Shawna) following child's lead	Mother (Shawna) expands on child's action
Pushes blue car forward	Pushes red car forward	Says "Rum rum"
Crashes blue car into red car	Crashes yellow car into red and blue cars	Says "Bang"
Lines red and yellow cars up	Adds blue car to line up	Sets up box as "garage" for cars

Step One: Selecting One to Two Activities Per Goal

The first step in the intervention process is to expand on the suggested activities listed on the Goal Development and Intervention Plan, written during the previous goal development process (described in Chapter 7). Authentic, culturally relevant activities are critical for effective intervention as are activities that are developmentally appropriate (i.e., neither too difficult nor too easy) and that are based on the particular child's interests. A variety of child-directed, routine, and planned activities should be selected.

If resources are needed in addition to the caregiver's suggestions on the Goal Development and Intervention Plan, numerous well-developed commercial curricula are available such as *Beautiful Beginnings: A Developmental Curriculum for Infants and Toddlers* (Raikes & McCall Whitmer, 2006), *The Creative Curriculum* (Dodge & Colker, 1992; Dombro, Colker, & Dodge, 2002), *High/Scope* (Hohmann & Weikart, 2004), *Ounce Assessment Scale* (Meisels, Dombro, Marsden, Weston, & Jewkes, 2003), and *Devereux Early Childhood Assessment* (Devereux Foundation, 1998). These curricula offer a variety of activities sequenced from easy to difficult, focus on the social emotional domain, and are described in more detail in Appendix C: Guide to Early Childhood Curricula at the end of this book.

Step Two: Identifying Embedding Opportunities

The second step in the intervening process is to specify two or three opportunities for embedding the targeted social emotional goal during the chosen activities. An Embedding Plan, like the blank one shown in Figure 8.3, can be written with embedding opportunities identified for each activity. A completed

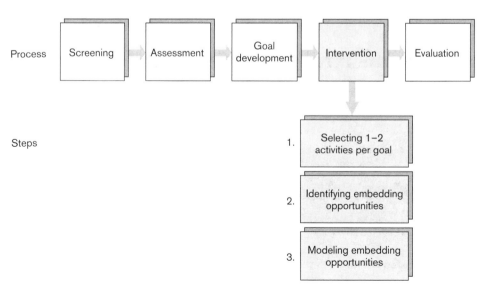

Figure 8.2.   Steps in the intervention process.

Embedding Plan can be found in Figure 8.4. One example of planning embedding opportunities is to provide a variety of foods for a toddler during mealtimes to foster SEAM:Toddler Goal C-10.1 (*Toddler eats and feeds self a variety of foods without problems*). Also during mealtimes, the toddler would have opportunities to practice self-regulation (C-8.1. *Toddler stays with motor activities for 5 minutes or longer*), such as when the caregiver very gradually increases the length of time the toddler stays in the highchair and the child learns to sit still to eat.

Using a form such as the Activity Matrix contained in Figure 8.5 may be helpful in classroom and group settings to assist with targeting, managing, and evaluating SEAM goals for groups of children. Children's names can be written across the top as column headings, and their targeted SEAM benchmarks and goals can be noted in the left-hand column. An example of a completed activity matrix is contained in Figure 8.6. If posted on a bulletin board, such a matrix can remind the classroom teachers to offer multiple opportunities for specific goals. For example, a teacher could use the Matrix as a reminder to provide Silvia, Hiro, Ean, and Eamon with opportunities to play cooperatively during a beanbag toss activity, or to ask Donna and Jacques to comply with demands, such to throw certain colored bags to specific children.

Embedding Plan

SEAM goals	Routine or activity	Embedding opportunities

Figure 8.3.   Blank Embedding Plan for SEAM goals.

Embedding Plan

SEAM goals	Routine or activity	Embedding opportunities
6.2 Toddler can separate from caregiver in familiar environment with minimal distress.	Morning good-bye at child care, at a friend's house, at church	Child has favorite toy and game; when mother leaves home on Saturday, vocalizes that father will return and bring popsicle from store
7.3 Toddler tells caregiver what he did or accomplished.	Home routines; after art, building, science activities	Verbally labels completed artwork, block designs Describes meal he has eaten
8.3 Toddler moves from one activity to another without problem.	Transitions in family child care	Visual prompts—child identifies next activity, goes to that location, and starts next activity immediately; visual prompts faded

Figure 8.4. Example of a completed Embedding Plan for SEAM goals (Toddler interval).

Activity Matrix

Children

Benchmark/goals											

Figure 8.5. Blank SEAM Activity Matrix.

Activity Matrix

Benchmark/goals	Silvia	Donna	Sue	Jacques	Paul	Hiro	Becca	Ean	Eamon
Regulates attention		×							
Demonstrates independence					×				
Shares	×		×			×	×	×	
Plays cooperatively	×					×	×	×	
Complies with demands		×		×					
Follows routines						×			

Figure 8.6. Example of a completed SEAM Activity Matrix.

In addition to Silvia, Ari has six other children in his preschool classroom with SEAM goals. So that he can keep in mind the children's goals and embedding opportunities, Ari completed the SEAM Activity Matrix (as shown in Figure 8.6) for the seven children. He also completed Activity Plans (see Pretti-Frontczak & Bricker, 2004, for a more detailed description) for each classroom activity so that he could anticipate what materials he will need and identify steps of the activity and possible variations if the activity was not of high interest to the children. Each Activity Plan included necessary materials; the environmental arrangement; a sequence of steps for introducing the activity (i.e., beginning, middle, end); opportunities for embedding learning; and planned variations (Pretti-Frontczak & Bricker, 2004). An example of one of Ari's completed Activity Plan can be found in Figure 8.7. The Activity Plan and Activity Matrix assists Ari by providing optimal, varied, and high-interest opportunities throughout the day so that he can practice his SEAM goals.

Step Three: Modeling Embedding Opportunities

During home visits, it may be necessary to model for caregivers how to embed learning opportunities during the targeted activities and events. Modeling two or three ways to embed a goal during one selected activity may be sufficient at

---

Activity Plan

Child's name: _Becca_

Name of person completing this plan: _Ari_

Date: _9/30_

1. **Activity name:** _Sponge Toss_

2. **Materials**
    - Sponges cut in shapes, such as triangles, squares, or circles
    - Large piece of newsprint (at least 6 ft × 6 ft), with 4 ft × 4 ft circle painted in the middle
    - Washable paints in large bowls
    - Large paint brushes

3. **Environmental arrangement**
    - Outdoors in quiet area of playground
    - Draw chalk lines in 8 ft × 8 ft square around newsprint as boundary for game and for children to stay inside of during activity

4. **Sequence of steps**

    Beginning
    The sponges in different shapes are presented in a "treasure chest" (painted cardboard box).
    Each child gets to take two sponges if he or can name the shapes.
    Each child paints one side of the sponge with a different color. Color and shape names can be embedded for practice.

    Middle
    Each child stands behind the boundary line (adjust distance as needed for skill of child) and tosses sponge so paint side lands on paper, making mark. Aim of Sponge Toss is for the children to make sponge marks along the drawn shape (e.g., circle, triangle) in different colors.

    End
    Children pick up sponges by color, wash and paint with different color, and toss again. Or children pick up sponges, clean them in a small bucket, then put them back in a treasure chest.

Figure 8.7. Example of an Activity Plan for Ari focused on cooperation, sharing, attention, and engagement.

5. **Embedded Learning Opportunities**
   Learns/practices cooperative skills:
   • Plays with other children
   • Shares and takes turns with other children

   Learns/practices sharing attention and engagement:
   • Focuses on events of others
   • Cooperates in play
   • Plays appropriately in group activities

   Learns/practices names of classmates, shapes, or colors:
   • Names shapes, colors
   • Uses names of classmates during activity

6. **Planned variations**
   1. Use different shapes.
   2. Use materials other than sponges, such as plastic horse shoes.
   3. Omit painting; use as water play on warm day.
   4. Omit painting and paper and do the activity in a sandbox.

7. **Peer Interaction Opportunities**
   Cooperation, taking turns (see also 5: Embedded Learning Opportunities)

8. **Caregiver involvement**
   • Include children's favorite items such as sticks, flat stones
   • Shapes and color names can also be practiced at home (as culturally appropriate)

Figure 8.7.   *continued*

first. Additional modeling of embedding can occur during subsequent home visits. Completing an Embedding Plan for caregivers like the one shown in Figure 8.4 may assist in reminding them of embedding opportunities that occur during daily routines.

Janina and Enrique chose to embed SEAM: Preschool-Age Goal C-5: Child focuses on event indicated by another, *with their 4-year-old twin daughters, Latisha and Mona, during art activities on weekend afternoons. Dan, the home visitor, is making his first visit with the family following the goal-developing process. Dan brought washable paints and some dried pasta for making pasta necklaces. Dan placed himself between Latisha and Mona and took the art materials out of the sack one by one, modeling suspense and surprise as he brought each material out of the sack. Enrique gave the pasta pieces to Janina and she showed Latisha and Mona how to dip the pasta into the red paint and put it on the newspaper to dry. Dan also modeled how to wait until the girls asked for a different pasta shape before giving it to them, practicing the second goal, C-1.4,* Child shares and takes turns with other children. *Dan left an activity sheet from the ASQ:SE containing suggestions for art and other developmentally appropriate activities that Janina and Enrique could do. Dan encouraged Janina and Enrique to join in the art activity and provided positive encouragement to the twins as they played.*

For the following home visit, Dan suggested that the 7-year-old neighbor Kim be invited to their house to play. Mona and Latisha do not regularly interact with other children and often communicate between themselves using their own invented language. Kim, an older peer, may provide opportunities for healthy interactions and engagement. Because Mona and Latisha enjoyed the pasta activity, Dan brought washable paints again and this time he also brought some pieces of cut cardboard shapes. During this visit, Janina and Enrique took the art materials from the sack one by one, and then had Kim bring out the pieces of cardboard. Enrique showed Latisha and Mona how to color the cardboard shapes and thread them on the string. Enrique and Janina waited until Mona and Latisha vocalized initial sounds and word approximations until they gave the twins the colored paints and materials that they wanted.

Toward the end of this home visit, Dan modeled additional embedding opportunities, showing how to make a game out of cleaning up materials from the cardboard and paint activity. Through the clean-up activity, he provided opportunities for Latisha and Mona to practice their compliance goals as well.

The number of embedding opportunities in each activity can be gradually increased as caregivers and children are successful in practicing the identified goals. Once goals are achieved, new Embedding Plans should be developed with caregivers.

In center-based programs, supervisors or lead teachers/interventionists may need to model the embedding of learning opportunities during child-directed, routine, and planned activities throughout the day for other staff members. For example, an interventionist might model for classroom aides and volunteers the embedding of learning opportunities for selected goals such as sharing of toys during free-play times. A Group Activity Matrix such as the one contained in Figure 8.5 can be placed on the classroom bulletin board to remind classroom staff of child goals and target activities. Again, embedding opportunities should be expanded and activities changed as children develop new skills in social emotional areas.

Step Four: Providing Multiple and Varied Learning Opportunities

Completing an Embedding Plan (Figure 8.3) and Activity Matrix (Figure 8.5) may assist in increasing the awareness of interventionists and caregivers in the provision of multiple and varied opportunities for children. Developmentally appropriate, child-directed activities can provide fun, repeated, and naturally reinforcing interventions. For example, for a preschool child, Jen, whose goals include describing the emotions of others (SEAM Goal C-2.3); she can be asked to describe the angry and frustrated feelings of her favorite character doll, the Little Mermaid, while she is reenacting a scene from the movie. Playtime with Mr. and Mrs. Potato Head might provide another opportunity for building happy, sad, and frustrated Potato Head figures and describing how these Potato Heads might feel. Finally, while waiting for a dental appointment, Jen can be asked how she feels about seeing the dentist for a checkup visit and how the other children might be feeling (e.g., boy who is crying, another who is sitting on his mother's lap playing with a toy).

In addition to high interest child-directed activities, routine activities are important to target for embedding learning and practice opportunities. These types of activities occur daily and can provide numerous opportunities for children and caregivers to practice their social emotional goals. Traveling on the bus, eating lunch, and washing hands and face are routine activities that may provide children and caregivers with multiple opportunities to practice SEAM goals. For example, Germano and his mother Alexandra may have many opportunities to practice SEAM Goal C-6.1: *Child explores new materials and settings* while traveling on a bus. Alexandra can encourage Germano to deposit money in the pay slot and then walk through the bus to their seat.

Activities in classroom and child care environments are often planned by adults to highlight a theme or topic. When these activities are based on themes and materials of high interest to children, they may offer more opportunities for embedding practice opportunities. For example, making vegetable prints with favorite colors and familiar vegetables may be more motivating to young preschool children than simply setting out watercolors and a small brush. Ean and Eamon can first gather vegetables from the classroom garden, eat some of these cut up vegetables for snack, and then use the stems and ends for vegetable printing with their favorite colored paints. Because they have helped plant, weed, and water the vegetables, they may be more involved with this art activity and find it more meaningful than painting a picture. If more involved and motivated, a child may be more likely to have multiple opportunities to practice Preschool-Age SEAM Goal C-8.1: *Child stays with motor activities for 10 minutes or longer,* and SEAM Goal C-1.4: *Child shares and takes turns with other children.*

FUNCTIONAL BEHAVIORAL ASSESSMENT

For some children with challenging behaviors, identifying opportunities to embed practice opportunities with naturally occurring consequences may not always be sufficient to create desired behavioral change. In order to decrease problem behaviors and increase appropriate social behaviors, a more in-depth assessment may be required than is outlined in the ABI:SE Approach, and a more formal structure for intervention may be needed. Function-based, or functional behavior assessment (FBA), is a more formal support procedure that uses the principles of applied behavior analysis. FBA focuses on several features: a) attention to environmental context and adult behavior, b) emphasis on the "purpose" or function of behavior, and c) focus on teaching appropriate behaviors (Carr et al., 2002; Koegel, Koegel, & Dunlap, 1996).

Children's problem behaviors occur for a reason and most always serve some function or purpose in children's lives. Most often, problem behaviors occur because children have been reinforced (i.e., obtained what they wanted) for these behaviors in the past. For example, if Marc's mother tells him that she won't buy him a candy bar and then gives him one when he begins to cry and tantrum in the grocery store, Marc has learned that crying and screaming in the grocery store will get him a candy bar or other treat. Most likely, Marc will use this behavior again in the future to get what he wants. Although we see this type of behavior as problematic, Marc has learned that it serves a function for him and allows him to get what he wants.

Challenging behavior can serve several functions for children, including attaining or escaping from attention, obtaining tangible items, accomplishing tasks, and receiving sensory stimulation (O'Neill et al., 1997). Consider the following examples:

Preschoolers Patty and John both begin to scream and cry when asked to go to circle time in their respective classrooms. In Patty's case, the teacher walks her through a calming routine and helps her to take slow breaths and count to 10. Patty enjoys this one-to-one time with her teacher and has learned that screaming and crying gives her access to this private time. John's teacher usually asks him to leave the circle and sit by himself at the table. John doesn't like circle time and enjoys this escape from the task. In both examples, the screaming and pouting behavior is serving a purpose or function, although it is a different function with a different consequence for each child.

In addition, problem behaviors may be manifestations of emotional problems or internal strife caused by events at home or in the community, such as the illness of a sibling or a divorce. Getting to know and understand the child's home environment through conducting home visits and completing environmental assessments such as the ESQ may be a helpful way for professionals to discover the origin and/or function of the child's troubling behaviors.

For children with challenging problem behaviors, it may be necessary to identify and then design interventions around the purpose or function of their behaviors. Interventions that are effective for some children may not work for others because the function of the behaviors and subsequent reinforcers or payoffs may differ.

Jim completed the Toddler SEAM for his 2½-year old son Robby and identified goals targeting benchmark C-8.0: Toddler regulates attention and activity level. *Jim reported that Robby has difficulty staying with an activity for more than several minutes and usually cries when asked to continue the activity. Jim and Brandy, the interventionist, developed a plan to provide Robby with more stimulating toys (e.g., books with textures, toys that make sound and light up) and more opportunities throughout the day to play with these toys. Jim did an excellent job of providing these toys and more opportunities for Robby to play independently, but Robby continued to cry, to which Jim responded with comforting. When Robby's behavior did not improve, Brandy suggested completing a functional assessment and developing some function-based supports.*

A functional assessment is an information-gathering process that assists in the identification of the purpose of a child's behavior as well as identification of events that may reliably predict the occurrence of problem behavior (Horner, 1994; Sugai, Horner, & Sprague, 1999). Information is typically gathered through interviews, observations, and a review of permanent products, such as intervention plans. Completion of a functional assessment yields several useful pieces of information, including 1) a clear and observable definition of the problem behavior(s); 2) a hypothesis statement identifying when behavior is most likely to occur, what the behavior is, and what usually takes place after the behavior; 3) identification of the purpose or function of the behavior; 4) observational data to support the developed hypothesis; and 5) strategies for implementing function-based interventions (Horner, 1994; Sugai et al., 1999). Interventions developed from a functional assessment focus on changing environments and adult behavior to provide opportunities for the child to learn appropriate behaviors and decrease problem behaviors.

Through further conversation with Jim, Brandy obtained more detailed information about Robby's problem behavior. Jim explained that Robby screamed and cried more often in the morning than he did in the evening. Brandy asked Jim about what typically happens after Robby begins to cry. Jim explained that he usually goes into the playroom to comfort him and then plays with him for a few minutes before leaving him alone again. Next, Brandy went to Jim's home to observe and noticed that Robby would stay with a task for more than 5 minutes without becoming upset when Jim was in the room, but that he would cry when he was left alone. Brandy and Jim discovered that Robby's problem behavior was most likely serving the function of getting attention, and they developed some new intervention strategies based on this understanding.

Brandy suggested that Jim make sure that he was in the room when Robby was engaged in an activity independently, and also to make sure that he paid frequent attention to Robby when he was playing appropriately. Initially, Brandy had Jim tell Robby that he was doing a good job, or to play with him for a few seconds every 2–3 minutes. As Robby began to play more independently, Jim withheld his attention for longer intervals (e.g., every 4–5 minutes). Brandy also suggested that Jim make sure that if Robby did cry, not to rush over and comfort him but to leave him alone as long as he was safe. After a couple of weeks, Robby was playing independently with less crying, and Jim was able to leave the room to take care of his other responsibilities.

In this example, Brandy and Jim discovered that the apparent function of Robby's crying behavior was to get his father's attention. They developed an intervention strategy that 1) prevented problem behavior from occurring by having Jim in the room while Robby was playing independently; 2) reinforced Robby for appropriate behavior by having Jim briefly play with him and give him verbal praise from time to time; and 3) removed Jim's reinforcement so that Robby was not given attention and comfort when he cried.

For children with more challenging problem behaviors and those who are not responding to activity-based intervention, it may be helpful to complete a functional assessment and develop a function-based intervention plan. This section has offered a brief introduction to function-based supports. A more thorough discussion of the process, including forms and examples, is provided in Appendix C at the end of this book. If goals have been developed to target challenging problem behavior and to teach appropriate replacement behaviors, completing a functional assessment and designing function-based supports may be helpful in achieving these goals.

SUMMARY

The intervention process involves providing multiple and varied opportunities for children and caregivers to practice their targeted SEAM goals. Activity-based intervention is the suggested intervention approach whereby learning opportunities are embedded in everyday routines and activities. These activities can be spontaneous such as doll and action figure play, activities planned by caregivers such as a picnic, and activities that are a part of everyday routines such as meal- and bedtime. An activity-based intervention approach allows great flexibility because it can be used in a variety of settings and under a variety of conditions. Varying developmental levels, economic backgrounds, values, experiences, and cultures can be easily incorporated into activity-based intervention activities. It is necessary that early childhood professionals carefully plan activities and embed opportunities in order to provide caregivers and children with multiple opportunities to practice and learn their targeted SEAM goals.

For children and families with particularly challenging behaviors, functional assessment and intervention strategies may be needed to identify the functions and consequences of the challenging behaviors. A functional assessment can help to identify alternate strategies to teach new behaviors to replace the challenging behaviors. Appendix C contains a discussion of FBA as well as forms to use when conducting a functional assessment.

Ongoing evaluation of intervention efforts are necessary in order to ensure the most effective intervention strategies are being used. Evaluation refers to documenting social emotional behaviors and comparing children's previous performance with their current performance. Knowing whether progress is being made toward social emotional goals and when to modify or replace existing goals is critical to effective intervention. Evaluation data should be gathered during all ABI:SE processes to monitor and alter screening and assessment strategies and to target goals and intervention efforts. The specific steps in the evaluation process are described next in Chapter 9.

9

Evaluating Intervention Outcomes

he fifth and final process in the ABI:SE Approach is *evaluation*. In the ABI:SE approach, two types of evaluation are deemed necessary: 1) monitoring child and caregiver progress toward individual and general curricular goals, and 2) assessing overall program impact on participating children and caregivers. For child and caregiver monitoring, evaluation refers to the systematic collection of data on child and caregiver progress toward targeted goals selected from the SEAM or other CBAs. Progress toward goals may be monitored weekly or monthly in order to determine if intervention strategies are providing appropriate and sufficient learning opportunities to attain targeted skills. Assessing overall program impact requires quarterly and annual evaluation data gathering, which may be more global than monitoring individual child and caregiver progress.

THE EVALUATION PROCESS IN THE ABI:SE APPROACH

The evaluation process requires professionals to gather comparative data at selected intervals (e.g., weekly, quarterly, annually) so that judgments can be made about the effectiveness of the ABI:SE Approach in assisting children and caregivers to achieve targeted social emotional outcomes and to measure general program outcomes. As described in earlier chapters, during the goal-developing process, functional and generative social emotional goals are selected from the SEAM. During the intervention process, practice or learning opportunities are embedded into daily routines and child and caregiver directed activities. If the appropriate goals have been targeted and adequate practice opportunities provided, weekly and monthly data on child and caregiver skills should reflect progress toward attaining these goals. Ongoing systematic data collection to monitor progress toward SEAM goals is critical to the appropriate use of the ABI:SE Approach.

As noted, gauging general program effectiveness is also important—for example, determining caregiver satisfaction, staff effectiveness, and children's overall acquisition of general curricular goals. However, this type of evaluation is

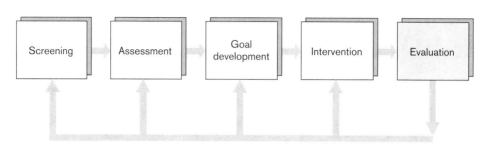

Figure 9.1. The role of evaluation in the ABI:SE Approach.

only briefly addressed in this chapter; the focus is on gathering data on child and caregiver behaviors to determine if progress is being made toward SEAM goals.

Consistent evaluation is essential to determine if the screening, assessment, goal development, and intervention processes of the ABI:SE Approach are being conducted effectively. If a child is not making progress toward targeted goals, it is necessary to review the previous processes to determine what type of modification might produce better outcomes.

The screening process needs to be evaluated and monitored to ensure that it meets established standards. These standards include acceptability to users (e.g., caregivers and staff), and acceptable levels of sensitivity and specificity.

Reviewing the assessment process and/or goal-developing process may reveal that inappropriate goals may have been selected; for example, the goals may turn out to have been too difficult or too easy. Consequently, portions of the SEAM may need to be re-administered and alternative goals selected. For example, a 4-year-old who is still unable to calm herself after periods of activity after 2 weeks of intervention may need a less-demanding goal focused on transitions between quiet classroom activities.

If goals appear appropriate, an analysis of the intervention process may be in order. If the same 4-year-old is not making progress toward her targeted goal of self-calming after periods of activity, modifications in the type of activities and increases in the frequency of embedding learning opportunities should be considered. A functional analysis may need to be completed and alternate interventions planned.

Finally, if adequate progress is still not being made, the evaluation process itself may need modification. Incomplete or inaccurate evaluation data may have been gathered, data may need to be collected more frequently, or different times and strategies may need to be targeted for data collection.

Only through ongoing progress monitoring during each of the ABI:SE processes, as shown in Figure 9.1, can appropriate decisions be made about child and caregiver progress toward their targeted social emotional goals.

STEPS IN THE EVALUATION PROCESS

The evaluation process has four steps, as shown in Figure 9.2.

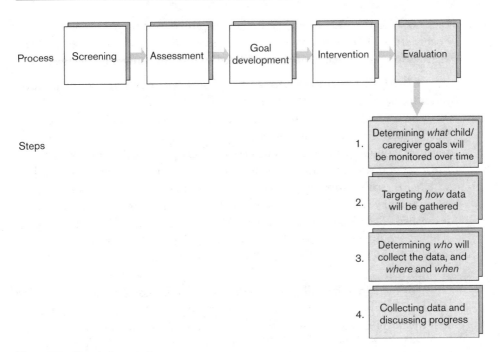

Figure 9.2. Steps in the evaluation process.

- Step One: Determining *what* child/caregiver goals will be monitored over time and the criteria for success (goal acquisition).

- Step Two: Targeting *how* data will be gathered.

- Step Three: Determining *who* will collect the data, and *where* and *when* data will be gathered.

- Step Four: Collecting weekly/monthly/quarterly data and discussing progress toward goals and overall program effectiveness with the intervention team, including the caregiver.

Each of the evaluation steps shown in Figure 9.2 is discussed next. The first three steps in the evaluation process involve planning for data collection, and should be done early in the intervening process. These planning steps are necessary to ensure that successful evaluation occurs, including gathering accurate data that reflect how a child and caregiver are interacting and the progress that they are making toward their SEAM goals. In addition, each step also addresses program effectiveness.

Step One: Determining *What* Child/Caregiver Goals Will Be Monitored Over Time

This step addresses which child and caregiver goals will be selected to be evaluated over time. In selecting goals to be monitored, it is essential to develop for each goal specific and objective criteria that can be used to determine when the goal is attained. This step is also used to select those questions or targets (e.g., staff performance) that are to be evaluated to monitor program effectiveness.

Child/Caregiver Progress   The *what* of child/caregiver progress refers to the selected goals that will be monitored over time to determine the effectiveness of intervention efforts. Each child/caregiver should have one to three SEAM goals that have been targeted as priorities for intervention. The caregiver together with the team needs to determine which goals will be monitored. The caregiver and team may first want to target only responding behaviors, such as whether the baby stops crying when picked up (*Baby responds to soothing when upset:* Infant SEAM C-3.1), or whether the baby turns toward his name when it is called (*Baby looks at or toward sounds and visual events* (C-5.2). After the infant has acquired these types of behaviors, initiating behaviors such as raising his arms to be picked up and waving "bye-bye" when leaving may be selected for monitoring.

For each goal, regardless of whether it is monitored, a criterion should be developed so that data collectors or evaluators (e.g., staff or caregivers) can agree that the targeted response (e.g., *The infant turns his head when her name is called*) occurred, partially occurred, or did not occur. Without specific, objective criteria for each goal, it will be difficult to obtain reliable information on child/caregiver progress.

Program Effectiveness   The *what* of program effectiveness refers to evaluation of selected questions (e.g., Are caregivers satisfied with offered services?) or variables (e.g., demographic information) that address more global aspects of program efficacy. Program effectiveness questions might focus on the number of children reaching at least one of their SEAM goals, general progress of all participating children, or staff satisfaction with the ABI:SE Approach.

Step Two: Targeting *How* Data Will Be Gathered

The *how* of data collection refers to the method of data collection such as anecdotal, narrative, intensity, or frequency counts. The focus in the ABI:SE Approach is on the collection of frequency data. Collected data can be used to monitor progress on child/caregiver goals and to monitor program effectiveness.

Child/Caregiver Progress   The most common method of data collection to monitor child/caregiver progress toward the acquisition of SEAM goals is frequency counts or tallies (i.e., event recording), whether recorded in the classroom, home, or other location. Counting the number of times a child engages in a certain behavior, such as participating in games with others, is usually straightforward and can be done by both caregivers and interventionists throughout the day, in a variety of settings. To take a frequency count, a tally is made each time a child (or caregiver) demonstrates a specified behavior. For example, the number of times that a preschooler shares materials with other children during an art activity can be counted and recorded on a sticky note at the art table. At home, the number of times an infant smiles and makes eye contact

Progress Monitoring Form

Child:

SEAM goal:

Data collection Setting	Time 1	Time 2	Time 3	Time 4	Time 5
#1					
#2					
#3					

Figure 9.3.   SEAM Progress Monitoring Form designed for use with individual child.

with caregivers while being fed can be marked on a wall calendar. A small note pad, piece of masking tape, or chart posted on the refrigerator can also be used for recording frequency counts.

More formalized data collection is preferred, if programs have the necessary resources. Such systems usually develop forms for individual child data collection, such as the one shown in Figure 9.3. This form has space to enter the child's SEAM goals as well as space for child responses across different settings. A classroom form to record the progress of several children toward their goals is contained in Figure 9.4. On this form, children's names can be written across the top row and at least two of their SEAM goals listed under each name. Settings (e.g., circle, outside, transitions) in which data collection is taking place can be written in the left-hand column, and progress data can be recorded in the appropriate box.

For some behaviors, a direct test probe procedure such as the one suggested by Wolery, Bailey, and Sugai (1988) may be used in which opportunities are provided for the child to perform the target behavior and both opportunities and responses are recorded. SEAM goals related to cooperation (e.g., Infant,

Progress Monitoring Form

	Child 1		Child 2		Child 3	
Data collection setting	SEAM Goal #1	SEAM Goal #2				
#1						
#2						
#3						

Figure 9.4.   SEAM Progress Monitoring Form designed for use with multiple children. (Suggested response key: + = correct response, − = incorrect response, N = no response)

Toddler, and Preschool-Age C-9.0) are well suited to using a direct test probe. For example, a child can be asked to comply with a targeted direction once a day, such as sitting on the floor for storytime. The child's opportunities for responding to the request and actual responses can be recorded on a form developed for that purpose. The following example illustrates this practice.

In 1 week, Jack is given five opportunities to respond to the request to sit on the floor. An appropriate response is considered sitting on the floor within 30 seconds without running away. In 1 week, Jack responds appropriately to the request four times, thereby displaying the behavior four out of five times, or 80% of the time.

Even if formal probes or trials are not used, the number of opportunities a child has to respond to a targeted goal should be noted as well as the number of responses. Collecting both number of opportunities and correct responses is essential to calculate rate data.

Larisa has a goal of "Greets familiar peers on the playground" (e.g., Preschool-Age SEAM Goal C-5.2: Child greets adults and peers*). Her teacher is asked to observe her for 1 week, and during that time, Larisa responds correctly (e.g., says "hi" to peers) in four out of eight opportunities for a response rate of 50%.*

Other examples of rate data would include the number of times a child becomes upset (i.e., opportunities) and the number of times she calms herself within 5–10 minutes (i.e., defined as a correct response).

In order to collect valid frequency data it is essential that goals be objectively defined. For example, a goal such as "Participates in simple games with others" (e.g., for Toddler SEAM Goal C-8.4) first will need to be operationally defined by the team so that everyone can identify and agree on "participating" behaviors as they observe them. "Participates in games" might be defined as staying in proximity to a peer and taking turns according to game rules for at least 5 minutes. "Follows routines and rules" (Preschool-Age SEAM Goal C-9.1) might be defined as 1) walking into the classroom, 2) putting coat in cubby, and 3) sitting on green carpet during circle time. If all team members including family members agree on the performance criteria (i.e., criteria for success), progress toward goals can be evaluated consistently, and the team will be unified in their intervention and evaluation efforts. Performance criteria for selected goals should be determined during Step One.

The child's goals as well as available resources should determine the data collection strategy. Other data collection methodologies (e.g., qualitative) apart from frequency counts are described elsewhere, including Alberto and Troutman (2002); Barnett, Bell, and Carey (1999); Bredekamp and Copple (1997); Kaiser and Rasminsky (1999); O'Neil and Schacter (1997); and Pretti-

Frontczak and Bricker (2004). Programs will need to determine the methods and systems that best fit their philosophy, evaluation questions, resources, and needs of children and families.

Program Effectiveness   When gathering data on program effectiveness, the type and amount of data collected will depend on the evaluation questions and available resources. For example, Head Start staff may wish to determine whether participating 4-year-old children were adequately prepared for kindergarten settings. They might observe the children in their new kindergarten classrooms to see if they are able to follow classroom rules, participate in group activities, and make new friends. The Head Start preschool may not have personnel available to conduct these observations, however, so the staff may have to develop simple questionnaires that can be sent to parents and kindergarten teachers. The questionnaires could ask about children's skills in their new classroom settings to ascertain if the children were able to successfully transition into kindergarten environments.

Evaluation questions and criteria also need to be objectively and clearly defined when collecting program effectiveness data. For example, how many caregivers/parents need to respond to a satisfaction survey to consider the feedback valid? What percent of caregivers/parents need to check "satisfied" and "very satisfied" to conclude caregivers are generally positive about program services? How is satisfactory staff performance to be defined?

Step Three: Determining *Who* Will Collect the Data, and *Where* and *When*?

This step addresses the *who, where,* and *when* of the data collection process. The *who* refers to those individuals who will actually record the data using some type of permanent record. The *where* refers to the physical location and/or activities of the data collection, and the *when* refers to the time of day or week that the data will be collected.

Child/Caregiver Progress   In classroom settings, the service delivery personnel (e.g., teacher, interventionists, therapists, aides) are most likely to be assigned the responsibility of data collection (i.e., the *who*). Many programs do not have sufficient resources to hire staff whose primary responsibility is to observe children and collect progress data, although this approach may be the best to assure accurate and efficient progress monitoring.

During the first weeks of the intervention process, a data collector should be identified for each child to monitor progress on selected SEAM goals. For classroom settings, the intervention team should adopt an overall classroom data collection plan and divide data collection duties among interventionists and caregivers, as appropriate. Figure 9.5 presents a sample classroom data collection plan.

Classroom Data Collection and Evaluation Form

Child goal	Data collector	Setting	Type of data	Frequency	Criteria

Figure 9.5.   Sample Classroom Data Collection and Evaluation Form.

In the home setting, the interventionist may want to serve as the data collector first, especially for SEAM goals related to child behaviors. The parent or caregiver may feel uncomfortable in a data collection role and may see this role as conflicting with his other caregiver responsibilities. Over time, the caregiver may be able to assume a more active role in monitoring her child's progress. For adult-related goals, such as removing dangers from the home environment, it may be more appropriate for the caregiver to self-monitor. For activities that the interventionist may not be able to routinely observe, such as certain adaptive behaviors (e.g., sleeping, toileting), the interventionist may need to rely on parent report.

For child/caregiver progress, the *where* refers to the specific settings (i.e., physical location) and may include the activities that provide opportunities to observe progress toward goals. For example, will circle time in the classroom, outdoor play, or snack time in the kitchen provide the best opportunities for observing sharing behaviors? When will it be easiest for the caregiver to note his or her child's communication responses—during storytime, breakfast, or on a morning walk?

The *when* of child/caregiver progress refers to the time of day or week when data will be collected. In a classroom setting, weekly data collection is ideal to provide timely feedback on child progress; however, for an interventionist who makes home visits twice a month, monthly data collection may be all that is possible. For goals that may require more frequent monitoring, the caregiver or other family member might be relied on to collect weekly data. For example, progress data on a toddler's acts of initiating and responding to communicative interactions (C-1.3) may need to be collected weekly because of the accelerated pace of acquiring language at this age. On the other hand, monthly progress toward accepting changes in routines and settings (C-10.3) may be adequate due to the greater complexity of this task and a typically slower pace for acquisition. Again, the caregiver and team should work together to decide the activities and schedule for data collection.

Program Effectiveness   In most cases, parameters of program effectiveness determine who will collect the data. For example, in determining caregiver/parent satisfaction, the lead teachers and/or supervising staff will most likely collect the information. Parents also may be selected to lead an evaluation of program effectiveness as specified by program goals and guidelines. Often, programs have policies that specify responsibilities as well as schedules and methodologies for conducting staff evaluations. External evaluators who may represent an outside, impartial viewpoint may also be appointed to conduct evaluations of program effectiveness. When controversial evaluations need to be made, such as determining if a director is fulfilling job responsibilities, a skilled external evaluator may be especially valuable.

In program evaluation efforts, the nature of the evaluation question will likely determine *where* the data are collected. For example, if parent/caregiver satisfaction data are being gathered, convenience should be considered such as at drop off and pick up areas or at parent meetings. For questions related to staff expertise, direct observations in the classroom and on home visits may be required.

When program effectiveness data are collected usually depends on the evaluation questions. For example, questions about the effectiveness of a preschool director may be asked of staff and parents at the middle and end of the school year. Caregiver satisfaction may only be evaluated annually through satisfaction surveys. Questions about whether a classroom of children is making adequate progress toward SEAM goals may be evaluated quarterly and annually. However, classroom progress data will depend on the weekly and monthly summaries of child progress data collected by interventionists.

The scenario with the home visitor, Cari, is continued to illustrate the first three steps in the evaluation process.

Shawna, LeBron's mother, has provided opportunities for LeBron to let her know his needs (Infant SEAM Goal C-1.4) during bath-, bed-, and mealtimes. After 1 month of intervention, Cari, the home visitor, and Shawna planned how they would evaluate LeBron's progress. Cari volunteered to observe their lunchtime routine and to count the number of times that LeBron expressed his needs, either through gestures or word approximations. Shawna felt that now LeBron was much better at letting her know what he needed, and that she would be happy to have Cari come at noon to observe. During her initial observation of Shawna and LeBron 4 weeks ago, Cari had noted that there was little communication between them, LeBron was difficult to understand, and Shawna sometimes misread or did not recognize LeBron's cues.

Cari arrived before lunchtime as they had agreed. She sat at the table and observed LeBron in his highchair. Shawna waited until LeBron gestured for his sippy cup and then gave it to him. She also waited until he said "hee" to give him a piece of cheese. He started to fuss when the cheese was gone, and Shawna asked him if he wanted some crackers. He nodded "yes" and Shawna gave him a few crackers. When he started to cry after the crackers were gone, Shawna gave him several more crackers.

Cari noted on her data sheet that LeBron had asked three times for what he wanted—cup, cheese, and crackers—and that Shawna had successfully embedded these opportunities for responding into his lunch routine. She also noted that Shawna had missed one opportunity—asking LeBron if he wanted more crackers— before giving him another portion.

As Shawna helped LeBron out of his highchair, Cari shared what she had ob-
served with Shawna and asked her if she had additional thoughts on how he was
doing with asking behaviors. Cari also mentioned the positive changes that she saw
in interactions between LeBron and Shawna and that Shawna seemed more confi-
dent in determining LeBron's needs.

On an earlier home visit, Cari and Shawna had discussed the SEAM caregiver/
adult goal—providing a safe environment for LeBron (Infant SEAM A-4.0)—
that had been chosen for Shawna. At the beginning of the third home visit, even
before Cari asked about safety issues, Shawna showed Cari the sturdy gate she had
put over the steep apartment stairs (replacing a lightweight aluminum outdoor
chair) and the covers on all the electrical sockets. Shawna also thanked Cari for help-
ing her find the baby consignment store in her neighborhood where she purchased
these gently used items. At this time, Cari noted on her progress report that the
adult/caregiver goal had been met.

During the next home visit, Cari will discuss with Shawna how she would like to
collect data on LeBron's second goal, Baby looks at books or pictures for several minutes or longer *(C-8.2). She will ask Shawna if she can bring some blocks to their home*
for LeBron while they observe together how long he stays with this motor activity.

Step Four: Collecting Data and Discussing Progress

This step addresses the actual weekly/monthly/quarterly data collection process.
This step also addresses the intervention team's discussion of progress toward
child/caregiver goals as well as program effectiveness with the intervention team
including the caregiver(s).

Child/Caregiver Progress

After planning *what, how, who, where* and *when,* evaluation data can be gathered according to the specified evaluation plan. Weekly, monthly, and quarterly
progress information should be summarized and reviewed in regularly scheduled meetings. For child progress data, monthly meetings with caregivers and
the intervention team are recommended. These meetings provide opportunities
to discuss if adequate progress is being made and to identify needed modifications in the assessment, intervention, and evaluation processes. Modified data
collection methods, revised frequency of collecting data, and different settings
and activities may need to be identified in order to collect accurate progress
data. In addition, modification to intervention strategies, such as the number of
embedding opportunities and how these are presented to children, may need
modification. Additional examples of evaluation issues and potential strategies
can be found in Table 9.1. Conducting thorough and accurate evaluations may
require ongoing reflection, staff discussion, and the development of problem-
solving strategies in order to pinpoint steps that need to be taken to improve
child/caregiver outcomes.

An example of weekly progress monitoring is described in this next scenario with Ean and his classroom teacher, Mirabelle.

Table 9.1. Evaluation issues and potential change strategies

Evaluation issues	Potential change strategies
Child cannot do targeted SEAM goal, such as calming self within 5–10 minutes.	Examine SEAM results. Selected SEAM items may need to be re-administered or an earlier (i.e., younger) interval used to target self-regulation goals.
Data on child progress is uneven—sometimes she seems to have the skills and sometimes she does not.	Discuss definitions of target behaviors—team might not agree on criteria for success. Look at settings where data collection occurred. Behaviors might not be generalizing to new environments.
Child and caregiver do not appear to be responding to intervention strategies and proposed activities.	Examine screening results. Environmental risks may have increased; the child's emotional needs may have expanded. Re-administer ASQ:SE and ESQ. If family appears appropriate for ABI:SE Approach, redo Goal Development and Intervention Plan.
Parents are responding on evaluation surveys that they are not satisfied with the classroom environment.	Have staff review overall results and suggest classroom changes. Check percent of caregivers who are responding to survey; may be only dissatisfied ones are answering. Conduct interviews with select parents to learn more about issues so that changes can be made.

Ean has been provided with at least three opportunities each day in the classroom to practice two goals, Child stays with motor activities for 10 minutes or longer *(Preschool-Age SEAM C-8.1) and* Shares and takes turns with other children *(C-1.4). To observe and record Ean's progress toward these goals, his teacher, Mirabelle, observed Ean in the classroom and recorded how long he stayed involved with or focused on a favorite activity, building with blocks. Mirabelle and her classroom team defined staying or focusing behaviors before data collection began (e.g., amount of time Ean is actively engaged with blocks, attending to and completing the building task), so that she was clear about what responses she could count as progress toward these goals.*

During the last data collection probe, Ean had increased his attending time from 5 to 6½ minutes. Today, Mirabelle sat near the block corner, in view of the classroom clock, and recorded a start and end time for the activity. While she timed how long he remained at circle time, Mirabelle also observed his progress toward his second goal, sharing and taking turns with his peers. *She counted the number of times during a 10-minute period that he shared and took turns with the blocks and other building materials used in the block corner.*

To record Ean's progress data, Mirabelle brought a small sticky note to the table. She wrote down the start and end times for the observation period (e.g., 10:15 A.M.— 10:25 A.M.) and marked tallies on the small sticky note each time she observed Ean sharing and taking turns. Finally, she noted when he left the block corner (e.g., 10:21 A.M.).

She also completed a 10-minute data collection period outdoors, tallying the number of times that he shared and took turns with shovels and trucks in the sand box. She marked these tallies on a sticky note she kept in her sweater pocket. When Ean achieves his targeted SEAM goals, Mirabelle will arrange a meeting with his parents to discuss his progress and decide which new goals to target. Mirabelle will also discuss his progress weekly with her teaching team during their classroom meetings.

Program Effectiveness In addition to the data Mirabelle is gathering on children's weekly and monthly progress, her teaching team is also interested in evaluating the overall effects that the program has had on children and their families. The preschool director, Manuel, will develop evaluation questions that link this overall evaluation to the preschool program's philosophy (or mission) and programmatic goals, as shown in Figure 9.6. Manuel will gather information from parents regarding their satisfaction with their children's daily classroom experiences as well as with their monthly home visits.

To answer the first two evaluation questions, a survey asking about parent/caregiver satisfaction with classroom activities, parent meetings, and home visits will be developed and given to parents/caregivers during one of the final home visits in the spring. Parents will complete the surveys anonymously and return them by mail in the pre-stamped envelopes. Results will be summarized and shared with parents, staff, and board of directors. Recommendations will be made for modifications based on parent/caregiver feedback. To answer the third evaluation question about child progress, the classroom teachers and home visitors will summarize progress that children have made toward SEAM goals over the school year. Each classroom teacher will calculate the number of children who have reached two or more SEAM goals during the preschool year and report this percentage (for example, 7 out of 10 children, or 70%). Teachers will

Little Amigos Preschool

Program Philosophy	Support diverse families and children in reaching their full potential
Program Goals	1. Provide safe and nurturing environment.
	2. Assist parents/caregivers in providing optimal caregiving for their children.
	3. Provide empirically-based intervention for children/families with identified needs.
Evaluation Questions	1. Do families feel that the staff at the Little Amigos Preschool provides a safe and nurturing environment for their children?
	2. Are caregivers/parents satisfied with the Little Amigos program, including classroom activities, parent meetings, and home visits?
	3. Are children with identified social emotional needs making progress towards their targeted goals?

Figure 9.6. Overall program evaluation plan for Little Amigos Preschool.

Progress Summary Form

Child	SEAM goal	Met/date	In progress	Modified

Figure 9.7. Progress Summary Form.

also report the percentage of children who have mastered at least one SEAM goal as well as those who have not made measurable progress.

Quarterly and annual meetings can be scheduled to discuss overall child and program progress toward goals and benchmarks as well as program effectiveness. A sample format for summarizing quarterly/annual progress toward child/caregiver goals and benchmarks is contained in Figure 9.7.

The evaluation of overall program effectiveness and individual child/caregiver progress often can be combined. For example, the number of goals targeted, how many caregivers/children met these goals, and the number of benchmarks targeted and attained can be determined and presented. For additional information, parent satisfaction surveys that ask parents how they feel about different aspects of the program can be completed and summarized. Qualitative or observational descriptions of behavior changes in children and caregivers over a year can also be summarized to capture changes that occur for families after targeted interventions. Some funding agencies prefer case studies or descriptions of selected children and caregivers in order to have concrete examples of what has transpired in the program and what the changes have meant for children and families. These case studies, as well as the quantitative progress data, can serve as powerful evidence of program effectiveness when additional funds for program operations are sought. Professional organizations such as the Division for Early Childhood of the Council for Exceptional Children (Sandall, Hemmeter, Smith, & Mclean, 2005) and National Association for the Education of Young Children (Bloom, 1997; Hyson, 2003) publish guidelines for conducting program evaluations in early childhood settings.

An excerpt from a completed annual program evaluation report from a fictional school, FoxPoint Preschool, can be found in Figure 9.8. In this scenario, the program director wrote the following summary that was based on the program description, weekly child progress data, and parent satisfaction questionnaires collected at the end of the school year. The report was distributed to parents and the board of directors.

SUMMARY

Evaluation is the fifth and final process in the ABI:SE Approach. This process is designed to provide caregivers, interventionists, and program administrators with information on how effective the ABI:SE Approach is in terms of children

---

FoxPoint Annual Evaluation

The philosophy of FoxPoint is based on developmentally appropriate practices (DAP) (Bredekamp & Copple, 1997) and a Reggio Emilia curriculum (Edwards, Gandini, & Forman, 1998). The foundation of the curriculum is art and writing, focused on long-term projects of interest to the children. During this past year, a sculptor and painter have been in residence in the FoxPoint studio and provided materials and guidance in sculpting with clay and painting with watercolors and oil paints. Other projects of interest included the birth of 10 kittens and 12 gerbils in the spring.

Four teachers participated in the FoxPoint annual evaluation, with a total of 82 children in their classrooms ranging in age from 3 to 5 years. The parents of these children were asked to complete a survey asking about their satisfaction with FoxPoint Preschool, the staff, and their children's program. Sixty-four parents completed the survey (78%) and indicated they were "satisfied" or "very satisfied" with their child's program and teachers; that their child had made significant progress during the year. Ninety percent of parent respondents indicated that they felt that FoxPoint teachers were extremely skilled and provided an enriching and stimulating environment for their child. In addition almost all parents made comments on their surveys, indicating how much their child had grown and changed in the last year and how much progress they felt they had made. All parents with 3- and 4-year-old children indicated that they planned to send their child to FoxPoint next year.

Following are examples of comments on the parent survey:

- My child wants to go to school every day this whole year. She cried and cried when she was sick or couldn't go for another reason. I feel so good about sending her to you every day.

- I love all the artwork that she makes at school. She is so proud of what she does. I thank you for having so many wonderful choices of things for her to do.

Parents were critical of only one part of FoxPoint—that there was no after-school care and that parents had to pick up their child often before the end of their work day. They suggested adding an after-school component next year. Several parents also suggested adding a hot lunch program, with an extra charge for the lunches.

Eighteen FoxPoint students received intensive services for behavioral and social emotional delays, in addition to the DAP approach. A curriculum-based measure, the Social Emotional Assessment/Evaluation Measure (SEAM), Experimental Edition, was used with these children. The SEAM was completed in the fall by the 18 parents, and they chose two to three goals for their child, such as participating in group activities, using words to express their emotions, and calming down within 5 minutes when upset. Thirteen of the 18 children successfully met the criteria for these targeted goals by the end of the school year. (One of the children moved in the spring to a different state, and the other four children were successful in reaching criteria for at least one of their SEAM goals.) Both staff and parents indicated on their surveys that these children had made substantial growth in social emotional areas and had gained several new skills that made it easier for them to get along in their preschool classroom.

Here are some examples of parent comments about their child's social-emotional progress.

- He has grown up so much. Thank you for making that happen. I never thought I'd see him be happy to go to school and proud of what he did there. What you did at school helped his attitude at home so much.

- He is using so much more language and seems so much more aware of the world. He is using his words so much more now to express himself. I think his teacher Ruth is the best in the world.

- You gave me invaluable help with what to do with him at home. Even though he still has tantrums, it doesn't happen half as much as it used to . . . .

Figure 9.8. Example of an annual evaluation incorporating information on children's social emotional development gathered from SEAMs.

improving in their social emotional competence by achieving targeted SEAM goals. Caregiver progress toward caregiver benchmarks can also be measured as well as overall program impact on staff, caregivers/parents, and children.

A closing perspective on what we believe to be the necessary commitment to young children with social emotional challenges and their families follows. This brief summary reviews our past intervention efforts with children and what we hope the future holds.

Afterword

Our Closing Perspective

The first three chapters of this book provide a carefully developed rationale for the need to address social emotional and mental health problems in young children who are at risk of or who have disabilities. Chapters 4 through 9 offer what we believe is a thoughtfully conceived, comprehensive framework for addressing social emotional problems in young children. The ABI:SE Approach, a linked systems framework, is composed of five important and connected processes: screening, assessment, goal development, intervention, and evaluation. In the preceding chapters, each process is defined, implementation steps are discussed, and examples are offered. The intent is to provide a clear and straightforward description of the approach so that it can be incorporated into programs that serve young children with disabilities or who are at risk. To augment the descriptions of each process, a variety of measures and forms are included as well as methods for their use.

The ABI:SE Approach can be used by a range of early intervention/early childhood special education and child development personnel who may have different philosophies and training backgrounds but who share the desire to prevent or remediate social emotional problems in young children. Little empirical data have yet been collected on the effectiveness of the ABI:SE Approach; however, two types of information have led us to believe that if used properly, the approach will assist professional staff in helping caregivers to move children toward acquisition of social emotional competence. As noted in Chapter 6, we define social emotional competence as based on 10 child benchmarks. The content of these benchmarks was derived from a rich theoretical and empirical literature addressing early social emotional development of children.

The first type of information that supports the ABI:SE Approach is derived from the empirical work examining activity-based intervention and the embedding of learning, or practice, opportunities. In general, these data support the effectiveness of the activity-based intervention approach (Pretti-Frontczak & Bricker, 2004) and the embedding of learning or practice opportunities into meaningful activities (Daugherty, Grisham-Brown, & Hemmeter, 2001; Horn, Leiber, Li, Sandall, & Schwartz, 2000). Second, we have preliminary findings from two research studies designed to assess the impact of elements of the ABI:SE Approach. These preliminary data suggest first that training personnel in early identification and screening for social emotional delays improves identification rates and enhances provider knowledge of social emotional development and potential delays (Squires, 2005). Second, preliminary data suggest that targeted social emotional interventions can improve selected aspects of parent–child interactions, including sensitivity to infants' cues in some mothers (Squires, 2005).

The careful delineation of the ABI:SE Approach and the associated data to support its effectiveness gives us hope that early intervention/early childhood special education and child care workers, in conjunction with parents and other caregivers, will be able to employ the five processes to assist children in acquiring and maintaining social emotional behaviors that make their lives satisfying to themselves and others.

This Afterword has a different purpose; its intent is threefold. First, it briefly reviews the history of early intervention/early childhood special education and its attention to the area of social emotional development and intervention. This review focuses on our perceptions rather than offering a carefully documented set of findings on how the field of early intervention/early childhood special education and child care has dealt with social emotional problems in young children with disabilities.

The second purpose is to describe what was occurring at the time this book was published in many programs that serve young children with disabilities or who are at risk for disabilities around the area of social emotional development and intervention. Again, we share our perceptions and personal experiences rather than present a carefully documented set of findings.

The third and final purpose is to share our intuitions about what the future may hold in terms of preventing the development of social emotional problems in young children and intervening with those children who already present with problems or potential problems.

A BRIEF HISTORY

Intervention programs for young children with disabilities became more apparent in the early 1970s. A few programs existed prior to this time but were focused primarily on children with birth defects (e.g., March of Dimes) or other physical disabilities (e.g., Easter Seals). Most infants and young children with serious communication, adaptive, and cognitive problems were institutionalized at an early age. Professionals who wanted to work with young children with moderate to severe disabilities usually were forced to work in the confines of large residential facilities. Working under the conditions that existed in most institutional settings proved to be exceptionally challenging. The only approach that appeared to produce change under such conditions was operant conditioning—an approach touted by noted psychologist and behaviorist B.F. Skinner that had been shown to be effective with adults and older children (see Bijou & Baer,

1961; Foxx & Arzin, 1973). Skinner's atheoretical approach was focused entirely on behaviors that could be observed and counted. The study of internal processes such as emotions was eschewed by Skinner and others.

Of interest, children with severe mental illness or psychoses were treated by an entirely different service system for the mentally ill that generally operated using very different theoretical positions from behavioral approaches. Of course, a few exceptions existed, including Ivar Lovaas and Todd Risley, who employed a behavioral approach with children diagnosed with autism. Also of interest were the many young children living in institutional settings who showed dramatic signs of serious emotional disturbance; however, in large measure these conditions were treated as part and parcel of their behavioral/cognitive disability.

Many of the people who developed the first early intervention programs for young children with disabilities conducted their early work with institutional populations using a stimulus–response–consequence paradigm that did not account for internal or physiological processes. It was not surprising then that when this group of investigators began developing community-based programs, the approach of choice was largely behavioral. For example, one of the very first community-based early intervention programs developed at Peabody College employed a highly structured approach that consisted of giving commands, specifying the child's response, and then delivering a tangible reward. This approach lent itself well to behaviors that could be easily observed and counted trial by trial (e.g., motor imitation, verbal imitation, naming pictures). Little thought was given to embedding learning opportunities in meaningful or authentic activities and even less attention was given to concepts such as self-image, emotional regulation, and the importance of satisfying and rewarding interactions. This highly mechanistic approach to intervention did not lend itself to more complex and hard-to-define social and emotional behaviors.

The highly structured, adult-guided behavioral approach continued to be used in many programs until personnel began to be influenced by theorists such as Piaget and by developmentalists who were studying early cognitive, communicative, and social behavior (e.g., Lois Bloom, Dante Cicchetti, Allan Sroufe). We begin to move from shaping one-to-one stimulus–response relationships to understanding that human behavior is complex, generative, and usually controlled by an array of triggering events (i.e., stimuli). We were yet to appreciate the enormous influence of emotions on the developing child.

From the beginning of intervention efforts with young children, aberrant and noncompliant behaviors were frequent and important targets to be eliminated. Little attention was devoted to understanding unwanted behaviors, such as how they developed and that they might be reflective of more complex emotional disabilities. And indeed, such behaviors were addressed only when they became so intolerable that drastic action had to be taken. Early childhood/early intervention professionals seemed not to understand the importance of attachment and bonding to children's development, the essential nature of trust, the development of human interactions, the critical phenomenon of self-worth and self-image, and the need to have and display a range of important emotions. The importance of these complex concepts has gradually seeped into our collective conscience so that today many of us realize the critical need to address social emotional behavior in young children. This realization is reflected in the current status of social emotional assessment and intervention for young children.

Beginning in the late 1980s and early 1990s, many early intervention/early childhood special education programs broadened their approaches by including group activities for children as well as individual behavioral tutoring to reach targeted goals. Curricular foci expanded to include motor, adaptive, social communication, cognitive, and social areas. Early childhood professionals got smarter about developing meaningful goals and intervention content. Both children and families benefited from more comprehensive approaches that recognized the importance of social communication and problem solving. Furthermore, early childhood professionals were beginning to recognize the value of embedding instruction into activities that had meaning for children.

Programs for children from poor environments, including Head Start and state funded pre-kindergartens, began with a focus on "catching" children up academically to their age peers from middle-income families. Literacy and number skills were generally the content focus of these programs, although Head Start is one of the few preventative intervention programs that emphasized a holistic approach from its inception, including mental health and medical and dental needs of children and families. Only after a number of research studies (e.g., Farran, 2000) pointed to the importance of social skills and readiness behaviors for success in public school settings did lawmakers, educators, and professionals working with children place a serious emphasis on individual and classroom behavioral programs in early childhood compensatory settings (Knitzer 2004; Ramey & Ramey, 2004). However, similar to programs for children with disabilities, aberrant and noncompliant behaviors were often emphasized, with a smaller concentration on preventative mental health and emotional wellness of children and families.

The rise in gun violence and shootings in schools that began in the 1990s prompted many educators to reconsider the importance of day-to-day social interactions and emotional well-being, including creating a positive social emotional climate in classrooms and schools. In addition, preventative programs for infants and toddlers developed in the mid- to late 1990s, such as Early Head Start and Healthy Start. These programs reflected the growing realization that positive social interactions, trust, and respect are largely rooted in parent–child interactions that take place during a child's first years of life.

Although many compensatory programs continue to emphasize literacy and standardized academic testing, which may compete with more holistic approaches, most early childhood educators and policy makers are beginning to realize how important it is for children (and families) to have positive relationships with teachers and peers and to feel connected to their schools in order to be successful at academic tasks and future vocations.

THE STATUS OF SOCIAL
EMOTIONAL ASSESSMENT TODAY

So where are early intervention/early child care professionals today in relation to successfully identifying children with social emotional or mental health problems or those with the potential to develop such problems? As mentioned, little objective survey data or published empirical data exist on the status of the ability of program personnel (i.e., those who serve children at risk and with disabilities) to identify, in a timely manner, social emotional problems and to provide effective interventions to children and their families. Rather, our information was gathered informally from a wide range of early intervention/early childhood special education, Head Start, and child care workers. We have formed two impressions from these data. First, many, but certainly not all, professionals and paraprofessionals serving populations of young children at risk and with disabilities recognize that many children they see have, or could develop, serious social emotional problems. Second, the majority of these personnel have little idea about how to work effectively with either the children or their caregivers to prevent or ameliorate such problems. Let us consider both of these impressions.

Our work and conversations with personnel who provide assessment and intervention services emphasizes the growing concern about young children with mental health challenges. This concern is certainly supported by the prevalence data that we reported earlier in Chapter 3. Furthermore, many program staff surmise or witness children living in "toxic" living conditions that continually threaten all aspects of healthy development. We know that children whose primary relationships are continually disrupted, who experience or witness physical or psychological violence, who rarely receive feedback about their goodness and worth, who are inhibited or dissuaded from exploration and experimentation, and who have little or no predictability either psychological or physically in their lives are children who are at extreme risk for developing serious mental health problems. Moreover, we know that once such problems become entrenched it becomes very difficult to undo the emotional damage (Reid, Patterson, & Snyder, 2002). Consequently, what program personnel see are growing numbers of young children who appear to be in great jeopardy of never becoming healthy, contributing adults.

In addition to concern over children who reside in punitive, nonsupportive environments, professionals working with children have voiced concerns about the impact of placing children with disabilities in natural settings with their peers without disabilities. In many of these settings (e.g., child care, general education kindergartens), only one or two children with disabilities are present in classrooms with peers who are typically developing, and often these children tend to be the least competent and least capable across a range of activities and skills. One may wonder what the emotional impact is of always being the least able child day after day. Add to this concern the fact that many community-based programs designed for children who are typically developing do not have staff with adequate training and experience to properly assist a child with disabilities, and often knowledgeable and experienced professionals are not able to offer satisfactory support to the staff or the child.

Thus, if the sample of professionals and paraprofessionals with whom we have conversed are representative, then it may be that many children at risk and who have disabilities face significant challenges to the development of healthy social emotional behaviors. This finding, if correct, has serious implications for our second impression—that many program personnel serving children at risk and those who have disabilities are ill equipped to address social emotional problems that these children may have.

Most personnel preparation programs offer courses on early development that cover several developmental areas, yet offer only one course focused on early social emotional development. In addition, most do not offer a single course that exclusively addresses assessment and intervention focused on the social emotional area. Most curricula are designed to cover assessment on a range of developmental domains, as are courses on intervention. Furthermore, students who participate in general preschool and elementary education programs in colleges and universities may have little exposure to children who are at risk or who have disabilities. Thus, it may be safe to say that early childhood/early intervention training programs do not offer extensive didactic or practical experience for helping children and families with social emotional problems or those who may be headed for the development of these types of problems. Is it then surprising that many personnel feel poorly prepared to assist children and families to deal with a range of potentially serious mental health problems? In fact, we have often observed that small problems are generally overlooked when solutions might be relatively easy and modest in cost. These problems often escalate until they evolve into serious confrontations that must be addressed. For example, a toddler's noncompliance might be consistently overlooked until he becomes a defiant preschooler who systematically ignores any adult direction. The problem is considerably more difficult to remedy at that point than if action had been taken at the onset of the toddler's noncompliant behavior.

THE FUTURE

Growing numbers of young children have, or are headed for, the development of social emotional problems. These problems may ultimately end in children developing significant disorders that could potentially result in seriously compromised development requiring intervention. Without early identification of these problems and effective intervention, the cost to us (i.e., society) may be the loss of significant human potential, not to mention the financial cost of incarceration in penal or mental health facilities. To not consider alternatives is unconscionable.

What does or should the future hold? Lacking a reliable crystal ball, we will confine ourselves to what we believe should occur or be offered: universal screening of very young children, a cascade of prevention/intervention services, empirically validated assessment and intervention materials, enhanced personnel preparation, and changes in federal and state policy.

Universal Screening for All Children

The first major change we advocate—the development of universal screening of all children—is a position supported by the American Academy of Pediatrics (2006). During the first few months of life, all infants should undergo developmental screens that can be conducted, in large measure, by primary caregivers, thus keeping costs within reasonable limits. In addition, all children's development should be monitored at least once per year to ensure early identification of problems or potential problems. A key to successful prevention and intervention is early detection, before problems evolve into serious disabilities. Of course, we believe that screening programs must include a focus on social emotional development along with other important areas of development.

Comprehensive and Connected Community Services

In Chapter 2 we offered a three-level pyramid model of hierarchical service options for families beginning with low-cost screening and intervention activities and moving on to more specialized and costly interventions. Communities, in conjunction with state and federal agencies, should develop comprehensive community plans that enable families to quickly access prevention/intervention services that will meet their needs. Community services should be connected and designed to eliminate overlap and use finite resources in the most efficient and effective way possible. Only when professionals and service agencies coordinate and complement each other will there be adequate resources to meet the diverse needs of families and children.

Development of Proven Assessment Measures and Intervention Materials

A third "should" for us is the development of assessment measures and intervention materials (e.g., curricula) that have been demonstrated to produce desired change in children's social emotional behavior and caregiver's responsive behavior. The few materials currently available, including the SEAM, have little data as yet to support their use. It is imperative that additional data be collected on the SEAM as well as on other available social emotional assessment measures and intervention materials. The psychometric properties and the treatment validity of assessment and intervention materials need to be verified in order to ensure that resources are being used wisely to assist young children and their families.

As many previous writers have noted, the quality of assessment and intervention services are highly dependent on the quality of the personnel who plan and deliver those services (Bricker & Widerstrom, 1999; Gilkerson & Cochran Kopel, 2005). The earlier chapters in this book have repeatedly remarked on the lack of input, training, and experience—particularly in the area of social emotional behavior—of many personnel currently serving young children and their families. Institutions of higher education should expand their training programs to include attention to the social emotional area. Changes in higher education alone will not be adequate because many personnel are already working in the field and will have little, if any, opportunity to return for an academic "retooling." Consequently, it is imperative that local and state agencies develop thoughtful and coordinated in-service training plans to address personnel needs focused on social emotional development, assessment, and intervention.

Changes in Federal and State Policy

A final "should" addresses the need for changes in federal and state policy. We believe that to ensure the development of universal screening, the provision of a cascade of services, validation of assessment and intervention materials, and the improvement of personnel preparation, federal and state policy will need expansion and refinement. Left to the good will of agencies and personnel, needed refinements will likely occur unsystematically, if at all; they may not endure if established; and they may omit critical dimensions of change. Clear and focused policy developed at the federal and state level could do much to ensure that change is systematically undertaken, is developed with the necessary infrastructure for maintenance, and addresses at least most areas of critical need. In addition, it will be important that federal and state policy is coordinated and complementary and that state personnel understand and support federal guidelines. Our experience with policies under the No Child Left Behind Act of 2001 (PL 107-110) clearly emphasizes the need for federal and state understanding and coordination.

A PARTING WORD

The development of the ABI:SE Approach was not a labor of love, but rather, what we perceived as a labor of necessity. As we have remarked throughout this volume, our work with the ASQ led us into the social emotional area; an area we had successfully avoided for many years. Based on extensive feedback from the field, we felt called to develop a screening measure focused on social emotional behavior. The ASQ:SE was developed and found to accurately identify most young children in need of further evaluation. That, in turn, forced us to face the reality that once children are identified with a social emotional problem, many personnel had little in the way of further assessment and intervention strategies to offer children and/or families. Our initial position was that others were much better prepared to address this significant need (we still feel that is accurate); however, we could see little or no action of the sort we felt would result in genuine assistance to interventionists, teachers, and child care workers. Thus, we jumped into the fray.

Time will tell whether our foray into social emotional assessment and intervention was an effort that will realize positive outcomes (however small). We can only hope that the final analysis shows that this volume and its content provided some small steps toward the development of comprehensive and coordinated systems, and that these systems consistently aid young children and their families in their search for social emotional competence.

References

Achenbach, T. (1991). *Child Behavior Checklist/2–3 years* (CBCL/2–3). Burlington: University of Vermont, Department of Psychiatry.

Achenbach, T., & Rescorla, L. (2000). *Manual for the Achenbach system of empirically based assessment preschool forms and profiles.* Burlington: University of Vermont, Department of Psychiatry.

Alberto, P., & Troutman, A. (2002). *Applied behavior analysis for teachers* (6th ed.). New York: Macmillan Publishing.

American Academy of Pediatrics (2006). Identifying infants and young children with developmental disorders in the medical home: An algorithm for developmental surveillance and screening. *Pediatrics, 118*(1), 405–420.

American Academy of Pediatrics Committee on Psychosocial Aspects of Child and Family Health. (2001). The new morbidity revisited: A renewed commitment to the psychosocial aspects of pediatric care. *Pediatrics, 108,* 1227–1230.

American Psychiatric Association. (1994). *Diagnostic and statistical manual of mental disorders* (4th ed.). Washington, DC: Author.

American Psychological Association. (1995). *Standards for educational and psychological tests.* Washington, DC: Author.

Aylward, G. (1990). Environmental influences on the developmental outcome of children at risk. *Infants and Young Children, 2*(1–9).

Bagnato, S.J., Neisworth, J.T., Salvia, J.J., & Hunt, F.M. (1999). *Temperament and Atypical Behavior Scale (TABS): Early childhood indicators of developmental dysfunction: Manual.* Baltimore: Paul H. Brookes Publishing Co.

Bailey, D., Bruer, J., Symons, F., & Lichtman, J. (Eds.), (2001). *Critical thinking about critical periods.* Baltimore: Paul H. Brookes Publishing Co.

Barnard, K. (1994). *Difficult life circumstances.* Seattle, WA: NCAST-AVENUW.

Barnett, D., Bell, S., & Carey, K. (1999). *Designing preschool interventions: A practitioner's guide.* New York: Guilford Press.

Beck, C. (1999, March). Maternal depression and child behavior problems: A meta-analysis. *Journal of Advanced Nursing, 29*(3), 623–629.

Behrman, R. (2004). Children, families, foster care: Analysis. *Future of Children, 14*(1).

Berk, L. (2003). *Infants, children, and adolescents.* Needham Heights, MA: Allyn & Bacon.

Berrick, J., Nedell, B., Barth, R., & Johnson-Reid, M. (1998). *Tender years.* Oxford, UK: Oxford University Press.

Bijou, S.W., & Baer, D.M. (1961). *Child development, Vol. 1: A systematic and empirical theory.* New York: Appleton-Century-Crofts.

Bilaver, L., Jaudes, P., Koepke, D., & George, R. (1999). The health of children in foster care. *Social Service Review 73,* 401–420.

Bishop, G., Spence, S., & McDonald, C. (2003). Can parents and teachers provide a reliable and valid report of behavioral inhibition? *Child Development, 74*(6), 1899–1917.

Bloom, P. (1997). *Great place to work: Improving conditions for staff in young children's programs.* Washington, DC: National Association for the Education of Young Children.

Bornstein, M., & Tamis-LeMonda, C. (2001). Mother–infant interaction. In T.B. Brazelton & S. Greenspan (2000). *The irreducible needs of children: What every child must have to grow, learn, and flourish.* Cambridge, MA: Perseus.

Bredekamp, S., & Copple, C. (Eds.). (1997). *Developmentally appropriate practice in early childhood programs.* Washington, DC: National Association for the Education of Young Children.

Bremmer, J.G., & Fogel, A. (Eds.), *Blackwell handbook of infant development* (pp. 269–295). Malden, MA: Blackwell Publishers.

Bricker, D. (1989). *Early intervention for at-risk and handicapped infants, toddlers and preschool children.* Palo Alto, CA: VORT Corp.

Bricker, D., & Cripe, J. (1992). *An activity-based approach to early intervention.* Baltimore: Paul H. Brookes Publishing Co.

Bricker, D., Schoen Davis, M., & Squires, J. (2004). Mental health screening in young children. *Infants and Young Children, 25*(1), 62–73, 129–144.

Bricker, D., & Widerstrom, A. (Eds.). (1996). *Preparing personnel to work with infants and young children and their families: A team approach.* Baltimore: Paul H. Brookes Publishing Co.

Bricker, D., Yovanoff, P., Capt, B., & Allen, D. (2003). Use of a curriculum-based measure to corroborate eligibility decisions. *Journal of Early Intervention, 26*(1), 20–30.

Briggs-Gowan, M., & Carter, A. (1998). Preliminary acceptability and psychometrics of the infant–toddler social and emotional assessment (ITSEA): A new adult-report interview. *Infant Mental Health Journal, 19,* 422–445.

Briggs-Gowan, M., & Carter, A. (2001). *Brief Infant–Toddler Social Emotional Assessment (BITSEA) Manual, version 1.0.* New Haven: The Connecticut Early Development Project. [Available from authors at ITSEA@yale.edu].

Briggs-Gowan, M., & Carter, A. (2006). *Brief Infant–Toddler Social and Emotional Assessment (BITSEA).* San Antonia, TX: Psychological Corp.

Briggs-Gowan, M., Carter, A., Irwin, J., Wachtel, K., & Cicchetti, D. (2004). The Brief Infant–Toddler Social and Emotional Assessment: Screening for social emotional problems and delays in competence. *Journal of Pediatric Psychology, 29*(2), 143–155.

Buscemi, L., Bennett, T., Thomas, D., & Deluca, D. (1995). Head Start: Challenges and training needs. *Journal of Early Intervention, 20,* 1–13.

Butterfield, P., Martin, C., & Pratt Prairie, A. (2004). *Emotional connections: How relationships guide early learning.* Washington, DC: Zero to Three.

Caldwell, B., & Bradley, R. (1984). *Home Observation for the Measurement of the Environment (HOME).* Little Rock: Center for Research on Teaching and Learning, University of Arkansas at Little Rock.

Caldwell, B., & Bradley, R. (2001). *Home Observation for the Measurement of the Environment (HOME) inventory administration manual* (3rd ed.). Little Rock: Center for Research on Teaching and Learning, University of Arkansas.

Campbell, S. (1995). Behavior problems in preschool children: A review of recent research. *Journal of Child Psychology and Psychiatry, 36,* 113–149.

Campos, J., Mumme, D., Kermoina, R., & Campos, R. (1994). A functional perspective on the nature of emotion. *Monographs of the Society for Research in Child Development, 59*(2–3, Serial No. 240), 284–303.

Carr, E.G., Dunlap, G., Horner, R.H., Koegel, R.L., Turnbull, A.P., Sailor, W., et al. (2002). Positive behavior support: Evolution of an applied science. *Journal of Positive Behavior Interventions, 4,* 4–16.

Carter, A., Little, C., Briggs-Gowan, M., & Kogan, N. (1999). The Infant–Toddler Social and Emotional Assessment (ITSEA): Comparing parent ratings to laboratory observations of task mastery, emotion regulation, coping behaviors and attachment status. *Infant Mental Health Journal, 20*(4), 375–392.

Catron, T. (1997). *School-based mental health services.* Kennedy Center News, No. 38. Vanderbilt University, Nashville, Tennessee.

Chan, B., & Taylor, N. (1998). The Follow-Along Program cost analysis in southwest Minnesota. *Infants and Young Children, 10*(4), 71–79.

Children's Defense Fund. (2002). *The state of children in America's union: A 2002 action guide to leave no child behind.* Retrieved August 20, 2002, from http://www.childrensdefense.org/pdf/minigreenbook.pdf

Children's Defense Fund. (2004). *Children's mental health resource kit.* (Retrieved on January 15, 2004, from http://www.childrensdefense.org/mentalhealthresourcekit.phpx

Children's Defense Fund (2005). *State of America's children.* Retrieved August 25, 2006, from www.children'sdefense.org/site/docserver.Greenbook

Cicchetti, D., & Cohen, D. (1995). Perspectives on developmental psychopathology. In D. Cicchetti & D. Cohen (Eds.), *Developmental psychopathology: Theory and methods* (pp. 3–20). New York: John Wiley & Sons.

Cicchetti, D., & Cohen, D. (2006). *Developmental psychopathology: Vol. 2, Developmental neuroscience* (2nd ed.). NY: John Wiley & Sons.

Cicchetti, D., Ganiban, J., & Barnett, D. (1991). Contributions from the study of high-risk populations to understanding the development of emotional regulation. In J. Garber & K. Dodge (Eds.), *The development of emotion regulation and dysregulation* (pp. 15–48). New York: Cambridge University Press.

Coons, C., Gay, E., Fandal, A., Ker, C., & Frankenburg, W. (1981). *The Home Screening Interview.* Denver: John F. Kennedy Child Development Center, School of Medicine, University of Colorado Health Sciences Center.

Conroy, M., & Brown, W. (2004). Early identification, prevention, and early intervention with young children at risk for emotional or behavioral disorders: Issues, trends, and a call for action. *Behavioral Disorders, 29*(3), 224–236.

Costello, E., Edelbrock, C., Costello, A., Dulcan, M., Burns, B., & Brent, D. (1988). Psychopathology in pediatric primary care: The new hidden morbidity. *Pediatrics, 82,* 415–424.

Crnic, K., Hoffman, C., Gaze, C., & Edelbrock, C. (2004). Understanding the emergence of behavior problems in young children with developmental delays. *Infants and Young Children, 17*(3), 223–235.

Culter, A., & Gilkerson, L. (2002). *Unmet needs project.* Illinois Council on Developmental Disability. Retrieved February 1, 2004, from http://www.erikson.edu.state.il.us/agency/icddx

Danaher, J., & Armijo, C. (2004). *Part C updates.* Chapel Hill: NECTAC. Individuals with Disabilities Education Act Amendments of 1997, PL 105-17, 20 U.S.C. §§ 1400 *et seq.*

Dawes, R. (1994). *House of cards: Psychology and psychotherapy built on myth.* New York: The Free Press.

Daugherty, S., Grisham-Brown, J., & Hemmeter, M.L. (2001). The effects of embedded skill instruction on the acquisition of target and non-target skills in preschoolers with developmental delays. *Topics in Early Childhood Special Education, 21,* 213–21.

Dawson, G., Frey, K., Panagiotides, H., Osterling, J., & Hessl, D. (1997). Infants of depressed mothers exhibit atypical frontal brain activity: A replication and extension of previous findings. *Journal of Child Psychology and Psychiatry, 38*(2), 179–186.

Devereux Foundation. (1998). *Devereux Early Childhood Assessment* (DECA). Lutz, FL: Psychological Assessment Resources.

Diamond, K., & Squires, J. (1993). The role of parental report in the screening and assessment of young children. *Journal of Early Intervention, 17,* 107–115.

Dodge, K. (1991). Emotion and social information processing. In J. Garber & K. Dodge (Eds.), *The development of emotion regulation and dysregulation* (pp. 159–181). New York: Cambridge University Press.

Dodge, D., & Colker, L. (1992). *The Creative Curriculum for early childhood.* Washington, DC: Teaching Strategies.

Dodge, K., & Garber, J. (1991). Domains of emotion regulation. In J. Garber & K. Dodge (Eds.), *The development of emotion regulation and dysregulation* (pp. 3–14). Cambridge, UK: Cambridge University Press.

Dombro, A., Colker, L., & Dodge, D. (2002). *The Creative Curriculum for infants and toddlers.* Clifton Park, NY: Delmar Thomson Learning.

Donahue, P., Falk, B., & Provet, A. (2000). *Mental health consultation in early childhood.* Baltimore: Paul H. Brookes Publishing Co.

Drotar, D. (2002). Behavioral and emotional problems in infants and young children: Challenges of clinical assessment and intervention. *Infants and Young Children, 14*(4), 1–5.

Dulcan, M., Costello, E., Costello, A., Edelbrock, C., Brent, D., & Janiszewski, S. (1990). The pediatrician as gatekeeper to mental health care for children: Do parents' concerns open the gate? *Journal of American Academy of Child and Adolescent Psychiatry, 29*(3) 453–458.

Duncan, B., Forness, S., & Hartsough, C. (1995). Students identified as seriously emotionally disturbed in school-based day treatment: Cognitive, psychiatric, and special education characteristics. *Behavioral Disorders, 20,* 238–252.

Durlak, J., & Wells, A. (1997). Primary prevention mental health programs for children and adolescents: A meta-analytic review. *American Journal of Community Psychology, (25)*2, 115–152.

Dworkin, R. (2000). *Sovereign virtue: The theory and practice of equality.* Cambridge: Harvard University Press.

Edwards, C., Gandini, L., & Forman, G. (Eds.) (1998). The hundred languages of children: The Reggio Emilia Approach—Advanced reflections (2nd ed.). Greenwich, CN: Ablex Publishing.

Eggbeer, L., Mann, T., & Gilkerson, L. (2003). Preparing infant–family practitioners: A work in progress. *Zero to Three 24*(1), 35–40.

Emde, R., Korfmacher, J., & Kubicek, L. (2000). Toward a theory of early relationship-based interventions. In J. Osofsky & H. Fitzgerald (Eds.), *WAIMH handbook of infant mental health: Early intervention, evaluation, and assessment* (Vol. 2, pp. 3–24). New York: John Wiley & Sons.

Farran, D. (1990). Effects of intervention with disadvantaged and disabled children. In S.J. Meisels & J.P. Sonkoff (Eds.) *Handbook of early childhood intervention* (pp. 501–539). New York: Cambridge University Press.

Farran, D. (2000). Another decade of intervention for children who are low income or disabled: What do we know now? In J. Shonkoff & S. Meisels (Eds.), *Handbook of early childhood intervention* (pp. 510–548). New York: Cambridge University Press.

Federal Interagency Coordinating Council. *FICC Summary Minutes.* (2002, December 12). Retrieved February 2, 2004, from http://www.fed-icc.org/quarterly-meetings/past-meetings/2002meetings.html#December

Feil, E., Walker, H., Severson, H., & Ball, A. (2000). Proactive screening for emotional/behavioral concerns in Head Start preschools. Promising practices and challenges in applied research. *Behavioral Disorders, 26,* 13–25.

Fenichel, E. (2000). Infant mental health and social policy. In J. Osofsky & H. Fitzgerald (Eds.), *WAIMH handbook of infant mental health: Infant mental health in groups at high risk* (Vol. 4, pp. 485–520). New York: John Wiley & Sons.

Fifer, W., Monk, C., & Grose-Fifer, J. (2004). Prenatal development and risk. In J.G. Bremner & A. Fogel (Eds.), *Blackwell handbook of infant development* (pp. 505–542). Malden, MA: Blackwell Publishing.

Filipek, P., Accardo, P., Ashwall, S., et al. (2000). Practice parameter: Screening and diagnosis of autism: Report of the quality standards subcommittee of the American Academy of Neurology and the Child Neurology Society. *Neurology, 55*(4), 468–479.

Fitzgerald, H., & Barton, L. (2000). Infant mental health: Origins and emergence of an interdisciplinary field. In J. Osofsky & H. Fitzgerald (Eds.), *WAIMH handbook of infant mental health: Perspectives on infant mental health* (Vol. 1, pp. 1–36). New York: John Wiley & Sons.

Fox, L., Dunlap, G., Hemmeter, M., Joseph, G., & Strain, P. (2003). The teaching pyramid: A model supporting social competence and preventing challenging behavior in young children. *Young Children, 58*(4), 48–52.

Foxx, R.M., & Arzin, N.H. (1973). The elimination of autistic self-stimulatory behavior by overcorrection. *Journal of Applied Behavior Analysis, 6,* 1–14.

Fraiberg, S., (1971). Intervention in infancy: A program for blind infants. *Journal of the American Academy of Child Psychiatry 3*(10), 381–405.

Fraiberg, S. (1974). Blind infants and their mothers: An examination of the sign system. In M. Lewis & L. Rosenblum (Eds.), *The effect of the infant on its caregiver* (pp. 215–232). New York: Wiley-Interscience.

Gilkerson, L., & Cochran Kopel, C. (2005). Relationship-based systems change: Illinois' model for promoting social-emotional development in Part C Early Intervention. *Infants and Young Children, 18*(4), 349–365.

Glascoe, F. (1991). Developmental screening: Rationale, methods, and application. *Infants & Young Children, 4,* 1–10.

Glascoe, F., & Byrne, K. (1993). The accuracy of three developmental screening tests. *Journal of Early Intervention 17*(4), 368–379.

Glascoe, F., Foster, M., & Wolraich, M. (1997). An economic analysis of developmental detection methods. *Pediatrics, 99*(6), 830–837.

Goldberg, I., Regier, D., McInerney, T., Pless, I., & Roghmann, K. (1979). The role of the pediatrician in the delivery of mental health services to children. *Pediatrics, 63,* 898–909.

Goldberg, I., Roghmann, K., McInerny, T., & Burke, J. (1984). Mental health problems among children seen in pediatric practice: Prevalence and management. *Pediatrics, 73*(3), 278–293.

Gottfried, A. (1984). *Home environment and early cognitive development: Longitudinal research.* Orlando, FL: Academic Press.

Greenberg, M.T., Domitrovich, C., & Bumbarger, B. (1999). *Preventing mental disorders in school-age children: A review of the effectiveness of prevention programs. Executive summary.* [Available from authors, Prevention Research Center, Penn State University, 109 S. Henderson Bldg., University Park, PA 16802.]

Greenspan, S., & Meisels, S. (1996). Toward a new vision for the developmental assessment of infants and young children. In S. Meisels & E. Fenichel (Eds.), *New visions for the developmental assessment of infants and young children* (pp. 11–26). Washington, DC: Zero To Three.

Gresham, F., & Elliott, S. (1990). *Social Skills Rating System: Ages 3–5 social skills interview.* Circle Pines, MN: American Guidance Service.

Harden, B., Winslow, M., Kendzioro, K., Shahinfar, A., Rubin, K., Fox, N. (2000). Externalizing problems in Head Start children: An ecological exploration. *Early Education and Development, 11,* 357–385.

Halfon, N., Regalado, M., Sareen, H., Inkelas, M., Peck Reuland, C., & Glascoe, F. (2004). Assessing development in the pediatric office. *Pediatrics, 113*(6), 1926–1933.

Harms, T., Cryer, D., & Clifford, R. (1997). *Infant/Toddler Environment Rating Scale* (ITERS) (Rev. ed.). New York: Teachers College Press.

Hart, B., & Risley, T.R. (1995). *Meaningful differences in the everyday experience of young American children.* Baltimore: Paul H. Brookes Publishing Co.

Hawkins, J., Catalano, R., Kosterman, R., Abbott, R., & Hill, K. (1999). Preventing adolescent health-risk behaviors by strengthening protection during childhood. *Archives of Pediatrics and Adolescent Medicine, 153,* 226–234.

Head Start National Survey. (2003, January). Early Head Start Research and Evaluation Project. *Research to practice: Depression in the lives of Early Head Start families.* Retrieved February 12, 2004, from http://www.acf.hhs.gov/programs/core/ongoing_research/

Hohmann, M., & Weikart, D. (2004). *Educating young children: Active learning practices for preschool and child care programs* (2nd ed.). Ypsilanti, MI: High/Scope Press.

Horn, E., Lieber, J., Li, S.M., Sandall, S., & Schwartz, I. (2000). Supporting young children's IEP goals in inclusive settings through embedded learning opportunities. *Topics in Early Childhood Special Education, 20,* 208–223.

Horner, R.H. (1994). Functional assessment: Contributions and future directions. *Journal of Applied Behavior Analysis, 27,* 401–404.

Horner, R., Sugai, G., Todd, A., & Lewis-Palmer, T. (2005). School-wide positive behavior support: An alternative approach to discipline in schools. In L. Bamabra & L. Kern (Eds.), *Indi-*

vidualized supports for students with problem behavior: Designing positive behavior support plans. New York: Guilford Press.

Horowitz, S., Leaf, P., Leventhal, J., Forsyth, B., & Speechley, K. (1992). Identification and management of psychosocial and developmental problems in community-based, primary care pediatric practices. *Pediatrics, 89,* 480–485.

Hyson, M. (2003). *Preparing early childhood professionals: NAEYC's Standards for Programs.* Washington, DC. National Association for the Education of Young Children.

Individuals with Disabilities Education Act Amendments of 1991, PL 102-119, 20 U.S.C. §§ 1400 *et seq.*

Jellinek, M. (1998). Pediatric psychosocial screening: Of sufficient benefit to encourage. *Developmental and Behavioral Pediatrics, 19,* 353–354.

Jellinek, M., & Murphy, J. (1999). *Psychosocial problems, screening, and the pediatric symptom checklist.* Retrieved August 21, 2001, from http://dpbeds.org/handouts

Jellinek, M., Patel, B., & Froehl, M. (2002). *Bright futures in practice: Mental health, Volume I, Practice Guide.* National Center for Education in Maternal and Child Health. Georgetown University.

Kaiser, B., & Rasminsky, S. (1999). *Meeting the challenge: Effective strategies for challenging behaviours in early childhood environments.* Ottawa, ON: M.O.M. Printing.

Kataoka, S., Zhang, L., & Wells, K. (2002, September). Unmet need for mental health care among U.S. children: Variation by ethnicity and insurance status. *American Journal of Psychiatry 159*(9), 15–48.

Kauffman, J. (1999). How we prevent the prevention of emotional and behavioral disorders. *Exceptional Children, 65,* 448–468.

Kelly, J., & Barnard, K. (1999). Parent education within a relationship-focused model. *Topics in Early Childhood Special Education, 19*(3), 151–157.

Kelly, J., & Barnard, K. (2000). Assessment of parent–child interaction: Implications of early intervention. In J. Shonkoff & S. Meisels (Eds.), *Handbook of early childhood intervention* (pp. 258–289). New York: Cambridge University Press.

Kemper, K., Osborn, L., Hansen, D., & Pascoe, J. (1994). Family psychosocial screening: Should we focus on high-risk settings? *Developmental and Behavioral Pediatrics, 15,* 336–341.

Knitzer, J. (2000). Early childhood mental health services: A policy and systems development perspective. In J. Shonkoff & S. Meisels (Eds.), *Handbook of early childhood intervention* (2nd ed., pp. 416–438, pp. 906–956). New York: Cambridge University Press.

Knitzer, J. (2004). The challenge of mental health in Head Start: Making the vision real. In E. Zigler & S.J. Styfco (Eds). *The Head Start debates* (pp. 179–192). Baltimore: Paul H. Brookes Publishing Co.

Knitzer, J., & Lefkowitz, J. (2006). *Pathways to early school success: Helping the most vulnerable infants, toddlers, and their families.* New York: National Center for Children in Poverty.

Kobe, F., & Hammer, D. (1994). Parenting stress and depression in children with mental retardation and developmental disabilities. *Research in Developmental Disabilities, 15,* 209–221.

Koegel, L.K., Koegel, R.L., & Dunlap, G. (Eds.) (1996). *Positive behavioral support: Including people with difficult behavior in the community.* Baltimore: Paul H. Brookes Publishing Co.

Kopp, C. (1989). Regulation of distress and negative emotions: A developmental view. *Developmental Psychology, 25*(3), 343–354.

Kupersmidt, J., Bryant, D., & Willoughby, M. (2000). Prevalence of aggressive behaviors among preschoolers in Head Start and community child care programs. *Behavioral Disorders, 26,* 42–52.

Lally, R. (2003). Infant–toddler child care in the United States: Where has it been? Where is it now? Where is it going? *Zero to Three, 24*(1), 29–34.

Landy, S. (2002). *Pathways to competence: Encouraging healthy social and emotional development in young children.* Baltimore: Paul H. Brookes Publishing Co.

Lavigne, J., Binns, H., Christoffel, K., Rosenbaum, D., Arend, R., Smith, K., et al. (1993). Behavior and emotional problems among preschool children in pediatric primary care: Prevalence and pediatricians' recognition. *Pediatrics, 91,* 649–655.

Lavigne, J., Gibbons, R., Christoffel, K., Arend, R., Rosenbaum, D., Binns, H., et al. (1996). Prevalence rates and correlates of psychiatric disorders among preschool children. *Journal of the American Academy of Child and Adolescent Psychiatry, 35,* 204–214.

Lichtenstein, R., & Ireton, H. (1984). *Preschool screening.* New York: Grune & Straton.

Liptak, G. (1996). Enhancing patient compliance in pediatrics. *Pediatrics in Review, 17*(4), 128–134.

Loeber, R., & Farrington, D., (1998). *Serious & violent juvenile offenders: Risk factors and successful interventions.* Thousand Oaks: CA: Sage Publications.

Lowenthal, B. (2001). *Abuse and neglect: The educator's guide to the identification and prevention of child maltreatment.* Baltimore: Paul H. Brookes Publishing Co.

Meisels, S., Dombro, A., Marsden, D., Weston D., & Jewkes, A. (2003). *Ounce Scale Assessment System.* New York: Pearson Early Learning.

Merrell, K. (2002). *Preschool and Kindergarten Behavioral Scale* (2nd ed.). Austin, TX: PRO-ED.

Merrell, K., & Holland, M. (1997). Social emotional behavior of preschool-age children with and without developmental delays. *Research in Developmental Disabilities, 18*(6), 393–405.

Merritt, K., Thompson, R., Keith, B., Johndrow, D., & Bennett Murphy, L. (1993). Screening for behavioral and emotional problems in primary care pediatrics. *Developmental and Behavioral Pediatrics, 14*(5), 340–343.

Metzler, C., Biglan, A., Rusby, J., & Sprague, J. (2001). Evaluation of a comprehensive behavior management program to improve school-wide positive behavior support. *Education and Treatment of Children, 24,* 448–479.

Mowder, B., Unterspan, D., Knuter, L., Goode, C., & Pedro, M. (1993). Psychological consultation and Head Start. *Journal of Early Intervention, 17,* 1–7.

Murray, L., Sinclair, D., Cooper, P., Docournau, P., & Turner, P. (1999). The socioemotional development of 5-year-old children of postnatally depressed mothers. *Journal of Child Psychology and Psychiatry and Allied Disciplines, 40,* 1259–1271.

National Alliance for the Mentally Ill. (2000). *Families on the brink—Executive summary: The impact of ignoring children with serious mental illness.* Retrieved October 30, 2000, from http://www.nami.org/youth/brink3/htmlx

National Association of School Psychologists (n.d.). *School based mental health services support improved classroom behavior and school safety.* Retrieved on February 5, 2004, from http://www.nasponline.org/advocacy/sbmhsvcs.html

National Center for Children in Poverty. (2002). Sept. 11th tragedies heighten need to address mental health issues facing low-income families. *News & Issues,* 7–8.

National Institutes of Health. (1999). *National Institute of Child Health and Human Development news alert: Maternal depression linked with social and language development, school readiness: Maternal sensitivity helps these children fare better.* Washington, DC. Retrieved July 21, 2000, from http://nichd.nih.gov/new/releases/depression.htmx

National Institutes of Mental Health, U.S. Public Health Service. (2000). *Report of the Surgeon General's conference on children's mental health: A national action agenda.* Washington, DC: U.S. Department of Health and Human Services.

Neisworth, J.T., & Bagnato, S. J. (2004). The mismeasure of young children: The authentic assessment alternative. *Infants and Young Children, 17*(3), 198–212.

Nickel R., & Desch, L. (Eds.) (2000). *The physician's guide to caring for children with disabilities and chronic conditions.* Baltimore: Paul H. Brookes Publishing Co.

Nickel, R., & Squires, J. (2000). Developmental screening and surveillance. In R. Nickel & L. Desch (Eds.), *The physician's guide to caring for children with disabilities and chronic conditions* (pp.15–30). Baltimore: Paul H. Brookes Publishing Co.

No Child Left Behind Act of 2001, PL 107-110, 115 Stat. 1425, 20 U.S.C. §§ 6301 *et seq.*x

O'Neill, R.E., Horner, R.H., Albin, R., Sprague, K., Storey, K., & Newton, J.S. (1997). *Functional behavioral assessment and program development for problem behaviors.* Belmont, CA: Wadsworth Publishing.

O'Neil, H., & Schacter, J. (1997). *Test specifications for problem-solving assessment.* Los Angeles, CA: National Center for Research on Evaluation, Standards, and Student Testing.

Osofsky, J., & Fitzgerald, H. (2000). *WAIMH handbook of infant mental health: Early intervention, evaluation, and assessment* (Vol. 2). New York: John Wiley & Sons.

Pessanha, M., & Bairrão, J. (2003). The home screening interview: A validation study. *International Journal of Child & Family Welfare, 6*(1/2), 27–32.

President's New Freedom Commission on Mental Health: *Report to the President.* (2003, July). Retrieved December 14, 2003, from http://www.mentalhealthcommission.gov/reports/Final Report/toc.html.

Pretti-Frontczak, K., & Bricker, D. (2004). *An activity-based approach to early intervention* (3rd ed.). Baltimore: Paul H. Brookes Publishing Co.

Qi, C., & Kaiser, A. (2003). Behavior problems of preschool children from low-income families: Review of the literature. *Topics in Early Childhood Special Education, 23*(4), 188–216.

Raikes, H.H., & McCall Whitmer, J. (2006). *Beautiful Beginnings: A developmental curriculum for infants and toddlers.* Baltimore: Paul H. Brookes Publishing Co.

Ramey, C., & Ramey, S. (1998). Early intervention and early experience. *American Psychologist, 53*(2), 109–120.

Ramey, C., & Ramey, S. (2004). Early educational interventions and intelligence: Implications of Head Start. In E. Zigler & S.J. Styfco (Eds.). *The Head Start debates* (pp. 3–18). Baltimore: Paul H. Brookes Publishing Co.

Raver, C. (2002). Emotions matter: Making the case for the role of young children's emotional development for early school readiness. *Social Policy Report, XVI*(3), 3–18.

Raver, C., & Zigler, E. (1997). Social competence: An untapped dimension in evaluating Head Start's success. *Early Childhood Research Quarterly, 12,* 363–385.

Reid, J., Patterson, G., & Snyder, J. (2002). *Antisocial behavior in children and adolescents.* Washington, DC: American Psychological Association.

Report of the Surgeon General's conference on Children's Mental Health: A national action agenda. Department of Health and Human Services. (1999, December). Retrieved February 5, 2004, from http://www.surgeongeneral.gov/topics/ch/childreport.htm

Roberts, C., Mazzucchelli, T., Taylor, K., & Reid, R. (2003). Early intervention for behaviour problems in young children with developmental disabilities. *International Journal of Disability, Development and Education 50*(3), 275–292.

Robinson, N., Weinberg, R., Redden, D., Ramey, S., & Ramey, C. (1998). Family factors associated with high academic achievement among former Head Start children. *Gifted Child Quarterly, 42,* 148–156.

Sandall, S., Hemmeter, M., Smith, B., & McLean, M. (2005). *DEC recommended practices: A comprehensive guide for practical application in early intervention/early childhood special education.* Longmont, CO: Sopris West.

Sameroff, A. (2000). Ecological perspectives on developmental risk. In J. Osofsky & H. Fitzgerald (Eds.), *WAIMH handbook of infant mental health: Infant mental health in groups at high risk* (Vol. 4, pp. 1–34). New York: John Wiley & Sons.

Sameroff, A., & Chandler, M. (1975). Reproductive risk and the continuum of caretaking casualty. In F. Horowitz (Ed.), *Review of child development research* (Vol. 4, pp. 187–244). Chicago: University of Chicago Press.

Sameroff, A., & Fiese, B. (1990). Transactional regulation: The developmental ecology of early intervention. In J. Shonkoff & S. Meisels (Eds.), *Handbook of early childhood intervention* (pp. 135–159). Cambridge: Cambridge University Press.

Sameroff, A., & Fiese, B. (2000). Models of development and developmental risk. In C. Zeanah (Ed.), *Handbook of infant mental health* (2nd ed., pp. 3–19). New York: Guilford Press.

Sameroff, A., & MacKenzie, M. (2003). A quarter-century of the transactional model: How have things changed? *Zero to Three, 24*(1), 14–22.

Sameroff, A., Seifer, R., Baldwin, A., & Baldwin, C. (1994). Stability of intelligence from pre-school to adolescence: The influence of social and family risk factors. *Child Development, 64,* 80–97.

Shinn, M., Walker, H., & Stoner, G. (2002). Etiology of youth antisocial behavior, delinquency, and violence and a public health approach to prevention. In *Interventions for academic and behavior problems II: Preventative and remedial approaches* (pp. 27–52). Bethesda, MD: NASP Publications.

Shonkoff, J., & Phillips, D. (Eds.) (2000). *From neurons to neighborhoods: The science of early childhood development.* Washington, DC: National Academies Press.

Shore, R. (1997). *Rethinking the brain: New insights into early development.* New York: Families and Work Institute.

Squires, J. (1996). Parent-completed developmental interviews: A low-cost strategy for child-find and screening. *Infants and Young Children, 9*(1), 16–28.

Squires, J. (2000, July 20). *Child-find strategies using the Ages & Stages Questionnaires® (ASQ).* [Web-based telephone conference/NEC*TAS North Carolina.

Squires, J. (2005). *Progress report: Early Head Start university partnerships.* Eugene, OR: Center on Human Development.

Squires, J., Bricker, D., Heo, K., & Twombly, E. (2001). Identification of social emotional problems in young children using a parent-completed screening measure. *Early Childhood Research Quarterly, 16,* 405–419.

Squires, J., Bricker, D., & Twombly, L. (2002). *Ages & Stages Questionnaires®: Social-Emotional* (ASQ:SE): A parent-completed, child-monitoring system for social-emotional behaviors. Baltimore: Paul H. Brookes Publishing Co.

Squires, J., Bricker, D., & Twombly, L., (2004). Parent-completed screening for social emotional problems in young children: The effects of risk/disability status and gender on performance. *Infant Mental Health Journal, 25*(1), 62–73.

Squires, J., & Nickel, R. (2003). Never too soon: Identification of social emotional problems in infants and toddlers. *Contemporary Pediatrics, 20*(3), 117–125.

Squires, J., Nickel, R., & Eisert, D. (1996). Early detection of developmental problems: Strategies for monitoring young children in the practice setting. *Developmental and Behavioral Pediatrics, 17*(6), 420–427.

Squires, J., Potter, L., & Bricker, D. (1999). *The ASQ user's guide for the Ages & Stages Questionnaires®: A parent-completed, child-monitoring system* (2nd ed.). Baltimore: Paul H. Brookes Publishing Co.

Sroufe, A. (1996). *Emotional development: The organization of emotional life in the early years.* Cambridge, UK: Cambridge University Press.

Stancin, T., & Palmermo, T. (1997). A review of behavioral screening practices in pediatric settings: Do they pass the test? *Journal of Developmental and Behavioral Pediatrics, 18*(3), 183–193.

Sugai, G., Horner, R.H., & Sprague, J. (1999). Functional assessment-based behavior support planning: Research-to-practice-to-research. *Behavioral Disorders, 24,* 223–227.

Thomas, A., & Chess, S. (1977). *Temperament and development.* New York: Brunner/Mazel.

Thompson, R. (1994). Emotion regulation: A theme in search of definition. *Monographs of the Society for Research in Child Development, 59*(2–3, Serial No. 240), 250–283.

Turnbull, A.P., Turbiville, V., & Turnbull, H.R. (2000). Evolution of family-professional partnerships: Collective empowerment as the model for the early twenty-first century. In J. Shonkoff & S. Meisels (Eds.), *Handbook of early childhood intervention* (pp. 630–650). New York: Cambridge University Press.

U.S. Department of Education (1999). *Twenty-first annual report to Congress on the implementation of the Individuals with Disabilities Education Act.* Retrieved March 10, 2004, from http://www.ed.gov/about/reports/annual/osep/1999/index.htmlx

U.S. Department of Health and Human Services (1999). *Mental health: A report of the surgeon general.* Rockville, MD: U.S. Department of Health and Human Services, Substance Abuse and Mental Health Services Administration, Center for Mental Health Services, National Institutes of Health, National Institute of Mental Health.

U.S. House of Representatives, Committee on Ways and Means. (1994). *Overview of entitlement programs: 1994 Greenbook.* Washington, DC: U.S. Government Printing Office.

U.S. Surgeon General. (2000). *Report of the Surgeon General's conference on children's mental health: A national action agenda.* U.S. Public Health Service. Washington, DC: 2000. Retrieved February 5, 2004, at http://www.surgeongeneral.gov/cmh/childreport.htm

Wagner, M. (1995). Outcomes for youths with serious emotional disturbance in secondary school and early adulthood. *The Future of Children, 5*(2), 90–112.

Walker, H., Horner, R., Sugai, G., Bullis, M., Sprague, J., Bricker, D., & Kaufman, M. (1996). Integrated approaches to preventing antisocial behavior patterns among school-age children and youth. *Journal of Emotional and Behavioral Disorders, 4,* 194–209.

Walker, H., Kavanagh, K., Stiller, B., Golly, A., Severson, H., & Feil, E. (1998). Early intervention for antisocial behavior. *Journal of Emotional and Behavioral Disorders, 6*(2), 66–80.

Walker, H., Nishioka, V., Zeller, R., Bullis, M., & Sprague, J. (2001). School-based screening, identification, and service. *Delivery Issues, 1*(3), 49–72.

Walker, H., Ramsey, E., & Gresham, F. (2003). *Heading off disruptive behavior.* Washington, DC: American Educator.

Webster-Stratton, C. (1995). *Parent training with low-income clients.* Paper presented at Association of Behavior Therapy, Washington, DC.

Webster-Stratton, C. (1997). Early intervention for families of preschool children with conduct problems. In M.J. Guralnick (Ed.), *The effectiveness of early intervention* (pp. 429–454). Baltimore: Paul H. Brookes Publishing Co.

Werner, E. (2000). Protective factors and individual resilience. In J. Shonkoff, & S. Meisels (Eds.), *Handbook of early childhood intervention* (2nd ed., pp. 115–132). New York: Cambridge University Press.

Wildman, B., Kinsman, A., Logue, E., Dickey, D., & Smucker, W. (1997). Presentation and management of childhood psychosocial problems. *The Journal of Family Practice, 44,* 77–84.

Wildman, B., Kizilbash, A., & Smucker, W. (1999). Physicians' attention to parents' concerns about the psychosocial functioning of their children. *Archives of Family Medicine, 8,* 440–444.

Witherington, D., Campos, J., & Hertenstein, M. (2001). Principles of emotion and its development in infancy. In G. Bremner & A. Fogel (Eds.), *Blackwell handbook of infant development* (pp. 427–464). Oxford, UK: Blackwell Publishers.

Wittmer, D., Doll, B., & Strain, P. (1996). Social and emotional development in early childhood: The identification of competence and disabilities. *Journal of Early Intervention, 20*(4), 299–318.

Wolery, M. (2000). Behavioral and educational approaches to early intervention. In J. Shonkoff & S. Meisels (Eds.), *Handbook of early childhood intervention* (pp. 179–203). New York: Cambridge University Press.

Wolery, M., Bailey, D., & Sugai, G. (1988). *Effective teaching: Principles and procedures of Applied Behavior Analysis with exceptional students.* Boston: Allyn & Bacon.

Yoshikawa, H. (1994). Prevention as cumulative protection: Effects of early family support and education on chronic delinquency and its risks. *Psychological Bulletin, 115*(1), 28–54.

Yoshikawa, H. (1995). Long-term effects of early childhood programs on social outcomes and delinquency. *The Future of Children, 5,* 51–75.

Zeanah, C. (1993). *Handbook of infant mental health.* New York: Guilford Press.

Zeanah, C. (Ed.). (2000). *Handbook of infant mental health* (2nd ed.). New York: Guilford Press.

Zeanah, C., Boris, N., & Larrieu, J. (1997). Infant development and developmental risk: A review of the past 10 years. *Journal of the American Academy of Child and Adolescent Psychiatry, 36,* 165–178.

Zero to Three. (1995). *Diagnostic Classification: 0–3, diagnostic classification of mental health and developmental disorders of infancy and early childhood.* Arlington, VA: National Center for Clinical Infant Programs.

Zigler, E., Taussig, C., Black, K. (2001). Early childhood intervention: A promising preventative for juvenile delinquency. *American Psychologist, 47*(8), 997–1006.

Appendices

Appendix A
Environmental Screening Questionnaire (ESQ), Experimental Edition

Appendix B
Social Emotional Assessment/Evaluation Measure (SEAM), Experimental Edition
  Infant
  Toddler
  Preschool-Age

Appendix C
Guide to Early Childhood Curricula
Guide to Social Emotional Screening Instruments
Functional Behavioral Assessment and Behavior Support Planning
  with Deborah Russell and Robert Horner

Appendix A

Environmental
Screening Questionnaire (ESQ™)

Experimental Edition

Environmental Screening Questionnaire (ESQ™)

The Environmental Screening Questionnaire (ESQ) was designed to identify risk and protective factors in a child's environment that might affect a parent or other caregiver's ability to support his or her child's social emotional development. Risk factors related to poverty, such as no telephone or transportation, frequent moves, and credit problems are included on the ESQ as well as emotional stresses such as an absent partner, children with behavior problems, and caregiver depression. Also assessed are the protective factors that may assist a family in providing a supportive and nurturing environment for their children, such as the availability of friends and family, educational assets, and reasonable living arrangements.

Administration

An explanation of the intent of the ESQ should be offered to caregivers before it is completed. The explanation should include the measure's purpose: *to look at factors in the child's environment that might affect caregivers' ability to support their child's social emotional development.* In addition, all caregiver questions and concerns should be addressed to ensure that maximum comfort levels and understanding have been reached.

The ESQ can be completed using a variety of strategies; however, if program resources permit, the preferred strategy for completing the measure is through caregiver interview. Program personnel can read and discuss each item with the caregiver. An interview format permits program personnel to explain items to caregivers, to answer questions that may arise, and to discuss issues that may surface for caregivers. The ESQ can also be completed independently by caregivers with a follow-up discussion with program personnel.

Caregivers should be encouraged to consider each item and select the "Yes" or "No" option depending on their situation. If participants believe the answer to be partly true or sometimes true (e.g., sometimes have telephone service, sometimes feels safe in the community), the "No" option should be checked. Caregivers may choose not to answer questions that they feel are too personal.

Scoring

Each question has a z or an x next to the "Yes" and "No" box options. The z answers receive 0 points and the x answers receive 10 points. Points are then summed to get an area score. **Scores of 30 and above in any area (e.g., housing, education) require follow-up assessment or referral.**

Prior to using the ESQ, personnel should have assembled a list of available resources and referral agencies so that caregivers who indicate a significant problem can be offered timely and appropriate referrals. The final page of the ESQ is a Summary of Scores/Referral Form that should be completed for any caregiver/family whose scores indicate a problem.

Environmental Screening Questionnaire (ESQ™)

Caregivers Name: _____

Date: _____

Please check "Yes" or "No" to answer the following questions. Caregivers may choose to omit questions they think are too personal.

Category	Yes	No
Education		
1. Are you a high school or GED graduate?	☐ z	☐ x
2. Are you taking classes or job training?	☐ z	☐ x
3. Do you have trouble communicating on the telephone?	☐ x	☐ z
4. Can you read English or another language?	☐ z	☐ x
5. Were you a teenager when you had your first child?	☐ x	☐ z
Total: _____		
Housing		
1. Have you moved three times or more in the last year?	☐ x	☐ z
2. Do you own or rent a home or apartment?	☐ z	☐ x
3. Do you rely on relatives or friends for housing?	☐ x	☐ z
4. Does your child have a safe outside play area?	☐ z	☐ x
5. Does your living arrangement satisfy your family's basic needs (e.g., heat, water)?	☐ z	☐ x
Total: _____		
Health/Behavior		
1. Do you have a child with a learning, behavioral, or emotional problem?	☐ x	☐ z
2. Do you, your partner, or children have a long-term health problem?	☐ x	☐ z
3. Are there mental health problems such as depression in your home?	☐ x	☐ z
4. Have you had contact with a child protection agency?	☐ x	☐ z
5. Does your child or children get along with other children?	☐ z	☐ x
Total: _____		
Economic		
1. Do you have health insurance?	☐ z	☐ x
2. Do you receive or need public assistance?	☐ x	☐ z
3. Are you currently employed?	☐ z	☐ x
4. Have you experienced credit problems?	☐ x	☐ z
5. Do you have regular telephone service?	☐ z	☐ x
Total: _____		

Category	Yes	No
Home		
1. Do you have a partner who lives with you most of the time?	☐ z	☐ x
2. Do you have frequent fights/arguments with your partner?	☐ x	☐ z
3. Have your children seen domestic or neighborhood violence?	☐ x	☐ z
4. Does anyone in your home have trouble with alcohol or drugs?	☐ x	☐ z
5. Do you feel free to visit friends and family?	☐ z	☐ x
Total: _____		
Community		
1. Do you feel safe in your neighborhood?	☐ z	☐ x
2. Do you have people to talk to about your problems?	☐ z	☐ x
3. Do you have friends or family members who can help you out?	☐ z	☐ x
4. Do you have regular transportation?	☐ z	☐ x
5. Do you use community resources?	☐ z	☐ x
Total: _____		

Environmental Screening Questionnaire
Summary of Scores/Referral Form

Circle the total score for each area.

Education	0	10	20	30	40	50
Housing	0	10	20	30	40	50
Health/behavior	0	10	20	30	40	50
Economic	0	10	20	30	40	50
Home	0	10	20	30	40	50
Community	0	10	20	30	40	50

Caregivers with scores of 30 or more should be referred to community agencies for further evaulation and supports.

Appendix B

Social Emotional Assessment/Evaluation Measure (SEAM™)

Experimental Edition

Infant
Child Benchmarks and Assessment Items
Child Benchmarks and Assessment Items (professional version with age intervals)
Adult/Caregiver Benchmarks and Assessment Items
Summary Form

Toddler
Child Benchmarks and Assessment Items
Child Benchmarks and Assessment Items (professional version with age intervals)
Adult/Caregiver Benchmarks and Assessment Items
Summary Form

Preschool-Age
Child Benchmarks and Assessment Items
Child Benchmarks and Assessment Items (professional version with age intervals)
Adult/Caregiver Benchmarks and Assessment Items
Summary Form

Social Emotional
Assessment/Evaluation Measure

INFANT

(for developmental range 3–18 months)

General Instructions

The Social Emotional Assessment/Evaluation Measure (SEAM): Infant is divided into two sections. The first section, Child Benchmarks and Assessment Items, is focused on the child. There are two versions of the Child Benchmark and Assessment Items: The first version does not include age intervals and is intended for parents/caregivers. The second, *for professional use only,* provides age intervals with each item to serve as guides for approximate ages at which children typically perform these skills. The second section, Adult/Caregiver Benchmarks and Assessment Items, is focused on the caregiver. These sections are then followed by a Summary Form for the professional to record observations that will assist in determining goals.

Social Emotional
Assessment/Evaluation Measure

SEAM™

INFANT

(for developmental range 3–18 months)

Child Benchmarks
and Assessment Items

Child's name: _____

Child's date of birth: _____

Family's name: _____

Name of person completing form: _____

Date of administration: _____

Instructions

Please read each benchmark and item carefully before selecting an answer. Each item is accompanied by several examples. Children may be able to successfully meet the item criterion in a variety of ways. Some items may be too difficult for the child; for example, a 4-month-old may not yet be able to imitate a parent's sounds. Professionals should ensure that caregivers understand that the SEAM may contain items that are developmentally too advanced for their child. Age norms should not be used with children with delays or developmental disabilities.

The three scoring options listed in the first three columns of the SEAM include "Most of the time," "Sometimes," and "Rarely or never" to indicate the frequency or likelihood of a child's behavior. For example, if an infant shows an interest in adults whom he knows well consistently over time, a check should be placed in the box under "Most of the time" for item C-1.1. Items marked "Most of the time" are generally considered strengths. If the infant shows interest in familiar adults inconsistently, the box under "Sometimes" should be checked. If the infant seldom shows an interest in familiar adults, the box under "Rarely or never" should be checked. The latter two columns allow participants to indicate whether a particular behavior is of concern and whether it should become an intervention goal, respectively. After you are finished with this SEAM and the corresponding Adult/Caregiver SEAM, record answers on the accompanying Summary Form.

Social Emotional Assessment/Evaluation Measure (SEAM): Infant, Experimental Edition. From *An Activity-Based Approach to Developing Young Children's Social Emotional Competence,* by Jane Squires & Diane Bricker.
© 2007 Paul H. Brookes Publishing Co., Inc., Baltimore. All rights reserved.

Child Benchmarks and Assessment Items
Infant

Please read each question carefully and
1. Check the box ■ that best describes your child's behavior.
2. Check the circle ● if this behavior is a concern.
3. Check the triangle ▲ if this will be an intervention goal.

		Most of the time	Sometimes	Rarely or never	Is a concern	Intervention goal
C-1.0	**Baby participates in healthy interactions.**					
1.1	**Baby shows interest in you and other familiar caregivers.**	■	■	■	●	▲
	Follows you with his eyes *Quiets when talked to* *Looks at you when touched* *Shows pleasure when you return*					
1.2	**Baby responds to you and other familiar caregivers.**	■	■	■	●	▲
	Reaches for you *Raises arms to be picked up* *Responds to her name* *Waves "bye-bye"* *Gives hugs*					
1.3	**Baby initiates and responds to communications.**	■	■	■	●	▲
	Coos, chuckles, smiles, or laughs at you *Coos or vocalizes when you talk to him* *Laughs aloud* *Imitates your coos and babbles*					
1.4	**Baby lets you know if she needs help or comfort.**	■	■	■	●	▲
	Lets you know when wet or hungry *Expresses emotions such as fear of loud sounds or new people, shyness, and surprise*					
C-2.0	**Baby expresses a range of emotions.**					
2.1	**Baby smiles at you.**	■	■	■	●	▲
	Smiles when you smile at her *Smiles when you talk to him*					

		Most of the time	Sometimes	Rarely or never	Is a concern	Intervention goal
2.2	**Baby smiles at familiar adults.**	☐	☐	☐	○	△
	Smiles when babysitter or familiar adult smiles at her					
	Responds by making sounds, faces, or wiggling hands and feet when familiar caregivers talk or play with him					
2.3	**Baby smiles and laughs at sights and sounds.**	☐	☐	☐	○	△
	Smiles or laughs at moving toy					
	Smiles or laughs when hearing funny noises					
C-3.0	**Baby regulates his social emotional responses, with caregiver support.**					
3.1	**Baby responds to your soothing when upset.**	☐	☐	☐	○	△
	Calms when soothed by you					
	Stops or reduces crying when picked up and talked to					
	Seeks comfort from you when upset					
	Stops crying or fussing when he sees you or hears your voice					
3.2	**Baby calms down after exciting activity.**	☐	☐	☐	○	△
	Calms when carried or rocked					
	Calms after active play such as tickling					
	Switches from a vigorous activity to a quiet activity					
3.3	**Baby soothes himself when distressed.**	☐	☐	☐	○	△
	Resumes playing with familiar adult after a brief period of fretting when you depart					
	Comforts self by holding a special blanket or sucking thumb or pacifier					
	Calms down within a few minutes when put to bed					
C-4.0	**Baby begins to show empathy for others.**					
4.1	**Baby mimics your facial expressions.**	☐	☐	☐	○	△
	Copies your actions such as opening mouth					

Social Emotional Assessment/Evaluation Measure (SEAM): Infant, Experimental Edition. From *An Activity-Based Approach to Developing Young Children's Social Emotional Competence,* by Jane Squires & Diane Bricker.

INFANT

		Most of the time	Sometimes	Rarely or never	Is a concern	Intervention goal
4.2	**Baby looks at and notices you and other familiar caregivers.**	☐	☐	☐	○	△
	Follows you or other familiar caregivers with eyes when they move around room					
4.3	**Baby looks at and notices others' emotional responses.**	☐	☐	☐	○	△
	Looks at person who enters the room *Stops activity and focuses on person speaking to him* *Laughs and smiles when others do so*					
4.4	**Baby responds to another's distress, seeking comfort for self.**	☐	☐	☐	○	△
	Seeks comfort from you when others are upset					
C-5.0	**Baby attends to and engages with others.**					
5.1	**Baby makes eye contact with you and others.**	☐	☐	☐	○	△
	Looks into your eyes when you look into her eyes while talking to her					
5.2	**Baby looks at or toward sounds and visual events.**	☐	☐	☐	○	△
	Looks toward you when he hears your voice *Turns toward your singing, or music playing on a radio*					
5.3	**Baby focuses on events shown by you and others.**	☐	☐	☐	○	△
	Follows your eyes *Looks at animal/person pointed at*					
5.4	**Baby shares attention and events with you.**	☐	☐	☐	○	△
	Looks at picture or points to toy or object *Points to gain your attention* *Takes part in games like Peekaboo and So Big*					

		Most of the time	Sometimes	Rarely or never	Is a concern	Interven- tion goal
C-6.0	**Baby explores hands and feet and surroundings.**					
6.1	**Baby explores his hands and feet.**	☐	☐	☐	○	△

Grabs foot when on back
Grasps hands together and wiggles fingers
Bangs objects together with both hands
Kicks or pushes a mobile to make it move

6.2	**Baby explores toys and materials.**	☐	☐	☐	○	△

Looks at object
Grabs objects or people within reach
Holds and explores toys
Crawls to his favorite toys or caregiver
Tries different actions with toys and objects

6.3	**Baby explores surroundings.**	☐	☐	☐	○	△

Rolls onto back
Turns head to see behind her
Crawls to look at and touch objects on floor
Moves to look behind doors and furniture
Begins to run, climb, and jump

6.4	**Baby crawls or walks a short distance away from you.**	☐	☐	☐	○	△

Crawls 10–20 feet away from you, looking back at you
Leaves your side to explore new toy, object or person and remains at a distance for a few minutes
Crawls or walks around living areas exploring people, locations, and objects

C-7.0	**Baby displays a positive self-image.**					
7.1	**Baby laughs at, or smiles at, her image or picture of self.**	☐	☐	☐	○	△

Smiles at reflection in a mirror
Laughs at self reflected in store window
Points to self in mirror or picture
Points to a picture of self

	Most of the time	Sometimes	Rarely or never	Is a concern	Intervention goal
7.2 Baby recognizes his name.	☐	☐	☐	○	△
Turns to face you when name is called					
7.3 Baby calls attention to herself.	☐	☐	☐	○	△
Coos and babbles when you enter room *Squeals to you* *Calls by using pronouns, "I want you," "Me hungry"*					
C-8.0 Baby regulates activity level.					
8.1 Baby participates in simple routines and games with you.	☐	☐	☐	○	△
Coos back and forth with you *Coos when feeding* *Looks in your eyes when you sing songs to him* *Plays Peekaboo, This Little Piggy, and other simple games* *Picks up items and puts them in container*					
8.2 Baby looks at books or pictures for several minutes or longer.	☐	☐	☐	○	△
Gestures or points to pictures in book *Looks at pictures in magazine or book* *Looks at book for 2–3 minutes* *Looks at "favorite" book*					
8.3 Baby engages in motor activities for several minutes or longer.	☐	☐	☐	○	△
Manipulates small toys with hands for several minutes *Rolls ball to you for several minutes*					
C-9.0 Baby cooperates with daily routines and requests.					
9.1 Baby opens her mouth for food.	☐	☐	☐	○	△
Opens mouth for breast or bottle					
9.2 Baby follows simple routines, with your help.	☐	☐	☐	○	△
Lifts arms to put on shirt					

	Most of the time	Sometimes	Rarely or never	Is a concern	Interven- tion goal
9.3 Baby cooperates with diaper and clothing changes.	☐	☐	☐	○	△
Remains on back for at least a short time *Does not fight or cry when diapers are changed*					
C-10.0 Baby shows a range of adaptive skills.					
10.1 Baby eats and gains weight on schedule.	☐	☐	☐	○	△
Breast or bottle feeds with few problems *Eats baby cereal, fruit* *Reaches for utensils when feeding* *Drinks from cup with help* *Uses a spoon and drinks from a sippy cup*					
10.2 Baby eats a variety of age- appropriate foods.	☐	☐	☐	○	△
Feeds himself finger foods (Cheerios, crackers) *Eats a variety of textures (e.g., baby food meat, bread, fruits, vegetables)*					
10.3 Baby sleeps with few problems.	☐	☐	☐	○	△
Calms self and goes to sleep *Falls asleep while rocked* *Falls asleep within 30 minutes at nap and bedtimes* *Sleeps about 14 hours a day with two daytime naps* *Sleeps about 10–12 hours a day*					
10.4. Baby eliminates (pees and poops) on regular schedule.	☐	☐	☐	○	△
Urinates several times daily *Has bowel movements daily or almost daily*					

Social Emotional
Assessment/Evaluation Measure

INFANT

(for developmental range 3–18 months)

Professional version with age intervals

Child Benchmarks
and Assessment Items

Child's name: _____

Child's date of birth: _____

Family's name: _____

Name of person completing form: _____

Date of administration: _____

Instructions

Please read each benchmark and item carefully before selecting an answer. Each item is accompanied by several examples. Children may be able to successfully meet the item criterion in a variety of ways. Some items may be too difficult for the child; for example, a 4-month-old may not yet be able to imitate a parent's sounds. Professionals should ensure that parents understand that the SEAM may contain items that are developmentally too advanced for their child. Age norms are provided on this version for professionals only and serve as approximate guidelines for children who are typically developing, primarily.

The three scoring options listed in the first three columns of the SEAM include "Most of the time," "Sometimes," and "Rarely or never" to indicate the frequency or likelihood of a child's behavior. For example, if an infant shows an interest in adults whom he knows well consistently over time, a check should be placed in the box under "Most of the time" for item C-1.1. If the infant shows interest in familiar adults inconsistently, the box under "Sometimes" should be checked. If the infant seldom shows an interest in familiar adults, the box under "Rarely or never" should be checked. The latter two columns allow participants to indicate whether a particular behavior is of concern and whether it should become an intervention goal, respectively. After you are finished with this SEAM and the Adult/Caregiver SEAM, record answers on the accompanying Summary Form.

Child Benchmarks and Assessment Items
Infant

Please read each question carefully and
1. Check the box ■ that best describes your child's behavior.
2. Check the circle ● if this behavior is a concern.
3. Check the triangle ▲ if this will be an intervention goal.

Approx. age in months		Most of the time	Sometimes	Rarely or never	Is a concern	Interven-tion goal
	C-1.0 Baby participates in healthy interactions.					
	1.1 Baby shows interest in you and other familiar caregivers.	■	■	■	●	▲
1–2	Follows you with his eyes					
1–3	Quiets when talked to					
3–6	Looks at you when touched					
7–12	Shows pleasure when you return					
	1.2 Baby responds to you and other familiar caregivers.	■	■	■	●	▲
4–7	Reaches for you					
7	Raises arms to be picked up					
6–9	Responds to her name					
10–12	Waves "bye-bye"					
10–12	Gives hugs					
	1.3 Baby initiates and responds to communications.	■	■	■	●	▲
2–4	Coos, chuckles, smiles, or laughs at you					
2–4	Coos or vocalizes when you talk to him					
7	Laughs aloud					
9–12	Imitates your coos and babbles					
	1.4 Baby lets you know if she needs help or comfort.	■	■	■	●	▲
0–6	Lets you know when wet or hungry					
8–12	Expresses emotions such as fear of loud sounds or new people, shyness, and surprise					
	C-2.0 Baby expresses a range of emotions.					
	2.1 Baby smiles at you.	■	■	■	●	▲
2–4+	Smiles when you smile at her					
2–4+	Smiles when you talk to him					

Approx. age in months		Most of the time	Sometimes	Rarely or never	Is a concern	Intervention goal
	2.2 Baby smiles at familiar adults.	■	■	■	●	▲
3–6+	Smiles when babysitter or familiar adult smiles at her					
9	Responds by making sounds, faces, or wiggling hands and feet when familiar caregivers talk or play with him					
	2.3 Baby smiles and laughs at sights and sounds.	■	■	■	●	▲
7+	Smiles or laughs at moving toy					
7+	Smiles or laughs when hearing funny noises					
	C-3.0 Baby regulates his social emotional responses, with caregiver support.					
	3.1 Baby responds to your soothing when upset.	■	■	■	●	▲
3+	Calms when soothed by you					
5	Stops or reduces crying when picked up and talked to					
7–12	Seeks comfort from you when upset					
7–12	Stops crying or fussing sometimes when he sees you or hears your voice					
	3.2 Baby calms down after exciting activity.	■	■	■	●	▲
0–3+	Calms when carried or rocked					
3–6	Calms after active play such as tickling					
6–9	Switches from a vigorous activity to a quiet activity					
	3.3 Baby soothes himself when distressed.	■	■	■	●	▲
2–6	Resumes playing with familiar adult after a brief period of fretting when you depart					
6–9+	Comforts self by holding a special blanket or sucking thumb or pacifier					
9+	Calms down within a few minutes when put to bed					

Approx. age in months		Most of the time	Sometimes	Rarely or never	Is a concern	Intervention goal
	C-4.0 Baby begins to show empathy for others.					
	4.1 Baby mimics your facial expressions.	■	■	■	●	▲
0–3	*Copies your actions such as opening mouth*					
	4.2 Baby looks at and notices you and other familiar caregivers.	■	■	■	●	▲
4–6	*Follows you or other familiar caregivers with eyes when they move around room*					
	4.3 Baby looks at and notices others' emotional responses.	■	■	■	●	▲
6–9+	*Looks at person who enters the room*					
6–9+	*Stops activity and focuses on person speaking to him*					
12–18+	*Laughs and smiles when others do so*					
	4.4 Baby responds to another's distress, seeking comfort for self.	■	■	■	●	▲
12–18+	*Seeks comfort from you when others are upset*					
	C-5.0 Baby attends to and engages with others.					
	5.1 Baby makes eye contact with you and others.	■	■	■	●	▲
3–4	*Looks into your eyes when you look into her eyes while talking to her*					
	5.2 Baby looks at or toward sounds and visual events.	■	■	■	●	▲
6	*Looks toward you when he hears your voice*					
9–12	*Turns toward your singing, or music playing on a radio*					
	5.3 Baby focuses on events shown by you and others.	■	■	■	●	▲
12	*Follows your eyes*					
12	*Looks at animal/person pointed at*					

Approx. age in months		Most of the time	Sometimes	Rarely or never	Is a concern	Interven-tion goal
	5.4 Baby shares attention and events with you.	■	■	■	●	▲
12	Looks at picture or points to toy or object					
12	Points to gain your attention					
13–18	Takes part in games like Peekaboo and So Big					
	C-6.0 Baby explores hands and feet and surroundings.					
	6.1 Baby explores his hands and feet.	■	■	■	●	▲
3–6	Grabs foot when on back					
3–6	Grasps hands together and wiggles fingers					
4–7	Bangs objects together with both hands					
7–12	Kicks or pushes a mobile to make it move					
	6.2 Baby explores toys and materials.	■	■	■	●	▲
1–2	Looks at object					
4–7	Grabs objects or people within reach					
4–7	Holds and explores toys					
7–12	Crawls to his favorite toys or caregiver					
12–18	Tries different actions with toys and objects					
	6.3 Baby explores his surroundings.	■	■	■	●	▲
4–7	Rolls onto back					
8–12+	Turns head to see behind her					
8–12+	Crawls to look at and touch objects on floor					
8–12+	Moves to look behind doors and furniture					
13–18+	Begins to run, climb, and jump					
	6.4 Baby crawls or walks a short distance away from you.	■	■	■	●	▲
7–10+	Crawls 10–20 feet away from you, looking back at you					
7–10+	Leaves your side to explore new toy, object or person and remains at a distance for a few minutes					
18+	Crawls or walks around living areas exploring people, locations, and objects					

Approx. age in months		Most of the time	Sometimes	Rarely or never	Is a concern	Interven-tion goal
	C-7.0 Baby displays a positive self-image.					
	7.1 Baby laughs at, or smiles at, her image or picture of self.	☐	☐	☐	●	▲
4–6	Smiles at reflection in a mirror					
4–6	Laughs at self reflected in store window					
10–18	Points to self in mirror or picture					
10–18	Points to a picture of self					
	7.2 Baby recognizes his name.	☐	☐	☐	●	▲
6–9	Turns to face you when name is called					
	7.3 Baby calls attention to herself.	☐	☐	☐	●	▲
6–9	Coos and babbles when you enter room					
10–18	Squeals to you					
18+	Calls by using pronouns, "I want you," "Me hungry"					
	C-8.0 Baby regulates activity level.					
	8.1 Baby participates in simple routines and games with you.	☐	☐	☐	●	▲
0–3	Coos back and forth with you					
0–3	Coos when feeding					
6–9	Looks in your eyes when you sing songs to him					
10+	Plays Peekaboo, This Little Piggy, and other simple games					
18+	Picks up items and puts them in container					
	8.2 Baby looks at books or pictures for several minutes or longer.	☐	☐	☐	●	▲
9–12	Gestures or points to pictures in book					
9–12	Looks at pictures in magazine or book					
12+	Looks at book for 2–3 minutes					
12+	Looks at "favorite" book					
	8.3 Baby engages in motor activities for several minutes or longer.	☐	☐	☐	●	▲
10+	Manipulates small toys with hands for several minutes					
10+	Rolls ball to you for several minutes					

Approx. age in months		Most of the time	Sometimes	Rarely or never	Is a concern	Intervention goal
	C-9.0 Baby cooperates with daily routines and requests.					
	9.1 Baby opens her mouth for food.	☐	☐	☐	●	▲
6+	Opens mouth for breast or bottle					
	9.2 Baby follows simple routines, with your help.	☐	☐	☐	●	▲
9+	Lifts arms to put on shirt					
	9.3 Baby cooperates with diaper changes and clothing changes.	☐	☐	☐	●	▲
4+	Remains on back for at least a short time					
4+	Does not fight or cry when diapers are changed					
	C-10.0 Baby shows a range of adaptive skills.					
	10.1 Baby eats and gains weight on schedule.	☐	☐	☐	●	▲
0–6	Breast or bottle feeds with few problems					
6	Eats baby cereal, fruit					
6+	Reaches for utensils when feeding					
6+	Drinks from cup with help					
8–14	Uses a spoon and drinks from a sippy cup					
	10.2 Baby eats a variety of age-appropriate foods.	☐	☐	☐	●	▲
9+	Feeds himself finger foods (Cheerios, crackers)					
9	Eats a variety of textures (e.g., baby food meat, bread, fruits, vegetables)					
	10.3 Baby sleeps with few problems.	☐	☐	☐	●	▲
0–6+	Calms self and goes to sleep					
0–6+	Falls asleep while rocked					
9	Falls asleep within 30 minutes at nap and bedtimes					
9	Sleeps about 14 hours a day with two daytime naps					
12	Sleeps about 10–12 hours a day					
	10.4 Baby eliminates (pees and poops) on regular schedule.	☐	☐	☐	●	▲
0–6+	Urinates several times daily					
0–6+	Has bowel movements daily or almost daily					

Social Emotional
Assessment/Evaluation Measure

INFANT

(for individuals with children in developmental range 3–18 months)

Adult/Caregiver Benchmarks
and Assessment Items

Child's name: _____

Child's date of birth: _____

Family's name: _____

Name of person completing form: _____

Date of administration: _____

The following questions are designed to obtain information that can determine the supports and resources needed for caregivers/parents to provide a safe and responsive environment for their children. The items focus on adult behaviors related to fostering infants' social emotional development and competence. The preferred method for completing this form is through interviewing the caregiver(s). Items that are not relevant or that caregivers do not want to answer can be omitted.

Items are written in easy-to-understand language and each item is accompanied by one or more examples to assist caregivers in understanding the item's intent. Caregivers can chose between a "Yes" or "Not yet" response. In addition, the form provides space for the professional and caregiver(s) to indicate if they would like to choose the item as an intervention goal and/or need information and resources related to goal and/or needs.

Instructions

1. Arrange a time and place to complete the form that is comfortable for the caregiver(s). Explain the purpose of the interview and the form.
2. Read each item and the examples. Then ask the caregiver(s) to indicate whether the "Yes" or "Not yet" response option best describes if he or she has the targeted skill. "Yes" should be checked if the caregiver(s) feels he or she has the information, resources, and/or skills indicated in the item. "Not yet" should be checked if the caregiver(s) feels that he or she does not have the information, resources, and/or skills indicated in the item.
3. Check the triangle ▲ next to an item if the caregiver(s) would like to target the content addressed in the item as an intervention goal, and/or if he or she needs resources or information from a professional (e.g., school, child's teacher/home visitor).
4. Consider the cultural appropriateness of each item for individual families and omit items that caregivers may find intrusive, disrespectful, or inappropriate.

Adult/Caregiver Benchmarks and Assessment Items
Infant

Please read each question carefully and
1.   Check the box ■ that best describes your behavior.
2.   Check the triangle ▲ if this will be an intervention goal.

	Yes	Not yet	Intervention goal
A-1.0 Caregiver responds positively to baby.			
1.1 Caregiver responds to baby's nonverbal communication appropriately.	■	■	▲
Watches how baby moves, such as kicking his arms and legs when excited, lying still as he falls asleep Smiles and gently touches or moves baby's arms and legs back and forth Soothes baby by cuddling or giving him a break from dressing when his body tenses and he seems frustrated or upset Responds to baby's upset by offering quiet time Responds when baby pushes caregiver's hand away by stopping or discontinuing feeding			
1.2 Caregiver responds to baby's verbal communication appropriately.	■	■	▲
Responds to baby's cries appropriately (i.e., can tell if baby is tired, hungry, cold, hot, sick, bored, scared, or wants to be held) Looks into baby's eyes and talks with her when she coos or gurgles Responds to baby's words, and helps him learn to use his words more to express himself			
1.3 Caregiver helps baby to calm down.	■	■	▲
Soothes baby when she is upset Finds a quiet activity to calm baby when she is too excited Sings or talks to baby, holding him close, using a soft, quiet voice			
A-2.0 Caregiver provides the developmentally appropriate type and level of activity for baby.			
2.1 Caregiver offers age-appropriate books, toys, and playthings for baby.	■	■	▲
Provides toys that baby enjoys and are safe for his age, such as board books, balls, blocks, wooden spoons			

	Yes	Not yet	Intervention goal
2.2 Caregiver plays with baby using age-appropriate games.	☐	☐	▲
Plays face games, Pat-a-Cake, and gently dances with baby *Plays both quiet and active games* *Plays games caregiver and baby enjoy together, such as Hide and Seek*			
A-3.0 Caregiver provides baby with predictable schedules/routines and appropriate environment.			
3.1 Caregiver creates and follows routines for baby's eating and sleeping.	☐	☐	▲
Offers baby food three times per day at similar times each day			
3.2 Caregiver provides a nap and sleeping schedule for baby that is predictable and appropriate for her age.	☐	☐	▲
Ensures baby's bedtime and naptime remain similar across days and weeks *Sings, reads, or gently talks to baby at bedtime to calm him and get baby ready to sleep*			
3.3 Caregiver provides times each day to play with baby.	☐	☐	▲
Sings, talks, and makes faces to baby when changing diaper *Shares a story or song with baby or shows her a favorite toy when she wakes up from nap* *Finds a quiet activity to calm baby when she is too excited* *Sings or talks to baby, holding her close, using a quiet, soft voice* *Takes turns using paints or crayons* *Takes turns when playing board games such as Chutes and Ladders*			
3.4 Caregiver helps baby regulate his emotional responses.	☐	☐	▲
Soothes baby if he becomes upset *Shifts to other activities to help baby calm down if he becomes excited, such as giving him a soft massage or reading a book*			
A-4.0 Caregiver provides baby with a safe home and play environment.			
4.1 Caregiver checks the home for things that may be dangerous to baby.	☐	☐	▲
Puts plug guards in electrical outlets *Installs guard rail for the staircase* *Obtains sides for baby's crib*			

	Yes	Not yet	Interven-tion goal
4.2 Caregiver transports baby safely.	☐	☐	▲
Uses a car seat that is appropriate for the height and weight of baby and fits safely in car *Uses a stroller that does not tip*			
4.3 Caregiver supervises baby or provides a way for baby to be safe.	☐	☐	▲
Puts baby in a playpen near the bathroom so caregiver can take a shower *Places baby so caregiver can see him play when cooking dinner*			
4.4 Caregiver has trusted person who can provide child care.	☐	☐	▲
Provides a safe environment for baby *Calls for "respite" care when necessary*			
4.5 Caregiver obtains regular medical care for baby.	☐	☐	▲
Takes baby to a well clinic at least two times per year, and as needed if sick			
4.6 Caregiver manages feelings of anger or frustration that may occur while with baby.	☐	☐	▲
Calls a trusted person for help or advice if baby cries for extended time and if unsure of what to do *Takes a short break by closing eyes and taking deep breaths or by going into a quiet room, when frustrated or angry with baby (knowing baby is safe)* *Takes time for self and relaxes while baby is napping*			

Social Emotional
Assessment/Evaluation Measure

SEAM™

INFANT

(for developmental range 3–18 months)

Summary Form

Child's name: _____

Adult/caregiver's name: _____

Instructions

The child (C) and adult/caregiver (A) benchmarks and their associated items are listed on the following pages. Beside each item is space to enter the administration date and whether the item has been identified as a strength (i.e., as indicated by checking "Most of the time" on an item on the the Infant SEAM and "Yes" on an item on the Adult/Caregiver SEAM), is considered of concern and needs monitoring (i.e., as indicated by a check on the ● for that item), or has been selected as an intervention goal (as indicated by a check on the ▲). The form can be used to enter data from three separate administrations over time.

CHILD	Admin date	Strength	Concern/continue monitoring	Identified as goal	Admin date	Strength	Concern/continue monitoring	Identified as goal	Admin date	Strength	Concern/continue monitoring	Identified as goal
Benchmark C-1.0												
Item 1.1												
Item 1.2												
Item 1.3												
Item 1.4												
Benchmark C-2.0												
Item 2.1												
Item 2.2												
Item 2.3												
Benchmark C-3.0												
Item 3.1												
Item 3.2												
Item 3.3												
Benchmark C-4.0												
Item 4.1												
Item 4.2												
Item 4.3												
Item 4.4												
Benchmark C-5.0												
Item 5.1												
Item 5.2												
Item 5.3												
Item 5.4												
Benchmark C-6.0												
Item 6.1												
Item 6.2												
Item 6.3												
Item 6.4												
Benchmark C-7.0												
Item 7.1												
Item 7.2												
Item 7.3												
Benchmark C-8.0												
Item 8.1												
Item 8.2												
Item 8.3												

	Admin date	Strength	Concern/continue monitoring	Identified as goal	Admin date	Strength	Concern/continue monitoring	Identified as goal	Admin date	Strength	Concern/continue monitoring	Identified as goal
Benchmark C-9.0												
Item 9.1												
Item 9.2												
Item 9.3												
Benchmark C-10.0												
Item 10.1												
Item 10.2												
Item 10.3												
Item 10.4												
ADULT/CAREGIVER												
Benchmark A-1.0												
Item 1.1												
Item 1.2												
Item 1.3												
Benchmark A-2.0												
Item 2.1												
Item 2.2												
Benchmark A-3.0												
Item 3.1												
Item 3.2												
Item 3.3												
Item 3.4												
Benchmark A-4.0												
Item 4.1												
Item 4.2												
Item 4.4												
Item 4.5												
Item 4.6												

Social Emotional
Assessment/Evaluation Measure

TODDLER

(for developmental range 18–36 months)

General Instructions

The Social Emotional Assessment/Evaluation Measure (SEAM): Toddler is divided
into two sections. The first section, Child Benchmarks and Assessment Items, is
focused on the child. There are two versions of the Child Benchmarks and Assessment Items: The first version does not include age intervals and is intended for
parents/caregivers. The second, for *professional use only,* provides age intervals
with each item to serve as guides for approximate ages at which children typically
perform these skills. The second section, Adult/Caregiver Benchmarks and Assessment Items, is focused on the caregiver. These sections are then followed by a
Summary Form for the professional to record observations that will assist in determining goals.

Social Emotional
Assessment/Evaluation Measure

TODDLER

(for developmental range 18–36 months)

Child Benchmarks
and Assessment Items

Child's name: _____

Child's date of birth: _____

Family's name: _____

Name of person completing form: _____

Date of administration: _____

Instructions

Please read each item carefully before selecting an answer. In some cases, observation of the child and/or caregiver may be necessary before scoring the measure. Each item is accompanied by several examples. Children may be able to successfully meet the item criterion in a variety of ways. Some items may be too difficult for the child; for example, an 18-month-old may not indicate when his diaper needs changing. Professionals should ensure that parents understand that the SEAM may contain items that are developmentally too advanced for their child. Age norms should not be used with children with delays or developmental disabilities.

The three scoring options include "Most of the time," "Sometimes," and "Rarely or never." For example, if a toddler talks and plays with adults he knows well consistently over time, a check should be placed in the box under "Most of the time" on item C-1.1. Items marked "Most of the time" are generally considered strengths. If a toddler talks and plays with familiar adults inconsistently, the box under "Sometimes" should be checked. If the toddler seldom talks and plays with familiar adults, the box under "Rarely or never" should be checked. The latter two columns allow participants to indicate whether a particular behavior is of concern and whether it should become an intervention goal, respectively. After you are finished with this SEAM and the corresponding Adult/Caregiver SEAM, record answers on the accompanying Summary Form.

Social Emotional Assessment/Evaluation Measure (SEAM): Toddler, Experimental Edition. From *An Activity-Based Approach to Developing Young Children's Social Emotional Competence,* by Jane Squires & Diane Bricker.
© 2007 Paul H. Brookes Publishing Co., Inc., Baltimore. All rights reserved.

Child Benchmarks and Assessment Items
Toddler

Please read each question carefully and
1. Check the box ▣ that best describes your child's behavior,
2. Check the circle ● if this behavior is a concern, and
3. Check the triangle ▲ if this will be an intervention goal.

	Most of the time	Sometimes	Rarely or never	Is a concern	Intervention goal
C-1.0 Toddler participates in healthy interactions.					
1.1 Toddler talks and plays with adults whom she knows well.	▣	▣	▣	●	▲
Points to show you things *Begins to include you or siblings in play; pretends to offer you or others food; tries to care for baby sibling* *Talks to you about her activities: "I push car"* *Uses one or two words to communicate with peers, such as "Car go?"*					
1.2 Toddler responds when you show him affection.	▣	▣	▣	●	▲
Hugs you; smiles back at you *Hugs and kisses people, pets, and stuffed animals* *Returns hugs, kisses, or other affectionate gestures* *Walks to you with arms out, wanting a hug*					
1.3 Toddler initiates and responds when you communicate with her.	▣	▣	▣	●	▲
Comes when you gesture for her to follow *Answers your questions with one word, such as "Juice"* *Asks questions: "Where mama?"; says, "Mama come" when she wants you to play* *Asks many questions (e.g., "why, what, how?")*					

TODDLER

		Most of the time	Sometimes	Rarely or never	Is a concern	Intervention goal
1.4	**Toddler lets you know if he needs help, attention, or comfort.**	☐	☐	☐	●	▲

Pulls on you or other adult or raises arms to be picked up
Asks for a drink of water by pointing or showing you
Goes to you or other familiar adults when hurt
Seeks attention from you and other familiar adults; babbles and "shows off" for you
Calls for you when he needs help, such as "Daddy help"

C-2.0	**Toddler expresses a range of emotions.**					
2.1	**Toddler smiles and laughs.**	☐	☐	☐	●	▲

Smiles when caregiver returns
Smiles and laughs at people and children
Kisses other children

2.2	**Toddler expresses a range of emotions using a variety of strategies.**	☐	☐	☐	●	▲

Expresses emotions physically and verbally, such as making faces and crying when frustrated; laughing and giggling when happy
Expresses a variety of feelings (happy, sad, frightened, surprised, angry)

2.3	**Toddler identifies her emotions, with your help.**	☐	☐	☐	●	▲

Can sing "Happy and You Know It" with you and makes the feeling faces
Answers accurately yes or no when asked if mad

2.4	**Toddler identifies his own emotions.**	☐	☐	☐	●	▲

Protests "No bath, Me sad"
Expresses why he is laughing, such as "Because I am happy"
Says, "I'm mad at you" when angry

TODDLER

	Most of the time	Sometimes	Rarely or never	Is a concern	Intervention goal
C-3.0 Toddler regulates her social emotional responses.					
3.1 Toddler responds to soothing when upset.	☐	☐	☐	○	△
Stops crying when picked up and comforted *Resumes playing after being hugged and kissed by caregiver when upset*					
3.2 Toddler can settle herself down after periods of exciting activity.	☐	☐	☐	○	△
Sits down and calms self with your help after a game of chase *Uses a favorite toy or game to distract herself when upset* *Signals you through expressions or words that she needs some assistance*					
3.3 Toddler can calm self when upset.	☐	☐	☐	○	△
Calms self after falling, within 5 to 10 minutes, with your help *Holds favorite doll or blanket to help calm self* *Stops crying a short time after you leave, with help*					
C-4.0 Toddler begins to show empathy for others.					
4.1 Toddler matches his response to others' emotional responses.	☐	☐	☐	○	△
Quiets when you are upset *Laughs and smiles when others do so* *Tries to help care for baby siblings*					
4.2 Toddler tries to comfort others when they are upset.	☐	☐	☐	○	△
Gives crying baby a hug; leads you to upset infant to soothe *Kisses your "owie" if you hurt yourself* *Hugs you if you are sad*					

	Most of the time	Sometimes	Rarely or never	Is a concern	Intervention goal
4.3 Toddler uses words to talk about another child's emotions.	☐	☐	☐	○	△
Says, "Baby cry, sad," when hearing a baby crying *Says "That boy is mad" about a child who is screaming* *Returns toy to stop crying of another child* *Describes a peer's feelings after watching him begin to cry when dropped off at child care: "He's sad because his mom is gone"*					
C-5.0 Toddler shares attention and engages with others.					
5.1 Toddler makes eye contact with you and other caregivers and peers.	☐	☐	☐	○	△
Plays simple games with you such as Peekaboo and This Little Piggy *Makes eye contact with teacher as he walks in room* *Looks at others at kitchen table during dinner*					
5.2 Toddler focuses on events that you show him.	☐	☐	☐	○	△
Looks at books with you and labels what pictures you point at *Follows your gaze* *Looks at things like fire trucks, animals noted by another*					
5.3 Toddler greets you and other familiar adults.	☐	☐	☐	○	△
Seeks attention from you and family members, but may act shy around strangers *Looks at and says "Hi" to other children* *Waves to familiar people* *Greets sibling by name when they get together* *Has a special friend he likes to play with*					
5.4 Toddler plays alongside other children.	☐	☐	☐	○	△
Plays side by side with other children without sharing toys or materials *Watches other children at play* *Will pass toys to other children when playing in the sandbox*					

TODDLER

		Most of the time	Sometimes	Rarely or never	Is a concern	Intervention goal
5.5	**Toddler shares in daily activities.**	☐	☐	☐	●	▲

Helps you put on shoes
Imitates household tasks and can put
*   some toys away with your help*
Helps put food in grocery cart

C-6.0	**Toddler begins to demonstrate independence.**					
6.1	**Toddler explores new environments, while maintaining some contact.**	☐	☐	☐	●	▲

Walks to sandbox but looks back at you,
*   making eye contact and checking in*
Walks with friend to see a new toy
*   while looking at your face to make*
*   sure it's okay*
Wants to do things by herself: "Me do it"

6.2	**Toddler can separate from you in familiar environment with minimal distress.**	☐	☐	☐	●	▲

Frets or cries only a few minutes when
*   you depart*
Lets you leave his sight for a few
*   minutes without showing distress*
Leaves you to join play with peers,
*   looking to make sure you are still*
*   around*
Gives Dad a hug and joins peers in play
*   when arriving at child care*

6.3	**Toddler tries new tasks before seeking help.**	☐	☐	☐	●	▲

Tries repeatedly to place block in hole or
*   stick in slot before seeking help*
Tries to reach toy on high shelf before
*   asking for help*
When taking lid off of sippy cup and Dad
*   reaches to help, toddler says "No"*
Wants to do things by herself

C-7.0	**Toddler displays a positive self-image.**					
7.1	**Toddler points to self in picture.**	☐	☐	☐	●	▲

Recognizes picture of self, or self in
*   mirror*
Points to self or locates his picture
Draws simple representation of self or
*   others*

		Most of the time	Sometimes	Rarely or never	Is a concern	Intervention goal
7.2	**Toddler knows personal information.**	☐	☐	☐	○	▲

Turns head or points to self when name is called
Calls herself by name or "Me"
Knows gender: "I'm a girl"

		Most of the time	Sometimes	Rarely or never	Is a concern	Intervention goal
7.3	**Toddler tells you what he did or accomplished.**	☐	☐	☐	○	▲

When you comment, "Wow, you climbed the ladder" at the park, toddler smiles
Begins calling attention to self by using pronouns, "I want you," "Me hungry"
Tells you that he made a house of blocks (may be in short form: "I build")
Tells about trip to store (may use incomplete sentences)

C-8.0	**Toddler regulates attention and activity level.**					
8.1	**Toddler stays with motor activities for 5 minutes or longer.**	☐	☐	☐	○	▲

Peddles trike outdoors for 5 minutes or longer
Plays with blocks 5 minutes or longer

		Most of the time	Sometimes	Rarely or never	Is a concern	Intervention goal
8.2	**Toddler looks at book or listens to a story for 5 minutes or longer.**	☐	☐	☐	○	▲

Sits with you and looks at a book for 5 minutes or longer
Listens to story being read for 5 minutes or longer

		Most of the time	Sometimes	Rarely or never	Is a concern	Intervention goal
8.3	**Toddler moves from one activity to another without problems.**	☐	☐	☐	○	▲

Moves on to another activity with help from you
Makes choices for play during free time
Follows familiar routine at child care

		Most of the time	Sometimes	Rarely or never	Is a concern	Intervention goal
8.4	**Toddler participates in simple games.**	☐	☐	☐	○	▲

Watches you and uses hands to sing "Twinkle Twinkle Little Star"
Sings nursery rhymes
Plays hide and seek with you

TODDLER

	Most of the time	Sometimes	Rarely or never	Is a concern	Interven-tion goal
C-9.0 Toddler cooperates with daily routines and requests.					
9.1 Toddler follows routines.	□	□	□	●	▲
Helps take off clothes, gets pajamas at bedtime *Helps get ready to travel by getting in car seat* *Follows hand-washing routine with some help* *Participates in activities with other children (singing and dancing, tumbling classes)*					
9.2 Toddler cooperates with simple requests.	□	□	□	●	▲
Comes near you when you wave "Come" with your hand *Responds when you say, "Bring me your shoes"* *Can follow two-step directions: "Shut the door and take off your coat"*					
C-10.0 Toddler shows a range of adaptive skills.					
10.1 Toddler eats and feeds self a variety of foods without problems.	■	■	■	●	▲
Uses fingers and tries to use spoon or fork to eat a variety of foods *Can use utensils to eat and drink from a cup*					
10.2 Toddler falls and remains asleep with few problems.	■	■	■	●	▲
Remains in bed with his favorite blanket or toy until asleep *Cries briefly before falling asleep at naptime* *Sleeps through the night (may be taking one or two daytime naps)* *Follows a routine such as calm activities after dinner, a warm bath, reading stories or singing songs to help get to sleep*					

	Most of the time	Sometimes	Rarely or never	Is a concern	Intervention goal
10.3 Toddler accepts changes in routines and settings.	■	■	■ -	●	▲
Adjusts to playing in a different area *Eats snack or lunch at picnic table* *Accepts changes in a familiar routine* * at school (field trips)*					
10.4 Toddler shows an interest in using the toilet.	■	■	■	●	▲
Indicates when diaper needs changing *Pulls down pants and sits on potty* *Uses potty as needed*					

TODDLER

Social Emotional Assessment/Evaluation Measure (SEAM): Toddler, Experimental Edition. From *An Activity-Based Approach to Developing Young Children's Social Emotional Competence,* by Jane Squires & Diane Bricker.

Social Emotional
Assessment/Evaluation Measure

SEAM ™

TODDLER

(for developmental range 18–36 months)
Professional version with age intervals

Child Benchmarks
and Assessment Items

Child's name: _____

Child's date of birth: _____

Family's name: _____

Name of person completing form: _____

Date of administration: _____

Instructions

Please read each item carefully before selecting an answer. In some cases, observation of the child and/or caregiver may be necessary before scoring the measure. Each item is accompanied by several examples. Children may be able to successfully meet the item criterion in a variety of ways. Some items may be too difficult for the child; for example, an 18-month-old may not indicate when his diaper needs changing. Age norms are provided on this version for professionals only and serve as approximate guidelines for children who are typically developing, primarily. Professionals should ensure that parents understand that the SEAM may contain items that are developmentally too advanced for their child.

The three scoring options include "Most of the time," "Sometimes," and "Rarely or never." For example, if a toddler talks and plays with adults he knows well consistently over time, a check should be placed in the box under "Most of the time" on item C-1.1. Items marked "Most of the time" are generally considered strengths. If a toddler talks and plays with familiar adults inconsistently, the box under "Sometimes" should be checked. If the toddler seldom talks and plays with familiar adults, the box under "Rarely or never" should be checked. The latter two columns allow participants to indicate whether a particular behavior is of concern and whether it should become an intervention goal, respectively. After you are finished with this SEAM and the corresponding Adult/Caregiver SEAM, record answers on the accompanying Summary Form.

Child Benchmarks and Assessment Items
Toddler

Please read each question carefully and
1. Check the box ■ that best describes your child's behavior.
2. Check the circle ● if this behavior is a concern.
3. Check the triangle ▲ if this will be an intervention goal.

TODDLER

Approx. age in months		Most of the time	Sometimes	Rarely or never	Is a concern	Intervention goal
	C-1.0 Toddler participates in healthy interactions.					
	1.1 Toddler talks and plays with adults whom she knows well.	■	■	■	●	▲
12–14	Points to show you things					
18–24	Begins to include you or siblings in play; pretends to offer you or others food; tries to care for baby sibling					
24–36	Talks to you about her activities: "I push car"					
24–36	Uses one or two words to communicate with peers, such as "Car go?"					
	1.2 Toddler responds when you show him affection.	■	■	■	●	▲
12–16	Hugs you; smiles back at you					
12–18	Hugs and kisses people, pets, and stuffed animals					
24	Returns hugs, kisses, or other affectionate gestures					
36	Walks to you with arms out, wanting a hug					
	1.3 Toddler initiates and responds when you communicate with her.	■	■	■	●	▲
12–16	Comes when you gesture for her to follow					
16–18	Answers your questions with one word, such as "Juice"					
18–36	Asks questions: "Where mama?"; says, "Mama come" when she wants you to play					
30–36	Asks many questions (e.g., "why, what, how?")					
	1.4 Toddler lets you know if he needs help, attention, or comfort.	■	■	■	●	▲
12+	Pulls on you or other adult or raises arms to be picked up					
14	Asks for a drink of water by pointing or showing you					

Social Emotional Assessment/Evaluation Measure (SEAM): Toddler, Experimental Edition. From *An Activity-Based Approach to Developing Young Children's Social Emotional Competence,* by Jane Squires & Diane Bricker.

Approx. age in months		Most of the time	Sometimes	Rarely or never	Is a concern	Intervention goal
18	Goes to you or other familiar adults when hurt					
24	Seeks attention from you and other familiar adults; babbles and "shows off" for you					
36	Calls for you when he needs help, such as "Daddy help"					
	C-2.0 Toddler expresses a range of emotions.					
	2.1 Toddler smiles and laughs.	■	■	■	●	▲
12	Smiles when caregiver returns					
18	Smiles and laughs at people and children					
18–24	Kisses other children					
	2.2 Toddler expresses a range of emotions using a variety of strategies.	■	■	■	●	▲
18–24	Expresses emotions physically and verbally, such as making faces and crying when frustrated; laughing and giggling when happy					
30–36	Expresses a variety of feelings (happy, sad, frightened, surprised, angry)					
	2.3 Toddler identifies her emotions, with your help.	■	■	■	●	▲
18–24	Can sing "Happy and You Know It" with you and makes the feeling faces					
18–24	Answers accurately yes or no when asked if mad					
	2.4 Toddler identifies his own emotions.	■	■	■	●	▲
18–30	Protests "No bath," "Me sad"					
25–30	Expresses why he is laughing, such as "Because I am happy"					
30–36	Says, "I'm mad at you" when angry					
	C-3.0 Toddler regulates her social emotional responses.					
	3.1 Toddler responds to soothing when upset.	■	■	■	●	▲
12	Stops crying when picked up and comforted					
18–24	Resumes playing after being hugged and kissed by caregiver when upset					

Social Emotional Assessment/Evaluation Measure (SEAM): Toddler, Experimental Edition. From *An Activity-Based Approach to Developing Young Children's Social Emotional Competence,* by Jane Squires & Diane Bricker.

Approx. age in months		Most of the time	Sometimes	Rarely or never	Is a concern	Intervention goal
	3.2 Toddler can settle herself down after periods of exciting activity.	☐	☐	☐	⬤	▲
12–18	Sits down and calms self with your help after a game of chase					
12–24	Uses a favorite toy or game to distract herself when upset					
12–24	Signals you through expressions or words that she needs some assistance					
	3.3 Toddler can calm self when upset.	☐	☐	☐	⬤	▲
12–24	Calms self after falling, within 5 to 10 minutes, with your help					
18–24+	Holds favorite doll or blanket to help calm self					
24–36	Stops crying a short time after you leave, with help					
	C-4.0 Toddler begins to show empathy for others.					
	4.1 Toddler matches his response to others' emotional responses.	☐	☐	☐	⬤	▲
12–24	Quiets when you are upset					
12–24	Laughs and smiles when others do so					
24–36	Tries to help care for baby siblings					
	4.2 Toddler tries to comfort others when they are upset.	☐	☐	☐	⬤	▲
18–24	Gives crying baby a hug; leads you to upset infant to soothe					
24–36	Kisses your "owie" if you hurt yourself					
24–36	Hugs you if you are sad					
	4.3 Toddler uses words to talk about another child's emotions.	☐	☐	☐	⬤	▲
12–18	Says, "Baby cry, sad," when hearing a baby crying					
18–24	Says "That boy is mad" about a child who is screaming					
24–30	Returns toy to stop crying of another child					
30–36	Describes a peer's feelings after watching him begin to cry when dropped off at child care: "He's sad because his mom is gone"					

Approx. age in months		Most of the time	Sometimes	Rarely or never	Is a concern	Intervention goal
	C-5.0 Toddler shares attention and engages with others.					
	5.1 Toddler makes eye contact with you and other caregivers and peers.	■	■	■	●	▲
13–18	*Plays simple games with you such as Peekaboo and This Little Piggy*					
18–24	*Makes eye contact with teacher as he walks in room*					
18–24	*Looks at others at kitchen table during dinner*					
	5.2 Toddler focuses on events that you show him.	■	■	■	●	▲
16+	*Looks at books with you and labels what pictures you point at*					
24	*Follows your gaze*					
24	*Looks at things like fire trucks, animals noted by another*					
	5.3 Toddler greets you and familiar adults.	■	■	■	●	▲
24	*Seeks attention from you and family members, but may act shy around strangers*					
30	*Looks at and says "Hi" to other children*					
30	*Waves to familiar people*					
30	*Greets sibling by name when they get together*					
36	*Has a special friend he likes to play with*					
	5.4 Toddler plays alongside other children.	■	■	■	●	▲
12–24	*Plays side by side with other children without sharing toys or materials*					
12–24	*Watches other children at play*					
24–36	*Will pass toys to other children when playing in the sandbox*					
	5.5 Toddler shares in daily activities.	■	■	■	●	▲
18	*Helps you put on shoes*					
24	*Imitates household tasks and can put some toys away with your help*					
30–36	*Helps put food in grocery cart*					

TODDLER

Approx. age in months			Most of the time	Sometimes	Rarely or never	Is a concern	Intervention goal
	C-6.0	**Toddler begins to demonstrate independence.**					
	6.1	**Toddler explores new environments, while maintaining some contact.**	■	■	■	●	▲
18–24		*Walks to sandbox but looks back at you, making eye contact and checking in*					
24		*Walks with friend to see a new toy while looking at your face to make sure it's okay*					
24–36		*Wants to do things by herself: "Me do it"*					
	6.2	**Toddler can separate from you in familiar environment with minimal distress.**	■	■	■	●	▲
12–18		*Frets or cries only a few minutes when you depart*					
12–18		*Lets you leave his sight for a few minutes without showing distress*					
18–30		*Leaves you to join play with peers, looking to make sure you are still around*					
30–36		*Gives Dad a hug and joins peers in play when arriving at child care*					
	6.3	**Toddler tries new tasks before seeking help.**	■	■	■	●	▲
18–24		*Tries repeatedly to place block in hole or stick in slot before seeking help*					
18–24		*Tries to reach toy on high shelf before asking for help*					
18–24		*When taking lid off of sippy cup and Dad reaches to help, toddler says "No"*					
24–30		*Wants to do things by herself*					
	C-7.0	**Toddler displays a positive self-image.**					
	7.1	**Toddler points to self in picture.**	■	■	■	●	▲
12–18		*Recognizes picture of self, or self in mirror*					
19–24		*Points to self or locates his picture*					
36		*Draws simple representation of self or others*					

TODDLER

Approx. age in months		Most of the time	Sometimes	Rarely or never	Is a concern	Intervention goal
	7.2 Toddler knows personal information.	■	■	■	●	▲
12–18	Turns head or points to self when name is called					
18–24	Calls herself by name or "Me"					
30	Knows gender: "I'm a girl"					
	7.3 Toddler tells you what he did or accomplished.	■	■	■	●	▲
18–24	When you comment, "Wow, you climbed the ladder" at the park, toddler smiles					
18–24	Begins calling attention to self by using pronouns, "I want you," "Me hungry"					
20–24	Tells you that he made a house of blocks (may be in short form: "I build")					
30–36	Tells about trip to store (may use incomplete sentences)					
	C-8.0 Toddler regulates attention and activity level.					
	8.1 Toddler stays with motor activities for 5 minutes or longer.	■	■	■	●	▲
14	Peddles trike outdoors for 5 minutes or longer					
14	Plays with blocks 5 minutes or longer					
	8.2 Toddler looks at book or listens to a story for 5 minutes or longer.	■	■	■	●	▲
18–30	Sits with you and looks at a book for 5 minutes or longer					
30–36	Listens to story being read for 5 minutes or longer					
	8.3 Toddler moves from one activity to another without problem.	■	■	■	●	▲
12–18	Moves on to another activity with help from you					
24–30	Makes choices for play during free time					
18–36	Follows familiar routine at child care					
	8.4 Toddler participates in simple games.	■	■	■	●	▲
18–24	Watches you and uses hands to sing "Twinkle Twinkle Little Star"					
24–30	Sings nursery rhymes					
30–36	Plays hide and seek with you					

TODDLER

Approx. age in months		Most of the time	Sometimes	Rarely or never	Is a concern	Interven- tion goal
	C-9.0 Toddler cooperates with daily routines and requests.					
	9.1 Toddler follows routines.	☐	☐	☐	○	△
12–18	*Helps take off clothes, gets pajamas at bedtime*					
12–18	*Helps get ready to travel by getting in car seat*					
19	*Follows hand-washing routine with some help*					
24–36	*Participates in activities with other children (singing and dancing, tumbling classes)*					
	9.2 Toddler cooperates with simple requests.	☐	☐	☐	○	△
18–24	*Comes near you when you wave "Come" with your hand*					
18–24	*Responds when you say, "Bring me your shoes"*					
24–36	*Can follow two-step directions: "Shut the door and take off your coat"*					
	C-10.0 Toddler shows a range of adaptive skills.					
	10.1 Toddler eats and feeds self a variety of foods without problems.	☐	☐	☐	○	△
18–24	*Uses fingers and tries to use spoon or fork to eat a variety of foods*					
30–36	*Can use utensils to eat and drink from a cup*					
	10.2 Toddler falls and remains asleep with few problems.	☐	☐	☐	○	△
12	*Remains in bed with his favorite blanket or toy until asleep*					
18	*Cries briefly before falling asleep at naptime*					
24–36	*Sleeps through the night (may be taking one or two daytime naps)*					
24–36	*Follows a routine such as calm activities after dinner, a warm bath, reading stories or singing songs to help get to sleep*					

Approx. age in months		Most of the time	Sometimes	Rarely or never	Is a concern	Interven- tion goal
	10.3 Toddler accepts changes in routines and settings.	■	■	■	●	▲
16–24	*Adjusts to playing in a different area*					
16–24	*Eats snack or lunch at picnic table*					
24	*Accepts changes in a familiar routine at school (field trips)*					
	10.4 Toddler shows an interest in using the toilet.	■	■	■	●	▲
18–24	*Indicates when diaper needs changing*					
24–36	*Pulls down pants and sits on potty*					
36	*Uses potty as needed*					

TODDLER

Social Emotional
Assessment/Evaluation Measure

TODDLER

*(for individuals with children in
developmental range 18–36 months)*

Adult/Caregiver Benchmarks
and Assessment Items

Child's name: _____

Child's date of birth: _____

Family's name: _____

Name of person completing form: _____

Date of administration: _____

The following questions are designed to obtain information that can determine the supports and resources needed for caregivers/parents to provide a safe and responsive environment for their children. The items focus on behaviors related to toddler social emotional development and competence. The preferred method for completing this form is through an interview of the caregiver(s). Items that are not relevant or that caregivers do not want to answer can be omitted.

Items are written in easy to understand language and each item is accompanied by one or more examples to assist caregivers in understanding the item's intent. Caregivers can chose between a "Yes" or "Not yet" response. In addition the form provides space for the caregiver(s) to indicate if he or she would like to choose the item as an intervention goal and/or needs information and resources related to goal and/or needs.

Instructions

1. Arrange a time and place to complete the form that is comfortable for the caregiver(s). Explain the purpose of the interview and the form.
2. Read each item and the examples. Then ask the caregiver(s) to indicate whether the "Yes" or "Not Yet" response option best describes if he/she has the targeted skill. "Yes" should be checked if the caregiver(s) feels he or she has the information, resources and/or skills indicated in the item. "Not yet" should be checked if the caregiver(s) feels he or she does not have the information, resources, and/or skills indicated in the item.
3. Check the triangle ▲ next to an item if the caregiver(s) would like to target the content addressed in the item as an intervention goal, and/or if he or she needs resources or information from a professional (school, child's teacher/home visitor).
4. Consider the cultural appropriateness of each item for individual families and omit items that caregivers may find intrusive, disrespectful, or inappropriate.

Adult/Caregiver Benchmarks and Assessment Items
Toddler

Please read each question carefully and
1. Check the box ■ that best describes your behavior.
2. Check the triangle ▲ if this will be an intervention goal.

		Yes	Not yet	Intervention goal
A-1.0	**Caregiver responds positively to toddler.**			
1.1	**Caregiver responds to toddler's nonverbal communication appropriately.**	■	■	▲
	Tells by watching toddler whether she is excited, tired, hungry, sick, or scared *Tries to respond when toddler is upset by talking to him or hugging him, then joining in a game or story* *Dances or jumps with toddler when she is happy* *Snuggles with toddler and helps him feel safe when he is scared or sick*			
1.2	**Caregiver responds to toddler's verbal communication appropriately.**	■	■	▲
	Listens to toddler's words and responds to her *Helps toddler learn more words to express herself* *Listens and responds to toddler's attempts to talk* *Answers toddler in words he can understand*			
1.3	**Caregiver supports toddler's emotional needs.**	■	■	▲
	Holds and soothes toddler when she is hurt, upset, or feeling frightened *Uses words that express toddler's feeling when caregiver can see she is mad, frustrated, unhappy, or excited* *Shows toddler how to calm down when upset by taking deep breaths* *Gives toddler choices about his daily routines, what he wears, what story to read, and what to play*			
1.4	**Caregiver uses positive comments and language with child.**	■	■	▲
	Caregiver comments on toddler's gentle petting of cat *Caregiver gives "high 5" when toddler picks up all toys* *Caregiver praises toddler when toddler ignores sibling's teasing*			
1.5	**Caregiver successfully redirects child's inappropriate behaviors.**	■	■	▲
	Caregiver gives favorite doll to toddler before toddler pokes infant sister *Caregiver takes toddler to outdoor play area when beginning to run indoors*			

TODDLER

		Yes	Not yet	Intervention goal
1.6	**Caregiver can recognize the function of a child's (negative) behaviors and, with assistance, can modify environment.**	■	■	▲
	Caregiver prepares toddler for long bus ride with art and other busy-work activities and appropriate clothing *Caregiver lets toddler choose one grocery item at store before tantrum occurs*			
A-2.0	**Caregiver provides the developmentally appropriate type and level of activity.**			
2.1	**Caregiver offers age-appropriate books, toys, and playthings for toddler.**	■	■	▲
	Buys or obtains toys that toddler enjoys and that are safe for his age *Offers materials and toys that encourage her thinking and problem-solving skills, such as sorting toys and buckets, puzzles, and stuffed animals*			
2.2	**Caregiver plays with toddler and has ideas for age-appropriate games.**	■	■	▲
	Plays simple action games with toddler like Simon Says and Ring Around the Rosie *Plays games that encourage the use of problem-solving skills, such as rhyming games and I Spy* *Plays games adult and child enjoy together, such as Hide and Seek*			
A-3.0	**Caregiver provides toddler with predictable schedule/routines and appropriate environment.**			
3.1	**Caregiver provides a mealtime routine for toddler that is predictable and appropriate for his age.**	■	■	▲
	Provides toddler with three meals per day at similar times each day *Provides a variety of foods for snacks and meals, such as different types of fruit and vegetables and foods the toddler can eat with her hands as well as foods needing utensils*			
3.2	**Caregiver provides a rest and sleeping schedule for toddler that is predictable and appropriate for his age.**	■	■	▲
	Provides bedtime and naptime at similar times across days and weeks *Follows a similar routine before bed, such as taking warm bath, brushing teeth, and reading stories*			

TODDLER

			Yes	Not yet	Interven-tion goal
3.3	**Caregiver provides toddler with predictable limits and discipline.**		☐	☐	▲
	Follows through consistently with limits and rules, such as no hitting or running in house *Notices and tells toddler the positive things she is doing* *Focuses on what toddler CAN do* *Uses "no" infrequently, and under similar conditions from day to day*				
3.4	**Caregiver provides time each day to play with toddler.**		☐	☐	▲
	Spends time at home playing with toddler, singing songs, looking at books together *Takes walks and goes to parks and stores with toddler* *Tries to make routine activities such as mealtimes, bath time, and potty time playful and fun*				
A-4.0	**Caregiver provides toddler with a safe home and play environment.**				
4.1	**Caregiver checks the home for things that can be dangerous to toddler.**		☐	☐	▲
	Keeps poisons (medications, cleaning supplies) and weapons in locked cupboard *Keeps sharp objects such as knives out of reach*				
4.2	**Caregiver is able to provide safe travel arrangements for toddler.**		☐	☐	▲
	Puts toddler in car seat that is appropriate for toddler's height and weight and fits safely in the car *Uses a stroller that does not tip*				
4.3	**Caregiver supervises toddler or provides a way for toddler to be safe.**		☐	☐	▲
	Supervises toddler's activities *Sits nearby at parks or outdoors to watch him play with peers in the sandbox*				
4.4	**Caregiver obtains regular medical and dental care for toddler.**		☐	☐	▲
	Takes toddler to well child clinic and dentist at least twice per year *Takes toddler for regular hearing and vision check-ups*				
4.5	**Caregiver manages feelings of anger or frustration that may come up while with toddler.**		☐	☐	▲
	Calls a trusted person for help or advice if toddler cries for extended time and if unsure of what to do *Takes a short break by closing eyes and taking deep breaths or by going into a quiet room, when frustrated or angry with toddler (knowing toddler is safe)* *Takes time for self and relaxes while toddler is napping*				

Social Emotional
Assessment/Evaluation Measure

SEAM™

TODDLER

(for developmental range 18–36 months)

Summary Form

Child's name: _____

Adult/caregiver's name: _____

Instructions

The child (C) and adult/caregiver (A) benchmarks and their associated items are listed on the following pages. Beside each item is space to enter the administration date and whether the item has been identified as a strength (i.e., as indicated by checking "Most of the time" on an item on the the Child SEAM and "Yes" on an item on the Adult/Caregiver SEAM), is considered of concern and needs monitoring (i.e., as indicated by a check on the ● for that item), or has been selected as an intervention goal (as indicated by a check on the ▲). The form can be used to enter data from three separate administrations over time.

TODDLER

TODDLER

	Admin date	Strength	Concern/continue monitoring	Identified as goal	Admin date	Strength	Concern/continue monitoring	Identified as goal	Admin date	Strength	Concern/continue monitoring	Identified as goal
CHILD												
Benchmark C-1.0												
Item 1.1												
Item 1.2												
Item 1.3												
Item 1.4												
Benchmark C-2.0												
Item 2.1												
Item 2.2												
Item 2.3												
Item 2.4												
Benchmark C-3.0												
Item 3.1												
Item 3.2												
Item 3.3												
Benchmark C-4.0												
Item 4.1												
Item 4.2												
Item 4.3												
Benchmark C-5.0												
Item 5.1												
Item 5.2												
Item 5.3												
Item 5.4												
Item 5.5												
Benchmark C-6.0												
Item 6.1												
Item 6.2												
Item 6.3												
Benchmark C-7.0												
Item 7.1												
Item 7.2												
Item 7.3												

	Admin date	Strength	Concern/continue monitoring	Identified as goal	Admin date	Strength	Concern/continue monitoring	Identified as goal	Admin date	Strength	Concern/continue monitoring	Identified as goal
Benchmark C-8.0												
Item 8.1												
Item 8.2												
Item 8.3												
Item 8.4												
Benchmark C-9.0												
Item 9.1												
Item 9.2												
Benchmark C-10.0												
Item 10.1												
Item 10.2												
Item 10.3												
Item 10.4												
ADULT/CAREGIVER												
Benchmark A-1.0												
Item 1.1												
Item 1.2												
Item 1.3												
Item 1.4												
Item 1.5												
Item 1.6												
Benchmark A-2.0												
Item 2.1												
Item 2.2												
Benchmark A-3.0												
Item 3.1												
Item 3.2												
Item 3.3												
Item 3.4												
Benchmark A-4.0												
Item 4.1												
Item 4.2												
Item 4.3												
Item 4.4												
Item 4.5												

TODDLER

Social Emotional
Assessment/Evaluation Measure

PRESCHOOL-AGE

(for developmental range 36–63 months)

General Instructions

The Social Emotional Assessment/Evaluation Measure (SEAM): Preschool-Age is divided into two sections. The first section, Child Benchmarks and Assessment Items, is focused on the child. There are two versions of the Child Benchmarks and Assessment Items: The first version does not include age intervals and is intended for parents/caregivers. The second, *for professional use only,* provides age intervals with each item to serve as guides for approximate ages at which children typically perform these skills. The second section, Adult/Caregiver Benchmarks and Assessment Items, is focused on the caregiver. These sections are then followed by a Summary Form for the professional to record observations that will assist in determining goals.

Social Emotional
Assessment/Evaluation Measure

SEAM™

PRESCHOOL-AGE

(for developmental range 36–63 months)

Child Benchmarks
and Assessment Items

Child's name: _____

Child's date of birth: _____

Family's name: _____

Name of person completing form: _____

Date of administration: _____

Instructions

Please read each item carefully before selecting an answer. Each item is accompanied by several examples. Children may be able to successfully meet the item criterion in a variety of ways. Some items may be too difficult for the child; for example, a 36-month-old may not wait for a parent or other adult before trying to cross a street. Professionals should ensure that parents understand that the SEAM may contain items that are developmentally too advanced for their child. Age norms should not be used with children with delays or developmental disabilities.

The three scoring options include "Most of the time," "Sometimes," and "Rarely or never." For example, if a preschool-age child shows affection to adults with regularity, a check should be placed in the box under "Most of the time" on item C-1.1. Items marked "Most of the time" are generally considered strengths. If a preschool-age child shows affection to familiar adults inconsistently, the box under "Sometimes" should be checked. If the preschool-age child rarely talks and plays with familiar adults, the box under "Rarely or never" should be checked. The latter two columns allow participants to indicate whether a particular behavior is of concern and whether it should become an intervention goal, respectively. After you are finished with this SEAM and the corresponding Adult/Caregiver SEAM, record answers on the accompanying Summary Form.

Child Benchmarks and Assessment Items
Preschool-Age

Please read each question carefully and
1. Check the box ■ that best describes your child's behavior.
2. Check the circle ● if this behavior is a concern.
3. Check the triangle ▲ if this will be an intervention goal.

		Most of the time	Sometimes	Rarely or never	Is a concern	Intervention goal
C-1.0	**Preschool-age child demonstrates healthy interactions with others.**					
1.1	**Child shows affection toward you and other familiar adults and children.**	■	■	■	●	▲
	Smiles at other children *Calls friends by name* *Hugs you and favorite friends* *Makes plans to sit by you or favorite friends at lunch*					
1.2	**Child talks and plays with you and adults he knows.**	■	■	■	●	▲
	Uses sentences to talk to others *Plays ball or other games with you* *Names a friend with whom she likes to play* *Plays favorite games* *Engages in back-and-forth conversations with you and other familiar adults*					
1.3	**Child uses words to let you know if she needs help, attention, or comfort.**	■	■	■	●	▲
	Asks for help to find a lost toy *Finds you when hurt* *Talks about recent experiences, such as, "At Granny's, I fell off my bike and hurt my foot"* *Can resolve some conflicts with words: "It's my turn with the fire hat"*					
1.4	**Child shares and takes turns with other children.**	■	■	■	●	▲
	Shares toys, such as rolling pins and shape cutters, when playing with playdough *Takes turns on swing with reminders from you* *Takes turns in simple games, such as tag* *Takes turns using paints or crayons* *Takes turns when playing board games such as Chutes & Ladders, and when playing other games such as Red Rover*					

		Most of the time	Sometimes	Rarely or never	Is a concern	Intervention goal
1.5	**Child plays with other children.**	☐	☐	☐	●	▲

Plays dress up with other children, sharing clothing
Plays in sandbox near other children
Plays imaginatively with peers for short times
Plays pretend games such as kitties, house
Plays imaginary games with peers that don't depend on objects, such as superheroes

C-2.0	**Preschool-age child expresses a range of emotions.**					
2.1	**Child smiles and laughs.**	☐	☐	☐	●	▲

Laughs when another child makes a funny face
Smiles when you come to pick her up from child care
Laughs at books during group time
Smiles and laughs when playing with peers

2.2	**Child expresses a range of emotions using a variety of strategies.**	☐	☐	☐	●	▲

Laughs, cries, shouts in excitement, shows anger physically such as crossing arms, stomping feet
Matches facial expression to many feelings such as happy, sad, mad, tired
Says, "I'm mad at you," or tells you or another adult rather than hitting a peer in anger

2.3	**Child describes emotions of others.**	☐	☐	☐	●	▲

Says "He is sad" when another child cries
Identifies others' emotions; says, "you're tired" when teacher yawns
Describes others' emotions and reason for the emotion, "Teacher, you are sad because the kids are noisy and not listening"

2.4	**Child identifies own emotions.**	☐	☐	☐	●	▲

Says she is mad or upset when angry
Tells you she is happy when given a desired toy
Identifies feelings and why she has them: "I am mad because I never get to be teacher helper"
Identifies some subtle feelings, such as frustration, disappointment, surprise

PRESCHOOL-AGE

	Most of the time	Sometimes	Rarely or never	Is a concern	Intervention goal
C-3.0 Preschool-age child regulates social emotional responses.					
3.1 Child responds to peer's or caregiver's soothing when upset.	■	■	■	●	▲
Quiets when physically comforted by you or a peer *Quiets in response to your attention: "Sebastian–you will have a turn next"* *Stops fretting when you explain why he needs to come inside*					
3.2 Child can calm self when upset within 5 minutes.	■	■	■	●	▲
Stops fussing after a minor fall within a few minutes *Finds another activity after conflict with peer*					
3.3 Child can calm self after periods of exciting activity.	■	■	■	●	▲
Calms down after a game of chase within 10 minutes, with some guidance from you *Stops laughing after funny event is over* *Transitions from outside to inside activities*					
3.4 Child remains calm in disappointing situations.	■	■	■	●	▲
Finds another game or toy when you remove a favorite toy, with some guidance from you *Says it's okay when she did not win a prize*					
C-4.0 Preschool-age child shows empathy for others.					
4.1 Child responds appropriately to others' emotional responses.	■	■	■	●	▲
Laughs when group of children are enjoying a game *Gives a toy back when another child shows distress* *Asks why a friend or caregiver is feeling sad or angry* *Understands that people have mixed emotions and may comment about peers, "She is sad and mad"*					

		Most of the time	Sometimes	Rarely or never	Is a concern	Intervention goal
4.2	**Child tries to comfort others when they are upset.**	☐	☐	☐	●	▲
	Comforts other child who is crying by offering a toy or reassuring words: "Are you okay?" *Asks why adult is sad and listens to response* *Expresses understanding of others' feelings: "It is sad that she doesn't have a bike"*					
C-5.0	**Preschool-age child shares and engages with others.**					
5.1	**Child focuses on event indicated by another.**	☐	☐	☐	●	▲
	Looks at a picture pointed out by another child *Helps you with household tasks, helps to feed the dog, wipe the table* *Joins peers in a family role play* *Chooses to play with peers, rather than adults*					
5.2	**Child greets adults and peers.**	☐	☐	☐	●	▲
	Says "Hi" to friend; says "Bye" when leaving preschool *Uses friends' and teachers' names*					
5.3	**Child cooperates in play or when completing a task.**	☐	☐	☐	●	▲
	Helps another child stack blocks to build a tall tower *Engages in dramatic role play: "You be the dad and I will be the baby"* *Can switch roles when playing: "Now I am the bus driver and you are the kid"*					
5.4	**Child participates appropriately in group activities.**	☐	☐	☐	●	▲
	Participates in group singing *Helps with cooking project, taking turns pouring ingredients and stirring with your guidance* *Sits quietly in a small group while a story is being read*					

PRESCHOOL-AGE

	Most of the time	Sometimes	Rarely or never	Is a concern	Intervention goal
C-6.0 Preschool-age child demonstrates independence.					
6.1 Child explores new materials and settings.	■	■	■	●	▲
Is becoming more independent and leaves your side for a short time at the park *Tries out equipment at new playground* *Explores new activity in the classroom, such as sensory table with shaving cream or dry beans*					
6.2 Child tries new task before seeking help.	■	■	■	●	▲
Tries to complete puzzle before seeking help *Tries to open jar before asking for assistance* *Tries spreading peanut butter on toast or muffin independently*					
6.3 Child stays with or returns to challenging activities.	■	■	■	●	▲
Asks to skate again after falling *Helps clean up until all objects are put away* *Builds a block tower again after it falls over*					
6.4 Child can leave caregiver without distress.	■	■	■	●	▲
Leaves you on park bench to play with friends in the playground *Tells you "Bye" and does not cry when left at familiar child care*					
C-7.0 Preschool-age child displays a positive self-image.					
7.1 Child knows personal information.	■	■	■	●	▲
Gives first name, age, and gender when asked *Tells you first and last name and siblings' first names* *Knows identifying information: phone number, address, birthday*					

PRESCHOOL-AGE

	Most of the time	Sometimes	Rarely or never	Is a concern	Intervention goal
7.2 Child shows off work, takes pride in accomplishments.	■	■	■	●	▲
Shows you a completed drawing *Says "Look at me" when painting* *Tells other adults, "Watch me run fast"* *Describes what she has done: "Mom, I cut this out, taped it, and put glitter on it. Isn't it beautiful?"*					
7.3 Child makes positive statements about self.	■	■	■	●	▲
Describes performance: "I made a huge dinosaur" *Describes traits: "I'm good at cutting"* *Describes work: "My tower is taller than Fernando's"* *Says, "I'm smart"*					
C-8.0 Preschool-age child regulates attention and activity level.					
8.1 Child stays with motor activity for 10 minutes or longer.	■	■	■	●	▲
Rides tricycle for 10 minutes *Plays games like Simon Says for 10 minutes*					
8.2 Child participates in early literacy activities.	■	■	■	●	▲
Holds book correctly and turns pages *Recognizes a few letters of the alphabet* *Copies and prints some letters and shapes* *Recognizes 20 letters of the alphabet, printed name and some words* *Writes first name and many letters*					
8.3 Child moves from one activity to another without problems.	■	■	■	●	▲
Shifts from group time to free play activities, with adult prompt, without problems *Moves from bath to bed with adult prompt*					
8.4 Child participates in games with others.	■	■	■	●	▲
Plays cars with other children *Plays card games such as Go Fish with others* *Plays board games with playmates*					

PRESCHOOL-AGE

	Most of the time	Sometimes	Rarely or never	Is a concern	Intervention goal
8.5 Child regulates his activity level to match setting.	☐	☐	☐	●	▲
Sits safely in the bath while bathing, with your supervision *Jumps and runs outside* *Participates in small and large group with guidance from you or other adult; sits and listens to story with group; dances with friends to music* *Plays with peers in sandbox with safety reminders* *Entertains self, such as taking book to reading corner to look at pictures* *Plays safely outside with peers or at parks, with your supervision*					
C-9.0 Preschool-age child cooperates with daily routines and requests.					
9.1 Child follows routines and rules.	☐	☐	☐	●	▲
Follows clean-up routine after meals with reminders *Helps get self dressed* *Follows simple rules at home and school* *Stays at table until excused* *Enjoys games with rules, such as Chutes and Ladders, Candyland* *Transfers rules from different settings: "My teacher says we walk outside"*					
9.2 Child does what he is asked to do.	☐	☐	☐	●	▲
Stops running when asked *Puts coat on when asked* *Remembers a rule when reminded, such as using a quiet voice, walking indoors*					
9.3 Child responds appropriately when corrected by adults.	☐	☐	☐	●	▲
Takes appropriate toy when prompted by adult *Returns too-large portion of food to serving plate when told*					
C-10.0 Preschool-age child shows a range of adaptive skills.					
10.1 Child feeds self and eats a variety of foods without problem.	☐	☐	☐	●	▲
Eats most offered foods *Eats small bites of new foods* *Eats with utensils and can pour juice from a pitcher or jug* *Prepares food for eating, such as opening bag of fruit snacks, using knife to spread peanut butter on crackers*					

	Most of the time	Sometimes	Rarely or never	Is a concern	Intervention goal
10.2 Child dresses self.	☐	☐	☐	●	▲
Undresses independently (not buttons or snaps) *Dresses and undresses independently* *Uses buttons and unzips* *Manipulates buttons, zippers, and shoes*					
10.3 Child goes to bed and falls asleep without a problem.	☐	☐	☐	●	▲
Goes to bed when prompted by you, without crying *Follows familiar routine at home, child care, or preschool* *Falls asleep shortly after going to bed*					
10.4 Child uses the toilet appropriately.	☐	☐	☐	●	▲
Indicates need and seeks bathroom when necessary *Uses toilet with little help from caregiver and remains dry at night* *Takes care of toileting needs independently*					
10.5 Child manages changes in settings and conditions.	☐	☐	☐	●	▲
Accepts changes in familiar routine, such as field trip at school, father picking her up instead of mom *Adjusts to sleeping in a strange bed* *Eats without problem in a restaurant*					
10.6 Child keeps himself safe in potentially dangerous conditions.	☐	☐	☐	●	▲
Waits for you or other adult before crossing a street *Climbs a jungle gym safely* *Follows rules when in public, such as stopping at crosswalks, not going away with strangers*					
10.7 Child solves problems to meet her needs.	☐	☐	☐	●	▲
Asks you for help when hungry or thirsty *Gets cup of water when thirsty* *Finds you when needs help with problems, such as opening outside door* *Negotiates with peer to design play or a game*					

PRESCHOOL-AGE

Social Emotional
Assessment/Evaluation Measure

SEAM™

PRESCHOOL-AGE

(for developmental range 36–63 months)

Professional version with age intervals

Child Benchmarks
and Assessment Items

Child's name: _____

Child's date of birth: _____

Family's name: _____

Name of person completing form: _____

Date of administration: _____

Instructions

Please read each item carefully before selecting an answer. Each item is accompanied by several examples. Children may be able to successfully meet the item criterion in a variety of ways. Some items may be too difficult for the child; for example, a 36-month-old may not wait for a parent or other adult before trying to cross a street. Age norms are provided on this version for professionals only and serve as approximate guidelines for children who are typically developing, primarily. Professionals should ensure that parents understand that the SEAM may contain items that are developmentally too advanced for their child. Age norms should not be used with children with delays or developmental disabilities.

The three scoring options include "Most of the time," "Sometimes," and "Rarely or never." For example, if a preschool-age child shows affection to adults with regularity, a check should be placed in the box under "Most of the time" on item C-1.1. Items marked "Most of the time" are generally considered strengths. If a preschool-age child shows affection to familiar adults inconsistently, the box under "Sometimes" should be checked. If the preschool-age child rarely talks and plays with familiar adults, the box under "Rarely or never" should be checked. The latter two columns allow participants to indicate whether a particular behavior is of concern and whether it should become an intervention goal, respectively. After you are finished with this SEAM and the corresponding Adult/Caregiver SEAM, record answers on the accompanying Summary Form.

Child Benchmarks and Assessment Items
Preschool-Age

Please read each question carefully and
1. Check the box ■ that best describes your child's behavior.
2. Check the circle ● if this behavior is a concern.
3. Check the triangle ▲ if this will be an intervention goal.

Approx. age in months		Most of the time	Sometimes	Rarely or never	Is a concern	Intervention goal
	C-1.0 Preschool-age child demonstrates healthy interactions with others.					
	1.1 Child shows affection toward you and other familiar adults and children.	■	■	■	●	▲
36	Smiles at other children					
36	Calls friends by name					
36+	Hugs you and favorite friends					
48–60+	Makes plans to sit by you or favorite friends at lunch					
	1.2 Child talks and plays with you and adults he knows.	■	■	■	●	▲
36	Uses sentences to talk to others					
36	Plays ball or other games with you					
36	Names a friend with whom she likes to play					
48	Plays favorite games					
48–60	Engages in back-and-forth conversations with you and other familiar adults					
	1.3 Child uses words to let you know if she needs help, attention, or comfort.	■	■	■	●	▲
36	Asks for help to find a lost toy					
36	Finds you when hurt					
36–48	Talks about recent experiences, such as, "At Granny's, I fell off my bike and hurt my foot"					
48	Can resolve some conflicts with words: "It's my turn with the fire hat"					
	1.4 Child shares and takes turns with other children.	■	■	■	●	▲
36	Shares toys, such as rolling pins and shape cutters, when playing with playdough					
36	Takes turns on swing with reminders from you					

PRESCHOOL-AGE

Approx. age in months		Most of the time	Sometimes	Rarely or never	Is a concern	Intervention goal
48	Takes turns in simple games, such as tag					
48	Takes turns using paints or crayons					
48–60	Takes turns when playing board games such as Chutes & Ladders, and when playing other games such as Red Rover					
	1.5 Child plays with other children.	■	■	■	●	▲
36	Plays dress up with other children, sharing clothing					
36	Plays in sandbox near other children					
36	Plays imaginatively with peers for short times					
48	Plays pretend games such as kitties, house					
48–60	Plays imaginary games with peers that don't depend on objects, such as superheroes					
	C-2.0 Preschool-age child expresses a range of emotions.					
	2.1 Child smiles and laughs.	■	■	■	●	▲
36	Laughs when another child makes a funny face					
36	Smiles when you come to pick her up from child care					
48	Laughs at books during group time					
36–60	Smiles and laughs when playing with peers					
	2.2 Child expresses a range of emotions, using a variety of strategies.	■	■	■	●	▲
36+	Laughs, cries, shouts in excitement, shows anger physically such as crossing arms, stomping feet					
36–48	Matches facial expression to many feelings such as happy, sad, mad, tired					
48–60	Says, "I'm mad at you," or tells you or another adult rather than hitting a peer in anger					
	2.3 Child describes emotions of others.	■	■	■	●	▲
36	Says "He is sad" when another child cries					
36–48	Identifies others' emotions; says, "you're tired" when teacher yawns					
48–60	Describes others' emotions and reason for the emotion, "Teacher, you are sad because the kids are noisy and not listening"					

PRESCHOOL-AGE

Approx. age in months		Most of the time	Sometimes	Rarely or never	Is a concern	Intervention goal
	2.4 Child identifies own emotions.	☐	☐	☐	○	▲
36	*Says she is mad or upset when angry*					
36	*Tells you she is happy when given a desired toy*					
48	*Identifies feelings and why she has them: "I am mad because I never get to be teacher helper"*					
54+	*Identifies some subtle feelings, such as frustration, disappointment, surprise*					
	C-3.0 Preschool-age child regulates his social emotional responses.					
	3.1 Child responds to peer's or caregiver's soothing when upset.	☐	☐	☐	○	▲
36	*Quiets when physically comforted by you or a peer*					
48	*Quiets in response to your attention: "Sebastian—you will have a turn next"*					
48–60	*Stops fretting when you explain why he needs to come inside*					
	3.2 Child can calm self when upset within 5 minutes.	☐	☐	☐	○	▲
36+	*Stops fussing after a minor fall within a few minutes*					
48–60	*Finds another activity after conflict with peer*					
	3.3 Child can calm self after periods of exciting activity.	☐	☐	☐	○	▲
36	*Calms down after a game of chase within 10 minutes, with some guidance from you*					
48+	*Stops laughing after funny event is over*					
48+	*Transitions from outside to inside activities*					
	3.4 Child remains calm in disappointing situations.	☐	☐	☐	○	▲
36	*Finds another game or toy when you remove a favorite toy, with some guidance from you*					
48+	*Says it's okay when she did not win a prize*					

Approx. age in months		Most of the time	Sometimes	Rarely or never	Is a concern	Intervention goal
	C-4.0 Preschool-age child shows empathy for others.					
	4.1 Child responds appropriately to others' emotional responses.	■	■	■	●	▲
36	Laughs when group of children are enjoying a game					
36	Gives a toy back when another child shows distress					
48	Asks why a friend or caregiver is feeling sad or angry					
48+	Understands that people have mixed emotions and may comment about peers, "She is sad and mad"					
	4.2 Child tries to comfort others when they are upset.	■	■	■	●	▲
36	Comforts other child who is crying by offering a toy or reassuring words: "Are you okay?"					
48	Asks why adult is sad and listens to response					
48+	Expresses understanding of others' feelings: "It is sad that she doesn't have a bike"					
	C-5.0 Preschool-age child shares and engages with others.					
	5.1 Child focuses on event indicated by another.	■	■	■	●	▲
36+	Looks at a picture pointed out by another child					
36	Helps you with household tasks, helps to feed the dog, wipe the table					
36+	Joins peers in a family role play					
48	Chooses to play with peers, rather than adults					
	5.2 Child greets adults and peers.	■	■	■	●	▲
36	Says "Hi" to friend; says "Bye" when leaving preschool					
40+	Uses friends' and teachers' names					

PRESCHOOL-AGE

Approx. age in months		Most of the time	Sometimes	Rarely or never	Is a concern	Intervention goal
	5.3 Child cooperates in play or when completing a task.	☐	☐	☐	○	△
36–48	*Helps another child stack blocks to build a tall tower*					
48	*Engages in dramatic role play: "You be the dad and I will be the baby"*					
48+	*Can switch roles when playing: "Now I am the bus driver and you are the kid"*					
	5.4 Child participates appropriately in group activities.	☐	☐	☐	○	△
36+	*Participates in group singing*					
48	*Helps with cooking project, taking turns pouring ingredients and stirring with your guidance*					
48+	*Sits quietly in a small group while a story is being read*					
	C-6.0 Preschool-age child demonstrates independence.					
	6.1 Child explores new materials and settings.	☐	☐	☐	○	△
36	*Is becoming more independent and leaves your side for a short time at the park*					
48–60+	*Tries out equipment at new playground*					
48–60+	*Explores new activity in the classroom, such as sensory table with shaving cream or dry beans*					
	6.2 Child tries new task before seeking help.	☐	☐	☐	○	△
36	*Tries to complete puzzle before seeking help*					
36	*Tries to open jar before asking for assistance*					
48+	*Tries spreading peanut butter on toast or muffin independently*					
	6.3 Child stays with or returns to challenging activities.	☐	☐	☐	○	△
36+	*Asks to skate again after falling*					
36+	*Helps clean up until all objects are put away*					
36+	*Builds a block tower again after it falls over*					

Approx. age in months		Most of the time	Sometimes	Rarely or never	Is a concern	Interven-tion goal
	6.4 Child can leave you without distress.	■	■	■	●	▲
36	Leaves you on park bench to play with friends in the playground					
48+	Tells you "Bye" and does not cry when left at familiar child care					
	C-7.0 Preschool-age child displays a positive self-image.					
	7.1 Child knows personal information.	■	■	■	●	▲
36	Gives first name, age, and gender when asked					
48	Tells you first and last name and siblings' first names					
60	Knows identifying information: phone number, address, birthday					
	7.2 Child shows off work, takes pride in accomplishments.	■	■	■	●	▲
36	Shows you a completed drawing					
36	Says "Look at me" when painting					
48+	Tells other adults, "Watch me run fast"					
48–60	Describes what she has done: "Mom, I cut this out, taped it, and put glitter on it. Isn't it beautiful?"					
	7.3 Child makes positive statements about self.	■	■	■	●	▲
48	Describes performance: "I made a huge dinosaur"					
54	Describes traits: "I'm good at cutting"					
60	Describes work: "My tower is taller than Fernando's"					
60	Says, "I'm smart"					
	C-8.0 Preschool-age child regulates his or her attention and activity level.					
	8.1 Child stays with motor activity for 10 minutes or longer.	■	■	■	●	▲
36+	Rides tricycle for 10 minutes					
36+	Plays games like Simon Says for 10 minutes					

PRESCHOOL-AGE

Approx. age in months		Most of the time	Sometimes	Rarely or never	Is a concern	Intervention goal
	8.2 Child participates in early literacy activities.	☐	☐	☐	○	△
36+	Holds book correctly and turns pages					
48	Recognizes a few letters of the alphabet					
48	Copies and prints some letters and shapes					
60	Recognizes 20 letters of the alphabet, printed name and some words					
60	Writes first name and many letters					
	8.3 Child moves from one activity to another without problems.	☐	☐	☐	○	△
48+	Shifts from group time to free play activities, with adult prompt, without problems					
48+	Moves from bath to bed with adult prompt					
	8.4 Child participates in games with others.	☐	☐	☐	○	△
36	Plays cars with other children					
48	Plays card games such as Go Fish with others					
48+	Plays board games with playmates					
	8.5 Child regulates his activity level to match setting.	☐	☐	☐	○	△
36+	Sits safely in the bath while bathing, with your supervision					
36–48	Jumps and runs outside					
36–48	Participates in small and large group with guidance from you or other adult; sits and listens to story with group; dances with friends to music					
36–48	Plays with peers in sandbox with safety reminders					
48–60	Entertains self, such as taking book to reading corner to look at pictures					
48–60	Plays safely outside with peers or at parks, with your supervision					
	C-9.0 Preschool-age child cooperates with daily routines and requests.					
	9.1 Child follows routines and rules.	☐	☐	☐	○	△
36	Follows clean-up routine after meals with reminders					
36	Helps get self dressed					
48	Follows simple rules at home and school					
48	Stays at table until excused					
48–60	Enjoys games with rules, such as Chutes and Ladders, Candyland					
48–60	Transfers rules from different settings: "My teacher says we walk outside"					

Approx. age in months		Most of the time	Sometimes	Rarely or never	Is a concern	Interven-tion goal
	9.2 Child does what he is asked to do.	☐	☐	☐	●	▲
36–48	*Stops running when asked*					
36–48	*Gets coat on when asked*					
48–60	*Remembers a rule when reminded, such as using a quiet voice, walking indoors*					
	9.3 Child responds appropriately when corrected by adults.	☐	☐	☐	●	▲
36–48	*Takes appropriate toy when prompted by adult*					
36–48	*Returns too-large portion of food to serving plate when told*					
	C-10.0 Preschool-age child shows a range of adaptive skills.					
	10.1 Child feeds self and eats a variety of foods without a problem.	☐	☐	☐	●	▲
36–60	*Eats most offered foods*					
36–60	*Eats small bites of new foods*					
48	*Eats with utensils and can pour juice from a pitcher or jug*					
48–60	*Prepares food for eating, such as opening bag of fruit snacks, using knife to spread peanut butter on crackers*					
	10.2 Child dresses self.	☐	☐	☐	●	▲
36	*Undresses independently (not buttons or snaps)*					
48	*Dresses and undresses independently*					
48	*Uses buttons and unzips*					
60	*Manipulates buttons, zippers, and shoes*					
	10.3 Child goes to bed and falls asleep without problem.	☐	☐	☐	●	▲
36+	*Goes to bed when prompted by you, without crying*					
36+	*Follows familiar routine at home, child care, or preschool*					
48+	*Falls asleep shortly after going to bed*					
	10.4 Child uses the toilet appropriately.	☐	☐	☐	●	▲
36	*Indicates need and seeks bathroom when necessary*					
48	*Uses toilet with little help from caregiver and remains dry at night*					
60	*Takes care of toileting needs independently*					

PRESCHOOL-AGE

Approx. age in months		Most of the time	Sometimes	Rarely or never	Is a concern	Intervention goal
	10.5 Child manages changes in settings and conditions.	■	■	■	●	▲
36	*Accepts changes in familiar routine, such as field trip at school, father picking her up instead of mom*					
36+	*Adjusts to sleeping in a strange bed*					
36+	*Eats without problem in a restaurant*					
	10.6 Child keeps himself safe in potentially dangerous conditions.	■	■	■	●	▲
36–48	*Waits for you or other adult before crossing a street*					
36–48	*Climbs a jungle gym safely*					
48–60	*Follows rules when in public, such as stopping at crosswalks, not going away with strangers*					
	10.7 Child solves problems to meet her needs.	■	■	■	●	▲
36	*Asks you for help when hungry or thirsty*					
48	*Gets cup of water when thirsty*					
48	*Finds you when needs help with problems, such as opening outside door*					
60	*Negotiates with peer to design play or a game*					

PRESCHOOL-AGE

Social Emotional
Assessment/Evaluation Measure

SEAM™

PRESCHOOL-AGE

(for individuals with children in developmental range 36–63 months)

Adult/Caregiver Benchmarks and Assessment Items

Child's name: _____

Child's date of birth: _____

Family's name: _____

Name of person completing form: _____

Date of administration: _____

The following questions are designed to obtain information that can determine the supports and resources needed for caregivers/parents to provide a safe and responsive environment for their children. The items focus on behaviors related to preschool-age children's social emotional development and competence. The preferred method for completing this form is through an interview of the caregiver(s). Items that are not relevant or that caregivers do not want to answer can be omitted.

Items are written in easy to understand language and each item is accompanied by one or more examples to assist caregivers in understanding the item's intent. Caregivers can chose between a "Yes" or "Not yet" response. In addition, the form provides space for the caregiver(s) to indicate if he or she would like to choose the item as an intervention goal and/or needs information and resources related to goal and/or needs.

Instructions

1. Arrange a time and place to complete the form that is comfortable for the caregiver(s). Explain the purpose of the interview and the form.
2. Read each item and the examples. Then ask the caregiver(s) to indicate whether the "Yes" or "Not yet" response option best described if he/she has the targeted skill. "Yes" should be checked if the caregiver(s) feels he or she has the information, resources and/or skills indicated in the item. "Not yet" should be checked if the caregiver(s) feels he or she does not have the information, resources, and/or skills indicated in the item.
3. Check the triangle ▲ next to an item if the caregiver(s) would like to target the content addressed in the item as an intervention goal, and/or if he or she needs resources or information from a professional (school, child's teacher/home visitor).
4. Consider the cultural appropriateness of each item for individual families and omit items that caregivers may find intrusive, disrespectful, or inappropriate.

Adult/Caregiver Benchmarks and Assessment Items
Preschool-Age

Please read each question carefully and
1. Check the box ■ that best describes your behavior.
2. Check the triangle ▲ if this will be an intervention goal.

		Yes	Not yet	Intervention goal
A-1.0	**Caregiver responds positively to preschool-age child.**			
1.1	**Caregiver responds to child's nonverbal communication appropriately.**	■	■	▲
	Tells by watching child whether she is excited, tired, hungry, sick, or scared *Responds when child is upset by joining him in a game or story* *Dances or jumps with child when she is happy* *Snuggles with child and helps him feel safe when he is frightened or sick*			
1.2	**Caregiver responds to child's verbal communication appropriately.**	■	■	▲
	Listens to child's words and tries to understand words he uses *Asks child questions about his day* *Talks to child about the surroundings—what they are doing; what they are cooking; what they see outside* *Answers child in words he can understand*			
1.3	**Caregiver supports child's emotional needs.**	■	■	▲
	Holds and soothes child when she is hurt or upset *Uses words that express child's feelings when caregiver can see she is hurt, frightened, frustrated, excited* *Encourages child to identify and talk about her feelings* *Gives child choices about his daily routines, what he wears, what story to read, and what to play* *Shows child how to calm down when upset by taking deep breaths, sitting down for a few minutes*			
1.4	**Caregiver uses positive comments and language with child.**	■	■	▲
	Caregiver comments on child's gentle petting of cat *Caregiver gives "high 5" when child picks up all toys* *Caregiver praises child when child ignores sibling's teasing*			
1.5	**Caregiver successfully redirects child's inappropriate behaviors.**	■	■	▲
	Caregiver gives favorite doll to child before child pokes infant sister *Caregiver takes child to outdoor play area when beginning to run indoors*			

PRESCHOOL-AGE

		Yes	Not yet	Intervention goal
1.6	**Caregiver can recognize function of child's behaviors and, with assistance, can modify environment.**	■	■	▲
	Caregiver prepares child for long bus ride with coloring paper activities and appropriate clothing *Caregiver lets child choose one grocery item at store before tantrum occurs*			
A-2.0	**Caregiver provides developmentally appropriate type and level of activity.**			
2.1	**Caregiver offers age-appropriate books, toys, and playthings for child.**	■	■	▲
	Provides a variety of different activities for child, such as games, art *Buys or obtains books and puzzles that child can complete and some that are challenging* *Provides toys that child uses for play, such as dress up clothes and toy dishes*			
2.2	**Caregiver plays with child and has ideas for age-appropriate games.**	■	■	▲
	Plays board games, card games, and puzzles with child *Plays simple action games with child, such as Simon Says and Red Rover* *Plays games that encourage the child's problem-solving skills, such as rhyming games and I Spy*			
A-3.0	**Caregiver provides preschool-age child with predictable schedule/routines.**			
3.1	**Caregiver provides a mealtime routine for child that is predictable and appropriate for his age.**	■	■	▲
	Provides child with three meals per day at similar times each day *Provides a variety of food for the child* *Includes child in meal preparation when possible, such as grocery shopping, picking out new vegetables, and measuring and stirring*			
3.2	**Caregiver provides a rest and sleeping routine for child that is predictable and appropriate for his age.**	■	■	▲
	Provides similar bedtime and nap times across days and weeks *Follows a similar routine before bed, such as taking warm bath, brushing teeth, and reading stories* *Provides time for child to look at books and rest after bath time*			

PRESCHOOL-AGE

			Yes	Not yet	Intervention goal
3.3	**Caregiver provides child with predictable limits and discipline.**		☐	☐	▲
	Sets limits for child, such as no hitting or running in the house				
	Notices and tells child the positive things she is doing				
	Tries to focus on what child CAN do				
	Uses "no" infrequently, and under similar conditions from day to day				
3.4	**Caregiver provides time each day to play with child.**		☐	☐	▲
	Plays a variety of different games with child, such as board games, catch				
	Takes time each day to laugh and be silly with child				
	Plays games that encourage the child's thinking skills, like I Spy and Matching				
A-4.0	**Caregiver provides preschool-age child with a safe home and play environment.**				
4.1	**Caregiver checks the home for things that can be dangerous to child.**		☐	☐	▲
	Keeps poisons (medications, cleaning supplies) and weapons in locked cupboard				
	Keeps sharp objects like knives out of reach				
4.2	**Caregiver is able to provide safe travel arrangements for child.**		☐	☐	▲
	Caregiver uses a car seat that is appropriate for child's height and weight and fits safely in the car				
	Uses a stroller that does not tip				
	Provides a bike helmet to wear while the child rides a bike				
4.3	**Caregiver supervises child.**		☐	☐	▲
	Supervises child's activities				
	Takes child to play yard that is fenced				
	Sits nearby at parks or outdoors to watch child play with peers in sandbox				
4.4	**Caregiver takes child for regular medical and dental care.**		☐	☐	▲
	Takes child to well child clinic and dentist at least twice per year				
	Takes child for regular hearing and vision check-ups				

Social Emotional
Assessment/Evaluation Measure

SEAM™

PRESCHOOL-AGE

(for developmental range 36–63 months)

Summary Form

Child's name: _____

Adult/caregiver's name: _____

Instructions

The child (C) and adult/caregiver (A) benchmarks and their associated items are listed on the following pages. Beside each item is space to enter the administration date and whether the item has been identified as a strength (i.e., as indicated by checking "Most of the time" on an item on the the Child SEAM and "Yes" on an item on the Adult/Caregiver SEAM), is considered of concern and needs monitoring (i.e., as indicated by a check on the ● for that item), or has been selected as an intervention goal (as indicated by a check on the ▲). The form can be used to enter data from three separate administrations.

PRESCHOOL-AGE

PRESCHOOL-AGE

	Admin date	Strength	Concern/continue monitoring	Identified as goal	Admin date	Strength	Concern/continue monitoring	Identified as goal	Admin date	Strength	Concern/continue monitoring	Identified as goal
CHILD												
Benchmark C-1.0												
Item 1.1												
Item 1.2												
Item 1.3												
Item 1.4												
Item 1.5												
Benchmark C-2.0												
Item 2.1												
Item 2.2												
Item 2.3												
Item 2.4												
Benchmark C-3.0												
Item 3.1												
Item 3.2												
Item 3.3												
Item 3.4												
Benchmark C-4.0												
Item 4.1												
Item 4.2												
Item 4.3												
Item 4.4												
Benchmark C-5.0												
Item 5.1												
Item 5.2												
Item 5.3												
Item 5.4												
Benchmark C-6.0												
Item 6.1												
Item 6.2												
Item 6.3												
Item 6.4												
Benchmark C-7.0												
Item 7.1												
Item 7.2												
Item 7.3												

	Admin date	Strength	Concern/continue monitoring	Identified as goal	Admin date	Strength	Concern/continue monitoring	Identified as goal	Admin date	Strength	Concern/continue monitoring	Identified as goal
Benchmark C-8.0												
Item 8.1												
Item 8.2												
Item 8.3												
Item 8.4												
Item 8.5												
Benchmark C-9.0												
Item 9.1												
Item 9.2												
Item 9.3												
Benchmark C-10.0												
Item 10.1												
Item 10.2												
Item 10.3												
Item 10.4												
Item 10.5												
Item 10.6												
Item 10.7												
ADULT/CAREGIVER												
Benchmark A-1.0												
Item 1.1												
Item 1.2												
Item 1.3												
Item 1.4												
Item 1.5												
Item 1.6												
Benchmark A-2.0												
Item 2.1												
Item 2.2												
Benchmark A-3.0												
Item 3.1												
Item 3.2												
Item 3.3												
Item 3.4												
Benchmark A-4.0												
Item 4.1												
Item 4.2												
Item 4.3												
Item 4.4												

PRESCHOOL-AGE

Appendix C

Resources

Guide to Selected Early Childhood Curricula
Guide to Selected Social Emotional Screening Instruments
Functional Behavioral Assessment and Behavior Support Planning
  with Deborah Russell and Robert Horner

Guide to Selected
Early Childhood Curricula

Appendix C1. Guide to early childhood curricula

Curriculum name	Description
Active Learning Series Cryer, D., Harms, T., & Bourland, B. (1988–1996) *Ordering information:* Dale Seymour Publications Kaplan (kaplanco.com) Pearson Learning Group 800-334-2017	Based on the Early Childhood Environment Rating Scales (ECERS–R) Series of seven curriculum guides More than 300 age-appropriate activities for listening and talking, activities for social growth and suggestions for physical development and creative learning Activities are designed to help children "develop their minds and bodies in a safe and healthful environment" Written for teachers of infants, toddlers and children from 2–5 years old and separate guide for children with disabilities Materials, required time, number of children, indoor/outdoor location are specified for each activity
Assessment, Evaluation, and Programming System (AEPS®)–2nd Edition Bricker, D. (Ed.). (2002) Curriculum for Birth–3 Years Curriculum for 3–6 Years *Ordering information:* Paul H. Brookes Publishing Co. www.brookespublishing.com 800-638-3775	Curriculum component of comprehensive curriculum-based assessment Psychometric data supporting the system exist Designed for children with disabilities but also appropriate for at risk populations Directly linked to assessment/evaluation and family participation components Developmentally sequenced activities that move from simple to more advanced skills Based on ecological and transactional theory
Beautiful Beginnings: A Developmental Curriculum for Infants and Toddlers Raikes, H.H., & Whitmer, J.M. (2006) *Ordering information:* Paul H. Brookes Publishing Co. www.brookespublishing.com 800-638-3775	Curriculum is divided into six age ranges between birth to age 3 Includes more than 350 photocopiable activities and forms Activities build on children's natural strengths and interests Fosters development in eight key areas, including communication, gross motor, fine motor, intellectual, discovery, social, self-help, and pretend Activities are low cost and easily implemented in Head Start and child care centers and homes Includes forms for tracking progress and stickers to celebrate accomplished goals Includes CD-ROM with all forms and activities

(continued)

Appendix C1. *(continued)*

Curriculum name	Description

The Carolina Curriculum for Infants and Toddlers with Special Needs–Third Edition
Johnson-Martin, N.M., Attermeier, S.M., & Hacker, B.J. (2004)
	Curriculum component of comprehensive curriculum-based assessment
	Curricular items follow the same format:
	  Title
	  Objective
	  Materials needed

The Carolina Curriculum for Preschoolers with Special Needs–Second Edition
Johnson-Martin, N.M., Attermeier, S.M., & Hacker, B.J. (2004)
Ordering information:
Paul H. Brookes Publishing Co.
www.brookespublishing.com
800-638-3775
	Teaching procedures
	    Integration strategies
	      Sensorimotor adaptations
	  Functional activities targeted
	Specific information on disabilities provided
	Adaptations for hearing, motor, visual impairments
	Designed for children with disabilities
	Directly linked to assessment/evaluation component
	Divided into 22 logical teaching sequences covering five developmental domains, including social adaptation
	Reliability, validity, and program efficacy data
	Effects of disabilities in classroom and classroom tips provided

Creative Curriculum for Infants and Toddlers Dombro, A., Colker, L., & Dodge, D. (2002)	Research-based preschool curriculum model based on Piaget's theories of child development Focus on 10 interest areas or activities in the environment (i.e., blocks, house corner, table toys, art, sand, water, library corner, music, movement, cooking, computers, and the outdoors)

Creative Curriculum for Early Childhood
Dodge, D., & Colker, L. (1992)
Ordering information:
Delmar Thomson Learning
Teaching Strategies
www.teachingstrategies.com
800-637-3652
	Helps teachers understand how to work with children at different developmental levels to promote learning
	Guides teachers in adapting the environment to make it more challenging
	Includes a parent component
	Infant curriculum includes
	  Comprehensive framework for planning and implementing quality activities,
	  Focus on building social relationships
	  Addresses what children learn during the first three years
	  Experiences to achieve learning goals
	  Staff and parents' guidelines for reaching goals
	Preschool (4th edition) curriculum components include
	  How Children Develop and Learn
	  The Learning Environment
	  What Children Learn
	  The Teacher's Role
	  The Family's Role

Devereux Early Childhood Assessment
Devereux Foundation (1998)
Ordering information:
www.devereuxearlychildhood.org
866-TRAIN US

- Strength-based system designed to promote "resilience" in children ages 2–5
- Includes assessment, family partnerships, and follow-up efforts that respond to children's individual characteristics and acknowledge the role of families
- Classroom focus
- Emphasis on social and emotional well-being
- Encourages partnerships between teachers and families
- Recommends classroom strategies that fit within an early childhood program's current
- Supports effective collaboration between home and school
- Stresses the importance of being data-driven early care and education professional

Hawaii Early Learning Profile for Infants and Toddlers (HELP) Assessment and Curriculum Guide
Vort Corporation. (1995).

- Curriculum component of comprehensive curriculum-based assessment
- Focuses on children's strengths as well as needs
- Provides adaptations for assessing and teaching each skill
- Provides clearly written intervention plans, activities
- Offers an easy-to-follow developmental sequence

Hawaii Early Learning Profile for Preschoolers (HELP) Assessment and Curriculum Guide
Vort Corporation. (1995).
Ordering information:
www.vort.com
650-322-8282

- HELP at home (B-3) includes parent handouts, curriculum resources
- HELP for preschoolers: Activities at Home includes parent handouts and curriculum resources

High Reach Learning
Mayberry, S., & Kelley, K.
Ordering information:
www.highreach.com
800-729-9988

- Learning materials for 3–12 months, 12–24 months, 2+ years, 3+ years, older 3's/4+, and pre-k/4+
- Theme-based curriculum with child-initiated and teacher-facilitated learning opportunities
- Activities designed to promote development of the whole child
- All support teaching tools and activities are built in
- Materials included for children and families to strengthen the school to home connection
- Addresses social, emotional, cognitive, and physical domains

High/Scope
High/Scope Educational Research Foundation
Ordering information:
www.highscope.org
734-485-2000

- Curriculum component of comprehensive, curriculum-based assessment
- Curricula focus on constructionist Piagetian activities for early childhood settings
- Small- and large-group instructional activities provided
- Children seen as active learners in classroom settings with rich materials
- Adult role is to challenge, support, and extend children's learning in social/academic development

(continued)

Curriculum name	Description

The Ounce Scale
Meisels, S. (2003)
Ordering information:
Pearson Early Learning
www.pearsonearlylearning.com
800-552-2259
	For infants/toddlers ages birth to 42 months
	Observational assessment tool that transforms developmental information into guidelines for intervention
	Focuses on observation of children's functional behaviors by both parents and service providers
	Measures children's performance measured within everyday routines and activities
	Three components include
	  Observation Record: For observing and documents behaviors
	  Family Album: For parents to record developmental observations
	  Developmental Profile: To evaluate developmental progress over time

Pathways to Competence for Young Children: A Parenting Program Landy, S., & Thompson, E. (2006) *Ordering information:* Paul H. Brookes Publishing Co. www.brookespublishing.com 800-638-3775	Ten-step program to teach parents how to foster children's social emotional development in nine key areas Demonstrates strategies on helping parents manage children's difficult behaviors Provides information on attachment, emotion regulation, and temperament Includes group discussions, lessons, activities and exercises, and role-play scenarios Looks at how a parent or caregiver's upbringing influences how they parent today Program is flexible for various group sizes and types Includes CD-ROM with more than 140 handouts
The New Portage Guides Birth to 3 years 3–6 years (2003) *Ordering information:* Portage Project www.portageproduct.org 800-862-3725	Curriculum component of comprehensive curriculum-based assessment Offers guidelines and tool for observing and planning activities Includes Activity and Routines Resource book with curriculum suggestions for each item Is functional and strength-based Provides suggestions for including parents in activities and assessment

Stop and Think Parent Program
Knoff, H. (2001)
Stop and Think for Teachers and Schools, Pre-K through First Grade
Knoff, H. (2001)
Ordering information:
Center for Improvement of Child Caring
www.ciccparenting.org
800-325-2422
	Teaches survival, interpersonal, problem-solving, and conflict resolution skills
	  Listening, following directions, waiting for your turn
	  How to interrupt, ask for help, apologize
	  How to deal with teasing, losing, rejection, fear, anger
	  How to accept a consequence, ignore distractions, ask to be included
	Includes
	  Teacher's Manual
	  Photocopiable forms with skill steps, lesson plans, teaching tools
	  Sets of cue cards for behavioral steps
	  Posters and "Stop and Think" stop sign
	  Book and DVD for parents for at-home activities

Guide to Selected Social Emotional Screening Instruments

Appendix C2. Guide to selected social emotional screening instruments meeting psychometric and utility standards.

Instrument name	Authors(s) and copyright year (if available)	Publisher/ordering information	Age range	Administration time	Number of items	Administrator	Psychometric Data Sensitivity 78% Specificity 95%	Meets standards[a] 1	2	3	4	5
Ages & Stages Questionnaires®: Social-Emotional (ASQ:SE)	Squires, J., Bricker, D., & Twombly, E. (2002)	Paul H. Brookes Publishing Co. 800-638-3775	6–60 months	10–15 minutes	Varies	Parent	Normative sample of 3,000. Test-retest validity data	✓	✓	✓	✓	✓
Behavioral Assessment of Baby's Emotional and Social Style (BABES)	Finello, K.M., & Poulsen, M.K. (1996)	California School of Professional Psychology-Los Angeles 818-284-2777	Birth–36 months	10 minutes	29	Parent	Limited; under development			✓	✓	✓
Brief Infant/Toddler Social Emotional Assessment (BITSEA)	Carter, A., & Briggs-Gowan, M. (2002)	Psychological Corporation 800-211-8378	12–36 months	10–15 minutes	43 Items taken from ITSEA-R. Areas: problem and competence including activity, anxiety, emotionality	Parent, child care provider	1,280 in normative sample; not geographically distributed (all subjects from Connecticut); internal consistency: Problem = .83–.89 Competence = .66–.75	✓	✓	✓	✓	✓
Conners' Rating Scale-Revised	Conners, C.K. (1997)	Multi-Health Systems, Inc. 800-456-3003	3–17 years	10 minutes	Parent Scale (long form): 80 Teacher Scale (short form): 59	Parent Teacher	Sample size = 8,000 multi-cultural	✓	✓	✓	✓	✓
Devereux Early Childhood Assessment Program (DECA)	Devereux Foundation (1998)	Kaplan Companies 800-334-2014	2–5 years	10 minutes	37	Administered and scored by highly trained individuals Uses parent report	Yes Inter-rater = .59–.77 Test-retest = .55–.94 2,000 normative sample sensitivity = .69	✓	✓	✓		✓

Instrument	Reference	Publisher/Contact	Age range	Time	Number of items	Administrator	Psychometrics	1	2	3	4	5
Early Screening Project (ESP)	Walker, H.M., Severson, H.H., & Feil, E. (1995)	Sopris West 303-651-2829	3–5 years	Stage 1: 1 hour Stage 2: 1 hour Stage 3: 40 minutes	Varies according to stages	Teacher Counselor Parent	Sensitivity = .80 Specificity = 94% Test-retest = .72 Inter-rater = .87	✓	✓		✓	✓
Eyberg Child Behavior Inventory (ECBI)	Eyberg, S. (1988)	Psychological Assessment Resources, Inc. 800-331-8378	2–16 years	10 minutes	36	Parent	Sensitivity = .80 Specificity = .86 Test-retest = .75–.86 Inter-rater = .79–.86	✓	✓		✓	✓
Functional Emotional Assessment Scale (FEAS)	DeGangi, G. & Greenspan, S. (2000)	Appendix B in DeGangi, G. (2000). *Pediatric Disorders of Regulation in Affect and Behavior*. Academic Press 301-320-6360	7 months–4 years	15–20 minutes	6 versions; 27–61 items	Professional	Yes Norms not naturally representative. Inter-rater reliability >.80				✓	
Infant-Toddler and Family Instrument (ITFI) & Manual	Provence, S. & Apfel, N.H. (2001)	Paul H. Brookes Publishing Co. 800-638-3775	6 months–3 years	Varies	35 in interview; 38 in concerns questionnaire	Professional with parent	No				✓	✓
Infant/Toddler Symptom Checklist	DeGangi, G., Poisson, S., Sickel, R., & Santman Wiener, A. (1999)	Therapy Skill Builders 800-872-1726	7–30 months	10 minutes	57	Parent	Limited Sensitivity = .78 Specificity = .84 Normative sample 94% white	✓			✓	✓
Parenting Stress Index (PSI), Third Edition-Short Form	Abidin, R.R. (1995)	American Guidance Service 800-328-2560	Birth–12 years	20–30 minutes	37	Parent	Yes Test-retest = .84 Small sample	✓	✓		✓	✓

[a]1 = Accuracy; 2 = Reliability; 3 = Utility; 4 = Low Cost; 5 = Parental Input/Cultural Sensitivity

(continued)

Appendix C2. *(continued)*

Instrument name	Authors(s) and copyright year (if available)	Publisher/ordering information	Age range	Administration time	Number of items	Administrator	Psychometric Data — Sensitivity 78% Specificity 95%	Meets standards[a] 1	2	3	4	5
Preschool and Kindergarten Behavior Scale (PKBS)	Merrell, K. (1994)	PRO-ED 800-897-3202	3–6 years	8–12 minutes	76	Parent and teacher	Yes Test-retest = .62–.87 Inter-rater = .36–.63	✓	✓	✓	✓	✓
Social Skills Rating System (SSRS)	Gresham, F.M., & Elliot, S.N. (1990)	American Guidance Service 800-328-2560	3–18 years	15–25 minutes	89	Parent and teacher	Yes Test-retest = .65–.93 4000 stratified norm sample	✓	✓	✓	✓	✓
Temperament and Atypical Behavior Scale (TABS) Screener	Bagnato, S.J., Neisworth, J.T., Salvia, J., & Hunt, F.M. (1999)	Paul H. Brookes Publishing Co. 800-638-3775	11–71 months	5 minutes	15	Parent Professional	Yes Validity r = .42–.64 .60 sensitivity	✓	✓	✓	✓	✓
Vineland Social-Emotional Early Childhood Scale (SEEC)	Sparrow, S. Ballas, D., & Cicchetti, D. (1998)	American Guidance Service 800-328-2560	Birth–5 years, 11 months	15–20 minutes	Varies	Professional	Yes, but based on 1984 data	✓	✓			✓

[a]1 = Accuracy; 2 = Reliability; 3 = Utility; 4 = Low Cost; 5 = Parental Input/Cultural Sensitivity

Functional Behavioral Assessment and Behavior Support Planning

For children with challenging problem behaviors who are not responding to initial activity-based intervention approaches, a more thorough assessment of their problem behavior and the context in which they are occurring may be helpful. Functional behavioral assessment (FBA) is a systematic process for developing hypotheses about factors that contribute to the occurrence and maintenance of problem behaviors. In addition, this approach assists in developing effective, function-based interventions and supports for decreasing problem behavior and increasing prosocial behaviors (O'Neill, Horner, Albin, Sprague, Storey, & Newston, 1997). This appendix outlines the processes and procedures for completing an FBA and planning for function-based behavioral support interventions. An FBA and a corresponding behavioral support plan (BSP) can be effective in targeting challenging problem behaviors such as noncompliance and defiance, disruption, inappropriate language, and minor aggressive behaviors. However, in the event that dangerous behaviors are occurring that may cause risk to the child for whom the intervention is targeted or other individuals, a behavior specialist should be consulted.

FEATURES OR GOALS

An FBA has three features or goals: 1) attending to environmental context and adult behavior, 2) determining the "purpose" or function of the behavior, and 3) teaching appropriate behaviors (Carr, et al., 2002; Koegel, Koegel, & Dunlap, 1996). Problem behavior often serves a function or purpose for the individual who exhibits it and therefore, it is important to examine the environments and context in which the behavior occurs. For example, when a child repeatedly engages in tantrums in the grocery store, the environmental context and his mother's behavior may need to be examined. The presence of candy bars in the checkout line, the disapproving looks given to his mother by other patrons, and his mother's tendency to acquiesce to the child's crying may serve to maintain this behavior. Completion of an FBA and corresponding BSP should assist

This appendix was developed with the assistance of Deborah Russell and Robert Horner, who created the Positive Behavioral Support materials specifically for this application.

the interventionist in identifying the eliciting factors and developing an intervention plan designed to eliminate the tantrums. The FBA/BSP process also addresses the importance of teaching appropriate replacement behaviors that a child can use instead of tantruming. Providing alternative behaviors, such as teaching the child to request the candy bar, should allow the child to obtain the desired object in a more socially acceptable manner.

STEPS OF THE FBA/BSP PROCESS

The FBA/BSP process is composed of five steps:

Step 1. Define the problem behavior.

Step 2. Develop a hypothesis statement identifying when the behavior is most likely to occur, what the behavior is, and what usually takes place after the behavior occurs.

Step 3: Identify the hypothesized purpose or function of the behavior

Step 4: Collect observational data to support the developed hypothesis

Step 5: Develop strategies for implementing function-based and contextually appropriate interventions.

The first three steps can be completed within the context of a functional assessment interview. A suggested interview format is contained in Figure AC.1: The Early Childhood Functional Assessment Interview (blank form). This form is divided into three sections (Parts A, B, and C) and should be completed through discussion with those who know the child well (e.g., teachers, parents) and who have had opportunities to observe the child engage in problem behaviors. It may also be beneficial to review personal and medical history information and academic records and other permanent products if the child has entered formal schooling.

Part A of the interview form addresses both child strengths and problem behaviors. Targeting the specific routines and activities when problem behaviors occur is the focus of Part B. The second page of the form provides space for recording specific information about the most disruptive or troubling of the child's problem behaviors. Part C is a summary section in which information can be recorded to support or refute the hypothesis. The next sections detail the five steps of the FBA/BSP process and the individual parts of each form.

Step 1. Define the Problem Behavior Using Objective, Observable Terms

The problem behavior should be defined using terms that are observable and measurable. Terms such as hyperactive and aggressive, for example, may seem descriptive but are not. "Aggressive" may mean a verbal assault to one observer, whereas to another observer, "aggressive" may mean hitting and kicking. A useful guideline for describing a problem behavior is to define it so that two independent observers can agree that the behavior (e.g., hitting) did or did not

Early Childhood Functional Assessment Interview (Blank Form)

Name: _____ Age: _____ Date: _____

Respondent(s): _____   _____

PART A

Child strengths (identify at least three strengths and contributions that the child brings to school and/or home):

_____

_____

Identify the problem behavior(s):

☐ Withdrawn   ☐ Physically aggressive   ☐ Disruptive   ☐ Steals

☐ Unresponsive   ☐ Verbally inappropriate   ☐ Does not do work   ☐ Tantrums

☐ Engages in self-injury ☐ Verbally harassing   ☐ Is noncompliant/Does not follow directions

☐ Other: _____

What does the problem behavior look like? _____

_____

What do you do now when problem behavior occurs? _____

_____

PART B

Daily routines and behavior analysis:

Activity/ routine	Type of problem behavior	How likely is problem behavior during this routine?	What strategies are you currently using?
		Low High 1 2 3 4 5 6	
		1 2 3 4 5 6	
		1 2 3 4 5 6	
		1 2 3 4 5 6	
		1 2 3 4 5 6	
		1 2 3 4 5 6	
		1 2 3 4 5 6	

(continued)

Figure AC.1.   Early Childhood Functional Assessment Interview (blank form). (Source: March et al. [2000]; adapted by permission.)

Figure AC.1. *(continued)*

Early Childhood Functional Assessment Interview Form (p. 2)

Problematic activity/routine #1: Choose the activity/routine that is the most problematic and complete the following section.

Activity/routine: _____

Behavior: _____

How often does problem behavior occur? _____

How long does it usually last when it does occur? _____

How concerned are you about this problem behavior?

	A little		Somewhat		Very	
1		2	3	4	5	6

What happens before the problem behavior (antecedents/triggers)?

☐ structured activity   ☐ unstructured time/transition   ☐ socially isolated

☐ with peers   ☐ reprimand/correction   ☐ physical demand

☐ difficult task   ☐ tasks too boring   ☐ activity too long

☐ other, describe _____

What happens after the problem behavior (response/consequence)?

☐ adult attention (including correction/reprimand)   ☐ peer attention

☐ preferred activity   ☐ gets money/things   ☐ escapes a hard task

☐ escapes an undesired activity ☐ escapes physical effort   ☐ escapes reprimand

☐ escapes adult attention   ☐ escapes peer negatives

☐ other, describe: _____

PART C

Summary

Antecedents/ triggers	Problem behavior	Response/ consequence	Maintaining function
			☐ Get peer attention ☐ Get adult attention ☐ Access preferred activity ☐ Access tangible ☐ Escape task item ☐ Escape peer attention ☐ Escape adult attention ☐ Sensory

How accurately does this summary describe your experience with this child?

Low					High
1	2	3	4	5	6

occur. For example, aggression may be more specifically defined as "hits other children with his fist." When defining problem behavior, it is helpful to consider various dimensions of the behavior, including the frequency, or how often it occurs; the duration, or how often it lasts; the intensity of the behavior; the latency of the behavior, or how long to onset after being triggered; and the function, or focus, of the problem behavior. Clarifying the description and definition of the problem behaviors will make observations and potential interventions more accurate and productive.

Step 2: Develop a Hypothesis Statement

Developing a hypothesis statement helps to clarify the context in which problem behavior is occurring and provides useful information for a BSP.

The first step in developing a hypothesis statement is to complete the problem behavior section of Part A of the Early Childhood Functional Assessment Interview form (see Figure AC.2 for an example for a case study involving Deirdre, a 4-year-old girl). This will assist the user in formulating a clear description for the hypothesis/summary statement.

Next, antecedent events that precede or trigger a problem behavior should be identified, using Part B of the interview form. Antecedents are events or other stimuli that occur before the problem behavior and signal or cause the problem behavior to occur. The daily routines and behavior analysis section of the interview form may be helpful in narrowing antecedent events and pinpointing times of the day or specific activities that elicit the problem behavior. For example, the teacher observes that Deirdre tends to kick and hit the teacher during the Free Choice activity. Also, when the teacher asks Deidre to put away her toys, Deidre kicks and hits the teacher. Asking her to clean up appears to be an antecedent or trigger that elicits the hitting and kicking behaviors. Identifying these events (i.e., antecedents) may provide insight about why the problem behavior is occurring and may help to identify strategies for removing triggering events and, therefore, decrease the likelihood of problem behavior occurring.

Once the problem behavior and antecedent event boxes of the hypothesis statement are completed, it is important to identify the response or consequence that usually follows the problem behavior. Consequences are events that follow the problem behavior and serve to maintain, increase, or decrease the likelihood of the behavior reoccurring. For example, when Deidre hits her teacher, she receives attention. In this case, the response or consequence is the teacher's attention. Understanding the response to problem behavior usually helps in understanding why problem behavior continues to occur and how to decrease these occurrences.

Step 3: Identify the Purpose
or Function of the Behavior

Part C on the Functional Assessment Interview form includes formulating a hypothesis statement of the problem behavior that identifies the function the

Early Childhood Functional Assessment Interview (Sample: Deidre)

Name: _____ Deidre _____ Age: __4__ Date: __9/30/2005__

Respondent(s): ___ Jane Smith, Teacher ___   Lisa Jones, Assistant

PART A

Child strengths (identify at least three strengths and contributions that the child brings to school and/or home):

Deidre likes to help the teachers in class (setting up lunch, cleaning up the room), she is aware

of the classroom routines/schedules, and is advanced in terms of knowing her letters.

Identify the problem behavior(s):

☐ Withdrawn   ☒ Physically aggressive   ☐ Disruptive   ☐ Steals

☐ Unresponsive   ☐ Verbally inappropriate   ☐ Does not do work   ☐ Tantrums

☐ Engages in self-injury   ☐ Verbally harassing   ☐ Is noncompliant/Does not follow directions

☐ Other: _____

What does the problem behavior look like? ___ Deidre kicks and hits teachers. ___

What do you do now when problem behavior occurs? _Teacher takes Deidre out of classroom into hall._

PART B

Daily routines and behavior analysis:

Activity/ routine	Type of problem behavior	How likely is problem behavior during this routine?	What strategies are you currently using?
Arrival	None	Low 　　　　 High ①　2　3　4　5　6	N/A
Circle Time	Pushing to get desired carpet square	1　2　3　4　⑤　6	Have her go back and come to circle again
Free Choice	Kicks, hits teacher	1　2　3　4　5　⑥	Separate Deidre
Lunch	None	①　2　3　4　5　6	N/A
Recess	Sticks with one activity	①　2　3　4　5　6	Encourage her to join in other activities
Circle Time	Pushing to get desired carpet square	1　2　3　4　⑤　6	Have her go back and come to circle again
Dismissal	None	①　2　3　4　5　6	N/A

Figure AC.2.   Early Childhood Functional Assessment Interview (Sample: Deirdre). (Source: March et al. [2000]; adapted by permission. © 2005 Deborah L. Russell & Robert H. Horner.)

Early Childhood Functional Assessment Interview Form (p. 2)

Problematic activity/routine #1: Choose the activity/routine that is the most problematic and complete the following section.

Activity/routine: _Free Choice_

Behavior: _Kicks and hits teachers_

How often does problem behavior occur? _1 time per Free Choice, almost daily_

How long does it usually last when it does occur? _Very brief, 1–3 seconds_

How concerned are you about this problem behavior?

A little		Somewhat		Very	
1	2	3	4	5	⑥

What happens before the problem behavior (antecedents/triggers)?

☐ structured activity   ☐ unstructured time/transition   ☐ socially isolated

☐ with peers   ☒ reprimand/correction   ☒ physical demand

☐ difficult task   ☐ tasks too boring   ☐ activity too long

☒ other, describe _Teacher asks Deidre to clean up toys_

What happens after the problem behavior (response/consequence)?

☒ adult attention (including correction/reprimand)   ☐ peer attention

☒ preferred activity   ☐ gets money/things   ☐ escapes a hard task

☒ escapes an undesired activity   ☐ escapes physical effort   ☐ escapes reprimand

☐ escapes adult attention   ☐ escapes peer negatives

☐ other, describe: _____

PART C

Summary

Antecedents/ triggers	Problem behavior	Response/ consequence	Maintaining function
During free choice time with peers, when teacher asks to clean up	Deidre hits/kicks teacher for 1–3 seconds, sometimes leaving marks but never breaking the skin	Teacher takes Deidre out of the room	☐ Get peer attention ☒ Get adult attention ☐ Access preferred activity ☐ Access tangible ☐ Escape task item ☐ Escape peer attention ☐ Escape adult attention ☐ Sensory

How accurately does this summary describe your experience with this child?

Low					High
1	2	3	4	5	⑥

problem behavior serves for the child. Challenging behaviors can serve several functions for children, including getting or escaping from attention, getting desired items, being able to do tasks, and sensory stimulation (O'Neill et al., 1997). These potential functions for problem behavior are listed in the final box in Part C of the interview form. In the case study for Deirdre, the response to or consequence of her hitting and kicking behavior was teacher attention. Under Part C of the interview form, the maintaining function of Deirdre's problem behavior falls into the category of "Get adult attention."

It is important to check only one box in Part C because interventions are defined by this statement. In choosing only one box, determine the function that is most likely or seems to be occurring the majority of the time. Keep in mind that for different children, the same problem behavior may be maintained by different consequences and functions. For example, another student in Deidre's preschool also engages in kicking and hitting behaviors when a peer tries to take a preferred toy from him. Typically, the peer gives the toy back after the child's aggressive response to having his toy taken away. For this child, the function of his hitting and kicking is getting to play with the preferred toy. This distinction between the kicking and hitting behaviors of Deidre and her peer provides important information for developing a BSP.

Step 4: Collect Observation Data to Support the Developed Hypothesis

Once a hypothesis statement about the child's behavior has been developed and noted in Part C of the Early Childhood Functional Assessment Interview, the child should be observed to verify the hypothesis. It is important to review the definition developed for the problem behavior contained in Part A of the interview form. What does the behavior look like? How often does the behavior occur and how long does it last? What is the focus or function of the behavior? Most important, what is the biggest concern? If a student is refusing to follow directions, the concern might be how frequently this child is refusing to do so, or if the problem is persisting over time. If, however, the student is refusing to follow directions that are meant to keep the student safe (e.g., stopping at a crosswalk), the concern might be focused on the type of directions not followed. Observations and data collection should be tailored to provide information about the behavior of concern. In the first instance, information can be collected on the number of times the student fails to follow directions. In the second instance, information about the type of direction given or by whom can be gathered. Collecting observational data in a consistent way allows for monitoring the student's progress over time. If a student is following only one out of every four directions given prior to intervention, and afterward she is following three out of every four directions, it can be seen that the behavior has improved.

The final question on the Early Childhood Functional Assessment Interview form asks the interviewee how accurately the hypothesis statement describes his or her experiences with the child. If the interviewee(s) rates the summary statement with a 5 or a 6 (i.e., high accuracy), it may not be necessary to collect additional observational information about the student's behavior in order to develop a BSP. Collecting observational information, however, can still provide useful information for making comparisons between behavior patterns before and after intervention. If the interviewee(s) rates the summary statement low in terms of accuracy (i.e., 1 or 2), observing the student's behavior patterns may provide clarification as to when and why problem behavior is occurring.

Step 5: Develop Strategies for Implementing Function-Based and Contextually Appropriate Interventions (BSP)

This final step involves identifying alternate, desirable behaviors that can replace the problem behaviors. A hypothesis or summary statement that accurately describes the child's problem behavior patterns should have been developed, and if needed, observation data collected to confirm that summary during Step 4. Information related to the description of problem behavior, identification of events that reliably predict problem behavior, and identification of the maintaining consequences or "function" of the problem behavior can be used to develop BSP. A blank Competing Behavior Pathway: Behavior Support Planning (BSP) form contained in Figure AC.3 has been included in this appendix to aid in this process, and is followed by an example for Deirdre (see Figure AC.4). First, the problem behaviors and antecedents and consequences identified in Steps one through three should be written in the corresponding boxes on the Competing Behavior Pathway: BSP form.

According to O'Neill and colleagues, "A fundamental rule of behavior support is that you should not propose to reduce a problem behavior without also identifying the alternative, desired behaviors the person should perform instead of the problem behavior" (1997, p. 71). In the development of a BSP, the desired behaviors that you would like the child to display are identified first. For example, if a student, Jenny, grabs toys from her peers, the desired behavior might be to ask to play with her peers, instead. This desired behavior would be written in the corresponding box on the top of the Competing Behavior Pathway: BSP form. The consequence that would take place following this desired behavior would go in the corresponding consequence box. In this case, the consequence might be making friends and playing cooperatively.

Having identified the desired behavior for Jenny, it is important to recognize that moving from grabbing and snatching behaviors to the desired sharing behaviors may not be a one-step process for Jenny. Identifying an acceptable alternative behavior can be viewed as one initial step toward the desired behavior. As noted, when identifying an alternative acceptable behavior, it is important to take into consideration the consequence or function that has been maintaining the child's behavior. In Jenny's case, getting access to a preferred toy appeared to be encouraging her to take toys from her peers. In order to eliminate toy taking, an alternative behavior that also provides her access to the

Early Childhood Competing Behavior Pathway:
Behavior Support Planning (Blank Form)

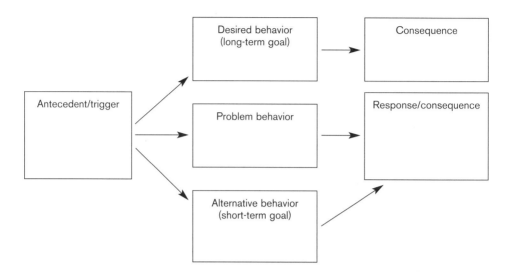

Antecedent strategies (prevention strategies)	Behavior teaching strategies (teaching new skills)	Consequence strategies (new adult responses)
Strategies to prevent antecedents/ triggers from occurring:	Strategies for teaching new skill #1 (replacement behavior):	Adult response to appropriate behavior (reward—access to desired consequence):
Strategies to alter antecedents to decrease the triggering effects:	Strategy for teaching new skill #2:	Adult response to problem behavior (minimize access to desired consequence):
Strategies to minimize effects of antecedents/triggers if they do occur:	Strategy for teaching new skill #3:	
		Punishment strategy (if needed):
		Safety procedures (if needed):

Figure AC.3. Early Childhood Competing Behavior Pathway: Behavior Support Planning (blank form). (Source: Crone & Horner [2003]; adapted by permission.)

Early Childhood Competing Behavior Pathway:
Behavior Support Planning (Sample: Deirdre)

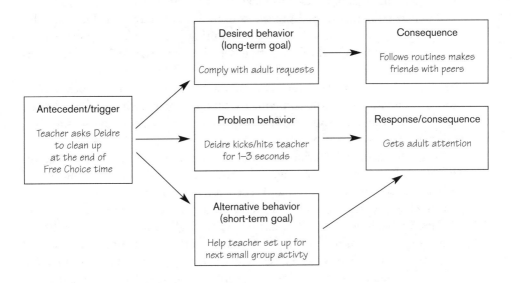

Antecedent strategies (prevention strategies)	Behavior teaching strategies (teaching new skills)	Consequence strategies (new adult responses)
Strategies to prevent antecedents/triggers from occurring: Teacher asks Deidre to help her set up next group activity before cleanup time. Strategies to alter antecedents to decrease the triggering effects: Have teacher help Deidre clean up and transition. Strategies to minimize effects of antecedents/triggers if they do occur: Teacher physically assists Deidre to clean up and transition.	Strategies for teaching new skill #1 (replacement behavior): Clean up, transition to next activity and help set up. Practice during clean up. Strategy for teaching new skill #2: Teach Deidre to ask teacher if she can be helper after she's cleaned up. Strategy for teaching new skill #3: Teach Deidre to clean up fast and be first in activity corner.	Adult response to appropriate behavior (reward—access to desired consequence): When Deidre engages in appropriate behavior, allow her to be teacher helper. Adult response to problem behavior (minimize access to desired consequence): When Deidre hits/kicks, tell her "no hitting" and physically prompt her to clean up and transition. Punishment strategy (if needed): Isolate in corner of room. Safety procedures (if needed): Standard safety procedures will apply.

Figure AC.4.   Early Childhood Competing Behavior Pathway: Behavior Support Planning (Sample: Deirdre). (Source: Crone & Horner [2003]; adapted by permission. © 2005 Deborah L. Russell & Robert H. Horner.)

preferred toy must be identified. For Jenny, an acceptable alternative behavior might be for her to offer the other child a different toy and trade for the toy that she wants. It is important to make this alternative behavior easy for Jenny and to make sure that it results in access to the preferred toy or activity. Initially, a staff person may need to be near Jenny during Free Choice time to facilitate the trading of toys. On the Competing Behavior Pathway: BSP form, the alternative behavior box is connected to the same consequence box as the problem behavior. Remember, it is important that the acceptable alternative behavior allows the child to access the consequence that was maintaining problem behaviors, so that more appropriate alternative behaviors result in getting the child what he or she wants, if possible.

The Competing Behavior Pathway: BSP form contains three columns for listing antecedent, behavior teaching, and consequences strategies. The "Antecedent/ Strategies" column focuses on antecedent events that predict and/or are triggered when problem behaviors occur. Strategies in this column focus on making the problem behavior irrelevant by preventing it from occurring, either by removing or decreasing the triggering antecedents or mediating their effects if they do occur. In Jenny's case, her problem behaviors may become irrelevant when more than one of each toy is available during Free Choice time. By preventing peers from having to fight over a desired toy, Jenny's grabbing behaviors will become irrelevant.

The second column, "Behavior teaching strategies," focuses on making the problem behavior inefficient by giving the child more appropriate behaviors that provide easier and quicker access to the desired consequence (e.g., obtaining the desired toy or activity). This column includes spaces to list new skills that will be taught. In some cases, there may be several precursor skills that need to be taught before the alternative behavior is addressed. In other cases, only one skill may be needed in the process of introducing the alternative behavior, and other skills will be needed for the transition from the alternative behavior to the desired behavior. In Jenny's case, she will need to be taught how to ask a peer to play. Other skills include teaching Jenny to ask the teacher for a desired toy rather than grabbing from peers. In either case, it is important to note that the child's behavior will have to be monitored and that the process of teaching the child the desired behavior is just that—a process. Several steps may be involved to move the child from engaging in problem behaviors to engaging in desired behaviors, with close monitoring of child behaviors throughout the process.

The final column on the Competing Behavior Pathway: BSP form, "Consequence strategies," focuses on strategies to make the problem behavior ineffective by developing adult-focused interventions. These interventions are designed to increase appropriate behaviors and appropriate consequences and decrease inappropriate behaviors. In Jenny's case, a reward for appropriate behavior might consist of extra time to play with the desired object when she plays with peers. A consequence for problem behavior might be to remove the desired toy when Jenny grabs it from her peers. In this column, it is important that the rewards for appropriate behaviors provide access to the consequence that was previously maintaining the problem behaviors. In addition, the consequences for problem behaviors must also remove access to the previous desired consequence. Examples for using the Early Childhood Functional Assessment Interview and Competing Behavior Pathway: Behavior Support Planning forms are included as Figures AC.5 and AC.6 at the end of this appendix for another child, Robby, who was described earlier in Chapter 8.

The Importance of Context

In the development of behavior support interventions, it is important to consider the context in which the behavior is occurring, not only to better understand the variables affecting the problem behavior but also to understand the variables that will affect implementation of the developed interventions. The goal in designing behavioral interventions is always to implement the least intensive interventions that will be effective. In other words, using the least amount of time, resources, and support for the desired effect is optimal. It is not always necessary to implement the most intensive strategy. The intensity level of the intervention should also match the values, skills, and resources of the interventionists and parents who will be implementing the plan. Intervention plans may not be successfully implemented if they are inconsistent with the views and beliefs of the interventionists and families.

This appendix was designed to help develop hypothesis statements and function-based interventions to eliminating problem behaviors. A brief introduction to the process and procedures that may help to develop comprehensive, function-based supports for young children exhibiting challenging behaviors was provided. Examples were offered to illustrate the process with some sample children. Equally important to developing an effective plan that is consistent with the values and beliefs of the teachers and families is monitoring the progress of that plan and the child's behavior. Teaching a child to use a desired behavior rather than to engage in problem behavior is not a one-step fix, but rather a process of teaching and reinforcing new, appropriate behaviors, removing reinforcement for inappropriate behaviors, and monitoring progress during the process.

REFERENCES

Carr, E.G., Dunlap, G., Horner, R.H., Koegel, R.L., Turnbull, A.P., Sailor, W., et al. (2002). Positive behavior support: Evolution of an applied science. *Journal of Positive Behavior Interventions, 4,* 4–16.

Crone, D.A., & Horner, R.H. (2003). *Building positive behavior support systems in schools: Functional behavioral assessment.* New York: Guilford Press.

Koegel, R.L., Koegel, & Dunlap, G. (Eds.) (1996). *Positive Behavioral Support: Including people with difficult behavior in the community.* Baltimore: Paul H. Brookes Publishing Co.

March, R., Horner, R.H., Lewis-Palmer, T., Brown, D., Crone, D., Todd, A.W., & Carr, E. (2000). Functional Assessment Checklist for Teacher and Staff (FACTS). Eugene: Department of Educational and Community Supports, University of Oregon.

O'Neill, R.E., Horner, R.H., Albin, R., Sprague, K., Storey, K., & Newston, J.S. (1997). *Functional behavioral assessment and program development for problem behaviors.* Belmont, CA: Wadsworth Publishing.

Early Childhood Functional Assessment Interview (Sample: Robby[a])

Name: _____Robby_____ Age: __2½__ Date: ___9/30/2005___

Respondent(s): ___Jim Monroe, Father___ _____

PART A

Child strengths (identify at least three strengths and contributions that the child brings to school and/or home):

Robby is very inquisitive and interested in things around him. He is affectionate toward me

(his father), and uses a lot of language for a child his age.

Identify the problem behavior(s):

☐ Withdrawn   ☐ Physically aggressive   ☐ Disruptive   ☐ Steals

☐ Unresponsive   ☐ Verbally inappropriate   ☐ Does not do work   ☒ Tantrums

☐ Engages in self-injury   ☐ Verbally harassing   ☐ Is noncompliant/Does not follow directions

☐ Other: _____

What does the problem behavior look like? ___Robby gets frustrated and upset and cries/whines.___

What do you do now when problem behavior occurs? _Go and comfort him._

PART B

Daily routines and behavior analysis:

Activity/ routine	Type of problem behavior	How likely is problem behavior during this routine?		What strategies are you currently using?
		Low	High	
Mealtime	None	① 2 3	4 5 6	N/A
Getting dressed	Gets frustrated without a lot of help	1 2 3	4 5 ⑥	Provide assistance as needed
Independent play time	Cries/whines/tantrums	1 2 3	4 5 ⑥	Comfort him
Independent play time	None	① 2 3	4 5 6	N/A
Bath time	None	1 ② 3	4 5 6	N/A
Bedtime	Sometimes cries a little before sleeping	1 2 3	4 5 ⑥	Read him another story/comfort him
Community visits	None	1 ② 3	4 5 6	N/A

[a] Presented in Chapter 8

Figure AC.5. Early Childhood Functional Assessment Interview (Sample: Robby) (Source: March et al. [2000]; adapted by permission. © 2005 Deborah L. Russell & Robert H. Horner.)

Early Childhood Functional Assessment Interview Form (p. 2)

Problematic activity/routine #1: Choose the activity/routine that is the most problematic and complete the following section.

Activity/routine: ___Independent play time___

Behavior: ___Cries and whines/tantrums___

How often does problem behavior occur? ___Always after being alone more than a few min.___

How long does it usually last when it does occur? ___1–5 minutes or until comforted___

How concerned are you about this problem behavior?

A little		Somewhat		Very	
1	2	3	4	5	(6)

What happens before the problem behavior (antecedents/triggers)?

☐ structured activity   ☐ unstructured time/transition   ☒ socially isolated

☐ with peers   ☐ reprimand/correction   ☐ physical demand

☐ difficult task   ☐ tasks too boring   ☐ activity too long

☐ other, describe _____

What happens after the problem behavior (response/consequence)?

☒ adult attention (including correction/reprimand)   ☐ peer attention

☐ preferred activity   ☐ gets money/things   ☐ escapes a hard task

☐ escapes an undesired activity   ☐ escapes physical effort   ☐ escapes reprimand

☐ escapes adult attention   ☐ escapes peer negatives

☐ other, describe: _____

PART C

Summary

Antecedents/ triggers	Problem behavior	Response/ consequence	Maintaining function
When left alone to play independently for more than a few minutes	Robby cries and whines and gets frustrated (stops playing, stomps feet, and so forth)	Dad comforts Robby until he stops crying and then plays along with him	☐ Get peer attention ☒ Get adult attention ☐ Access preferred activity ☐ Access tangible ☐ Escape task item ☐ Escape peer attention ☐ Escape adult attention ☐ Sensory

How accurately does this summary describe your experience with this child?

Low					High
1	2	3	4	5	(6)

Early Childhood Competing Behavior Pathway:
Behavior Support Planning (Sample: Robby[a])

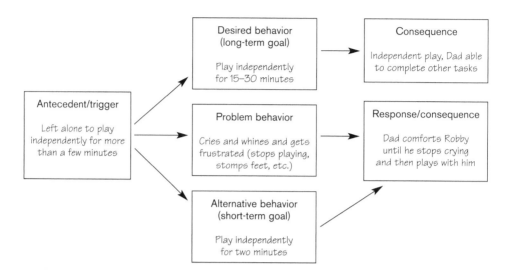

Antecedent strategies (prevention strategies)	Behavior teaching strategies (teaching new skills)	Consequence strategies (new adult responses)
Strategies to prevent antecedents/triggers from occurring: Leave Robby alone only for up to 2 minutes at a time initially (set a timer to signal to go and check on him). Strategies to alter antecedents to decrease the triggering effects: Have Dad work nearby rather than leaving the room. Strategies to minimize effects of antecedents/triggers if they do occur: Have another adult available to play with Robby, leave something of Dad's in the room with Robby, or set timer so that Robby learns when buzzer goes off that Dad will be back.	Strategies for teaching new skill #1 (replacement behavior): Teach Robby to play independently for two minutes. Initially, engage Robby in an activity, leave the room for only two minutes and then come back. Slowly fade time to longer and longer durations. Strategy for teaching new skill #2: Teach Robby to come and ask for help/ask to play with Dad. Strategy for teaching new skill #3: Consider leaving a timer with Robby so that he can learn that when the buzzer goes off, Dad will be back	Adult response to appropriate behavior (reward—access to desired consequence): When Robby has played independently for 2 minutes (longer as fading occurs) go and engage with him and give him attention. Adult response to problem behavior (minimize access to desired consequence): When Robby becomes upset, do not go and comfort him/give him attention until he stops crying/whining. Punishment strategy (if needed): Timeout—remove Robby from access to attention. Safety procedures (if needed): N/A

Figure AC.6.   Early Childhood Competing Behavior Pathway: Behavior Support Planning (Sample: Robby) (Source: Crone & Horner [2003]; adapted by permission. © 2005 Deborah L. Russell & Robert H. Horner.)

Index

Page numbers followed by "*f*" indicate figures; those followed by "*t*" indicate tables.

ABI:SE, *see* Activity-Based Intervention: Social
  Emotional Approach
Abuse, *see* Child abuse
Activities
  appropriateness of, 48*t*, 50–51
  child-directed, routine, and planned activities,
    102, 103*t*
  embedding opportunities, 99–100, 106–107
  modeling, 105, 109, 111–112
  selecting, 106, 112–113
  sponge toss activity plan, 110*f*–111*f*
  see also Intervention
Activity levels, regulation of
  case examples, 105, 114–116, 127
  as child benchmark, 48*t*, 49–50
  intervention activities, 103*t*, 107, 108*f*, 113, 122
Activity Matrix, 107, 108*f*, 109 109*f*, 112
Activity Plans, 109, 110*f*–111*f*
Activity-Based Intervention, *see* Intervention
Activity-Based Intervention: Social Emotional
    Approach (ABI:SE)
  adult/caregiver benchmarks, 48*t*, 50–51, 78*t*,
    79*t*, 80*t*–81*t*
  case example, 53–54
  child benchmarks, 47–50, 48*t*, 77*t*–79*t*, 80*t*
  empirical support for, 131–132
  historical perspective, 132–134
  linked system framework, 42–45, 43*f*, 51–54, 52*f*
  overview, 7–8, 10, 41–42
  target populations, 8, 10, 14–18, 45–47
  underlying principles, 27–29, 27*t*, 28*f*
  who should use, 7, 8, 41–42, 131
  see also specific processes
Adaptive skills
  case examples, 102
  as child benchmark, 48*t*, 50
  intervention activities, 107
Adolescents, mental health disorders and, 22
Adult benchmarks, *see* Caregivers

Ages & Stages Questionnaires®: Social Emotional
    (ASQ:SE), 21, 138
Aggression
  case examples, 67–68
  in preschool-age children, prevalence, 13, 14
  professional referrals for, 46
American Academy of Pediatrics, 137
ASQ:SE, *see* Ages & Stages Questionnaires®:
    Social Emotional
Assessment
  age considerations, 75, 76–77
  benchmarks, 51, 77*t*–81*t*
  case examples, 73–74, 84, 85*f*, 86*f*, 87
  need for development of materials, 137
  overview, 43*f*, 44, 51, 72–74
  process and steps, 52*f*, 74–76, 74*f*
  purpose, 71, 72
  review and evaluation of, 118
  target groups, 46
  see also Evaluation, child/caregiver; Functional
    behavioral assessment
Attention
  case examples, 111–112, 114–116, 126, 127
  as child benchmark, 48*t*, 49–50
  intervention activities, 99–100, 105, 113
Autism, children with, 46, 133
Autonomy, *see* Independence

Behavior problems
  case examples, 114–116
  children from low-income families, 14–15
  functional behavioral assessment, 113–116
  historical perspective, 133–134
  under Individuals with Disabilities Education
    Act (IDEA), 22
Benchmarks
  adult/caregiver, 48*t*, 50–51, 78*t*, 79*t*, 80*t*–81*t*
  age considerations, 75, 76–77
  child, 47–50, 48*t*, 77*t*–79*t*, 80*t*

271

Benchmarks—*continued*
   content focus, 48*t*, 81–82, 84
   ·*see also* Social Emotional
      Assessment/Evaluation Measure
Biological risks for children, 3, 4
BITSEA, *see* Brief Infant–Toddler Social and
     Emotional Assessment
Brain imaging research, 56–57
Brief Infant–Toddler Social and Emotional
     Assessment (BITSEA), 21, 61

Caregivers
   assessment, participation in, 75–76
   benchmarks and assessment items, 48*t*, 50–51,
     78*t*, 79*t*, 80*t*–81*t*
   evaluation process, participation in, 120, 124
   goal development, participation in, 97
   home environment screening and, 62
   modeling activities for, 105, 109, 111–112
   screening, participation in, 56, 57, 60–61
Case studies, as evidence of program
     effectiveness, 129
Census data, *see* United States Census data
Challenging behaviors, *see* Behavior problems
Child abuse
   children in foster care, 16
   children with disabilities, 18
Child-directed activities, 102, 103*t*
Children
   benchmarks, 47–50, 48*t*, 77*t*–79*t*, 80*t*
   biological and environmental risks, 3–5
   child strengths, examples, 94*f*, 95*f*
   with disabilities, 16–18
   foster care, 15–16, 18
   mental health problems, prevalence, 12–13
   poverty and, 14–15
   quality of care, 3–4, 11–12
Children's Defense Fund report, 11
Classrooms
   Classroom Data Collection and Evaluation
     Form, 124*f*
   environmental screening, 62–63
Cognitive skills, need for improvement in, 4
Communication skills, *see* Language skills
Community services, 19–20, 19*f*, 137
Concurrent validity, 59
Context, effect on screening outcomes, 57
Cooperation skills, 102, 121–122
Costs
   of lack of early identification and intervention,
     136
   of screening measures, 60
Council for Exceptional Children, 129
Crying behavior, 114–116
Cultural sensitivity, 56, 57, 61
Curriculum-based assessment, 71
   see also Assessment; Social Emotional
     Assessment/Evaluation Measure (SEAM)

Daily activities, 102, 103*t*
Data collection
   Classroom Data Collection and Evaluation
     Form, 124*f*
   methods of, 120–123, 121*f*
   planning, 123–125
   summary and review, 126–129, 127*t*, 129*t*
   see also Evaluation, child/caregiver; Program
     evaluation
Demands, *see* Requests, compliance with
Department of Health and Human Services, *see*
     United States Department of Health and
     Human Services
Depression, maternal, 15, 56
Development
   brain imaging and, 56–57
   screening challenges and, 57–59
   theories of, 25–29
Developmental psychopathology, *see* Mental
     health disorders
*Diagnostic and Statistical Manual of Mental
     Disorders–Fourth Edition,* 13
Difficult Life Circumstances (DLC) assessment, 62
Direct test probe procedures, 121–122
Directions, ability to follow, 48*t*, 50
Disabilities, children with
   eligibility for services, 45, 46
   historical perspective, 132–134
   mental health and, 10, 16–18, 45, 135–136
   screening process, 65*f*
Division for Early Childhood of the Council for
     Exceptional Children, 129
DLC, *see* Difficult Life Circumstances (DLC)
     assessment

Early Childhood Environment Rating
     Scale–Revised (ECERS-R), 62–63
Early childhood mental health, *see* Mental health
     disorders
Early Childhood Screener, 21
Early childhood special education programs, 6–7,
     133–134
Early Head Start, 134
Early identification
   barriers to, 20–22
   importance of, 18–19, 22–23, 56, 136
   pyramid of service options, 19–20, 19*f*, 137
   see also Screening
Early intervention programs
   historical perspective, 59, 133–134
   lack of resources, 6–7
ECERS-R, *see* Early Childhood Environment
     Rating Scale–Revised
Embedding intervention opportunities
   Embedding Plans, 106–107, 107*f*, 108*f*
   empirical support for, 131–132
   examples, 99–100
   modeling of, 105, 109, 111–112

Emotion regulation
as child benchmark, 48t, 49
definitions, 33–34
examples, 34–35, 35t
intervention activities, 104t
Emotional competence, 32
Emotions
brain imaging research, 56
case examples, 73–74, 125–126
child benchmarks, 48–49, 48t
definitions, 9, 10, 30–31
developmental considerations, 31–32
intervention activities, 100, 104t, 112–113
Empathy
as child benchmark, 48t, 49
intervention activities, 103t
Engagement
case examples, 111–112, 122
as child benchmark, 48t, 49
intervention activities, 99–100, 104t
see also Attention
Environmental context
assessment of, 72
brain imaging research and, 56–57
case examples, 68, 89–90, 97, 126
emotional responses and, 31–32
risk factors, 3–5
safety, 48t, 50
as underlying principle of development,
27–29, 27t, 28f
Environmental screening, 62–64
Environmental Screening Questionnaire (ESQ):
Experimental Edition, 63–64
see also Appendix A
Evaluation, child/caregiver
case examples, 122, 125–126, 127
Classroom Data Collection and Evaluation
Form, 124f
data collection methods, 120–123, 121f
data collection plans, 123–126
frequency of, 124
overview, 43f, 45, 52, 52f, 117–118
Progress Monitoring Form, 121f
Progress Summary Form, 129f
selecting goals to monitor, 119–120
summary and review of data, 126–129, 127t,
129t
see also Assessment; Program evaluation

FBA, see Functional behavioral assessment
see also Appendix C
Fear reactions, 29, 31
Federal policy
focus on children, 4
need for change, 138
Feedback and consequences, 103–104, 104t
Forms
Activity Matrix, 107, 108f, 109 109f, 112

Activity Plans, 109, 110f–111f
Data Collection and Evaluation Form, 124f
Embedding Plans, 106–107, 107f, 108f
Goal Development and Intervention Plan,
90–91, 91f, 93–95, 94f, 95f
Progress Monitoring Form, 121f
Progress Summary Form, 129f
Summary Form: Infant Interval, 86f
Foster care, children in, 15–16, 18
Frequency data, collecting, 120–122, 121f
Functional behavioral assessment (FBA), 113–116

Goal development
case examples, 73–74, 89–90, 92, 93–95, 97, 98
evaluation of, 118
functional and generative goals, 101
overview, 43f, 44–45, 51, 52f
steps, 52f, 90–93, 90f
types of goals, 72
Goal Development and Intervention Plan
blank form, 91f
completing with caregivers, 90–91, 93–95
examples, 94f, 95f
Goodness of fit principle, 27, 27t, 28f, 29
Government policy, see Federal policy
Graduation rates, and children with severe
emotional disturbances, 13
Group Activity Matrix, 107, 108f, 109 109f, 112

Head Start
children with social emotional problems in,
14–15
historical perspective, 134
screening mandate, 59
Health and Human Services, see United States
Department of Health and Human
Services
Health insurance, 11
Healthy interactions, see Interactions and
relationships
Healthy Start, 134
Home Observation for Measure of the
Environment (HOME), 62
HOME Screening Questionnaire (HSQ), 62
Homes
environmental screening measures, 62–64
safety of, 48t, 50
House of Representatives, see United States
House of Representatives
HSQ, see HOME Screening Questionnaire

IDEA, see Individuals with Disabilities Education
Act
Identification, see Early identification; Screening
Independence
as child benchmark, 48t, 49
children with disabilities, 17
intervention activities, 108f, 113

Individuals with Disabilities Education Act
    (IDEA) Amendments of 1991 (PL 102-
    119), 13, 22
Individuals with Disabilities Education Act
    (IDEA) Amendments of 1997 (PL 105-
    17), 59
Infant Toddler Environment Rating
    Scale–Revised (ITERS-R), 62–63
Infants
    age interval, 76
    benchmarks and assessment items, 77*t*–78*t*
    with disabilities, 17
    reach-and-grasp response, 26
    smiling response, 26–27
Institutionalization of children, 132–133
Interactions and relationships
    case examples, 73–74, 98, 101, 104–105,
        111–112
    child benchmarks, 48, 48*t*
    intervention activities, 102, 103*t*, 113
Intervention
    Activity Matrix, 107, 108*f*, 109 109*f*, 112
    Activity Plans, 109, 110*f*–111*f*
    case examples, 101, 103, 104–105, 105*t*, 109,
        111–112
    child-directed, routine, and planned activities,
        102, 103*t*
    components of, 101–104
    embedding opportunities, 99–100, 106–107,
        109, 111–112
    Embedding Plans, 106–107, 107*f*, 108*f*
    evaluation of, 118
    feedback and consequences, 103–104, 104*t*
    functional behavioral assessment (FBA),
        113–116
    historical perspective, 132–134
    multiple and varied opportunities, provision
        of, 103, 112–113
    need for development of materials, 137
    overview, 43*f* 116, 45, 52, 52*f*
    referral for, 64, 65*f*, 68–69
    steps, 52*f*, 106–107, 106*f*, 109, 111–113
    types of, 19*f*, 20
    see also Goal Development and Intervention
        Plan; *specific goals*
Intervention teams
    goal selection, 92
    progress meetings, 127
ITERS-R, *see* Infant Toddler Environment
    Rating Scale–Revised

Kindergarten, preparation for, 123

Language skills
    children with disabilities, 17
    need for improvement in, 4
Low birth weight, 11
Low income and families, *see* Poverty

Magnetic Resonance Imaging (MRI), *see* Brain
    imaging research
Maltreatment, *see* Child abuse
Maternal health disorders, *see* Mothers
*Meaningful Differences in the Everyday Experience
    of Young American Children* (Hart and
    Risley), 14
Mental health disorders
    awareness of, 6, 58–59, 135–136
    definitions, 8–9
    early identification, 18–22, 19*f*
    groups at risk, 10, 14–18, 45–47, 135
    historical perspective, 132–134
    maternal depression, 15, 56
    need for intervention, 4–5, 9–10, 12, 21–22, 23
    prevalence, 12–13, 18, 22
    recommended initiatives, 9
    risk factors, 11–12
Milestones, *see* Benchmarks
Modeling intervention activities, 105, 109,
    111–112
Monitoring progress
    as component of evaluation, 117
    rescreening, 64, 65*f*, 67–68
    see also Evaluation, child/caregiver
Morbidity, mental health disorders and, 11
Mortality, mental health disorders and, 11–12
Mothers
    maternal depression, 15, 56
    parent–child interactions, 5, 17
    social emotional responses, 36–37
    substance abuse and smoking, 56–57
    teenage mothers, 11
    see also Parents
MRI, *see* Brain imaging research

National Association for the Education of Young
    Children, 129
National Center on Child Abuse and Neglect,
    children with disabilities, 18
National Institute of Mental Health, report on
    children, 13
Neglect, *see* Child abuse
No Child Left Behind Act of 2001 (PL 107-
    110), 4, 138
Normative studies, screening measures, 59–60

Operant conditioning, 132–133
Organizational theories of development, 25–29,
    27*t*, 28*f*

Parents
    assessment, participation in, 75–76
    benchmarks and assessment items, 48*t*, 50–51,
        78*t*, 79*t*, 80*t*–81*t*
    evaluation process, participation in, 120, 124
    goal development, participation in, 97
    home environment screening and, 62

modeling activities for, 105, 109, 111–112
parent–child interactions, 5, 17, 104–105
poverty and, 15
screening, participation in, 56, 57, 60–61
single and teenage parents, 11
social emotional responses, 36–37
see also Mothers
Pediatricians
identification of mental health disorders, 21, 58–59
universal screening, 137
Personnel preparation programs, 136, 137–138
PET, *see* Brain imaging research
Physicians, identification of mental health disorders, 21, 58–59
PL 102-119, *see* Individuals with Disabilities Education Act (IDEA) Amendments of 1991
PL 105-17, *see* Individuals with Disabilities Education Act (IDEA) Amendments of 1997
PL 107-110, *see* No Child Left Behind Act of 2001
Planned activities, 102, 103*t*
Play
case examples, 69, 73–74, 101, 105
development of skills, 33
Positron Emission Tomography (PET), *see* Brain imaging research
Poverty
community-based programs, 134
influence on child development, 3–4
as mental health risk factor, 11, 14–15
Practitioners, *see* Professionals
Predictability of schedules, 48*t*, 50
Preschool-age children
age interval, 76
benchmarks and assessment items, 80*t*
mental health problems, prevalence, 13, 22
social competence, 32–33
Prevention strategies
community-based programs, 19*f*, 134
low-cost options, 20
Probe procedures, 121–122
Problem behaviors, *see* Behavior problems
Professionals
identification of mental health disorders, 21, 58–59
practitioner-completed screening measure, 61
referrals to, 46, 47, 64, 65*f*, 68
training needs, 15, 136, 137–138
Program evaluation
annual evaluation report example, 130*f*
data collection issues, 123, 124–125, 128–129
evaluation plan example, 128–129, 128*f*
external evaluators, 125
Progress Summary Form, 129*f*
questions to address, 117, 120

Progress Monitoring Form, 121*f*
Progress Summary Form, 129*f*
Protective factors, identification of, 63, 72–73
Psychological/psychiatric disorders, *see* Mental health disorders
Psychometric data, development of screening measures, 60

Range of emotions, *see* Emotions
Reach-and-grasp response, development of, 26
Referrals to professionals, 46, 47, 64, 65*f*, 68
Relationships, *see* Interactions and relationships
Reliability of screening measures, 60
Requests, compliance with
case examples, 102
as child benchmark, 48*t*, 50
intervention activities, 121–122
Responsivity of caregivers, 48*t*, 50
Risk factors
assessment of, 72–73
biological and environmental risks, 3–5
groups at risk for mental health problems, 10, 14–18, 45–47, 135
prevalence of, 11–12
screening process, 63, 64, 65*f*
as underlying principle of development, 27–29, 27*t*, 28*f*
Routine activities, 97, 102, 103*t*
Rules, ability to follow, 48*t*, 50, 122

Safety, of child
as adult/caregiver benchmark, 48*t*, 50
case examples, 68, 89–90, 97, 126
Schedules and routines, 48*t*, 50
School-age children, social emotional disturbances, 13, 22
Screening
case examples, 67–68, 69
challenges of, 57–59
environmental screening, 62–64
evaluation of, 118
general developmental screening, 55–56, 57, 137
outcomes, 55, 57, 64, 67
overview, 19*f*, 43*f*, 44, 51, 52*f*
process and steps, 52*f*, 64, 65*f*, 66–69, 66*f*
purpose and importance of, 51, 52*f*, 55–57
recommended practices, 56, 57
screening instruments, 21, 59, 61, 62–63
standards, 59–61
target groups, 46
universal screening, 137
SEAM, *see* Social Emotional Assessment/ Evaluation Measure
Self-image
as child benchmark, 48*t*, 49
intervention activities, 108*f*
Sensitivity of screening measures, 59
Single parents, 11

Smiling response, development of, 26–27
Smoking, maternal, and children's brain
    development, 56–57
Social Emotional Assessment/Evaluation Measure
        (SEAM)
    Activity Matrix, 107, 108*f*, 109*f*
    benchmarks and assessment items, 51, 77*t*–81*t*
    case examples, 84, 85*f*, 86*f*, 87, 96*f*
    Data Collection and Evaluation Form, 124*f*
    Embedding Plans, 106–107, 107*f*, 108*f*
    Goal Development and Intervention Plan,
        90–91, 91*f*, 93–95, 94*f*, 95*f*
    Infant benchmarks, 77*t*–78*t*
    overview, 75–77, 81–82, 83*f*, 84, 89
    Preschool-Age benchmarks, 80*t*–81*t*
    sample cover page, 83*f*
    Summary Form: Infant Interval, 86*f*
    Toddler benchmarks, 78*t*–79*t*
Social emotional development
    challenges to defining, 29–30
    definitions, 9, 10, 32
    lack of emphasis on, 4, 134
    learning model, 35–36, 36*f*
    need for intervention, 4–5
    parent responses and, 36–37
    screening challenges, 57–59
    social competence, 32–33
    see also Mental health disorders
Social Skills Rating Scale (SSRS), Ages 3–5, 61
Socioeconomic status, *see* Poverty
SSRS, *see* Social Skills Rating Scale (SSRS),
        Ages 3–5
State policies, need for change, 138
Substance abuse, maternal, effect on brain
        development, 56–57
Supports
    identification of, 63
    need for, 4

Surgeon General, *see* United States Surgeon
        General

TABS, *see* Temperament and Atypical Behavior
        Scale
Teachers
    practitioner-completed screening measure, 61
    training needs, 15, 136, 137–138
    see also Professionals
Teenage mothers, as child risk factor, 11
Temperament and Atypical Behavior Scale
        (TABS), 21
Test–retest reliability, 60
Time lines, goal attainment, 97–98
Toddlers
    age interval, 76
    benchmarks and assessment items, 73–74,
        78*t*–79*t*
Transactional theories of development, 25–29,
        27*t*, 28*f*

United States Census data, psychometric
        evaluations, 60
United States Department of Health and Human
        Services, emotional and behavioral
        problems in children, 13
United States House of Representatives Report,
        children in foster care, 16
United States Surgeon General, on mental health
        disorders in children, 13
Universal screening, 127
Utility of screening measures, 60

Validity of screening measures, 59–60
Violence, children exposed to, 46–47

World Health Organization (WHO), on mental
        health disorders, 11–12